CGR $20

AROUND THE
BIG BLUE MARBLE

AROUND THE
BIG BLUE MARBLE

THE BOC CHALLENGE 1994-95 SINGLE-HANDED
RACE AROUND THE WORLD

NIGEL ROWE

Foreword by
Sir Robin Knox-Johnston

AURUM PRESS

To the spirit of The BOC Challenge
and the memory of Harry Mitchell

First published 1995 by Aurum Press Limited
25 Bedford Avenue, London WC1B 3AT

A catalogue record for this book is available from the British Library.

ISBN 1 85410 354 7

Additional text material by Herb McCormick

Cover and interior design by Design/Section, Frome
Printed and bound in Great Britain by Hartnoll Ltd, Bodmin

Published in association with Good Books

CONTENTS

~~~~~~~~~~~~~~

ACKNOWLEDGEMENTS

~~~~~~~~~~~

A handful of people encouraged me in my ambition to sail alone around the world. Others helped me actually put the project together and turn the dream into a practical proposition. Still others helped me on my way and in the ports of call. To this extent mine was anything but a solo effort, and they all deserve thanks for giving me the greatest and most memorable experience of my life.

My friend Mark Schrader was in on the plan from the beginning, and was there throughout with sound advice and encouragement. My fiancée Julia became increasingly involved in the planning, preparation and provisioning; she also helped to pick up the pieces along the way and afterwards. *Sky Catcher* would not have been the delight she was to sail and live aboard if it had not been for designer Skip Miller, who remodelled the boat, became a friend and then my shore crew along with Andy Darwent. I may not have made it to the start line, let alone beyond, without them. My greatest debt is owed to these four.

It would not have happened at all, of course, if Dick Giordano (as chairman and chief executive of The BOC Group) had not gone along with my idea for BOC to sponsor the event in the first place, back in 1981. Nor if his successor Pat Rich had not agreed to continue sponsoring the event and to me taking a leave of absence from the company to follow my dream. Nor if Pat's successor as chief executive, Pat Dyer, had not gone along with the idea as well.

Sponsorship support from the Carbide Graphite Group Inc helped to fund my BOC Challenge campaign, thanks to Jim Baldwin and Nick Kaiser. Thanks also to Sally Baldwin and the C/G Group staff and customers who helped to give *Sky Catcher* and me such a terrific send off from Charleston. Thanks are also due to Hunter Marine, who designed and built *Sky Catcher* in the first place and who gave us house-room at their Florida facility during her substantial refit.

The event itself would not have existed for me to compete in without the support of sponsors beyond The BOC Group. Key amongst them were IBM as presenting sponsor, and satellite communications provider COMSAT. Significant support for the event came from other sponsors and suppliers too: Omega, Champagne Mumm, Helly-Hansen, Alden, Trimble Navigation, Medical SeaPak, CompuServe, Edson International, Hertz, Rosenbluth Travel, and *Yachting* magazine.

The four ports of call helped to make the event a success both for sponsors and competitors, and none more so than Charleston, South Carolina.

This book would not be as it is without Graham Tarrant of Good Books, its editor and midwife — or without the contributions from my friend Herb McCormick who watched events unfold from race headquarters — or without its generous foreword from Sir Robin Knox-Johnston who did so much to create the character of The BOC Challenge in the first place when he was its race director.

Above all, my thanks to my fellow competitors in The BOC Challenge 1994-95 who gave me help, friendship, and many fine tales.

Nigel Rowe
July 1995

FOREWORD

~~~~~~~~~~~

Amongst long distance sailing events The BOC Challenge is unique. This is not so much due to the course, although a sail around the world is arguably the toughest natural challenge available to man on this planet; it is due to the spirit that has imbued the competitors since the race began. It was the first of the regular singlehanded around-the-world races and its appeal always has been to both the professional sailor and the romantic adventurer. Each time this unlikely combination of out-and-out ambition and just doing their own thing has coalesced into a tightly knit group of individuals striving to win, of course, but recognizing that the real struggle is not amongst themselves – it is with the sea. This is the unique spirit of the BOC.

At first glance Nigel Rowe was not an obvious entrant. Jetting around the globe in the hard, realistic world of commerce hardly seems the nursery for dreams of becoming a solo circumnavigator. Yet the signs were always there. The enthusiasm to support the race in the first place in 1982, certainly for strong commercial reasons, slowly changed to a fascination with the sailors and their motives, and I don't think many of us were surprised when he started to talk about entering the OSTAR (Singlehanded Trans Atlantic Race), with the BOC as his ultimate objective. Like a spectator on the sidelines, the more he watched, the more he wanted to get into the game. Like so many others, he had become obsessed.

Characteristically, he built up his own experience to the point where he felt he was ready for his ultimate ambition and then eased out of the corporate world to conduct his personal odyssey. The perceptions, experiences and conclusions are not those of the professional sailor; they are of an educated amateur and give a far greater insight into the solitary world of the singlehander as a result.

Nigel's unusual background and long history with the event give him a unique understanding of the race and those who compete in it. *Around the Big Blue Marble* is, of course, the story of the 1994-95 BOC – but above all it is an adventure story, an unusual competitor's enthralling tale, exceptionally well told.

Robin Knox-Johnston.

Torbryan, July 1995

~~~~~~~~~~~~

From space, according to one of the early astronauts,

the oceans of Planet Earth made it look like a "big blue marble".

These oceans connect with each other to form the perfect arena for

the longest race on earth for an individual in any sport —

The BOC Challenge.

CHRISTMAS DAY 1994

It began as a gale. Within two days it was a full-blown Force 12 storm. The Giant of the Southern Ocean was in a black rage, determined this time to claim a victim.

Perhaps I should have known disaster was about to strike. The warning would certainly have been heeded by sailors of old. It came at dawn on Christmas morning. I was brewing a cup of coffee in the galley when a loud crash on deck brought me up into the cockpit to see what had happened. A huge black-brown gull lay dead and dangling from the lines on the foredeck guardrail. I could not bring myself to touch the poor creature, so I prayed for its soul and cut it away.

The wind began to rise and by afternoon it was around 40 knots. It was out of the north, pushing ever larger folds of ocean in mounting waves across the strong and unstoppable westerly swell. I noted in my diary: "Very confused and uncomfortable sea. Scary stuff."

By the following morning the wind speed wandered between 50 and 60 knots. We had four reefs in the main, and no headsails, but we were still surfing on the waves at close to 20 knots at times. Sleep was impossible as we rolled and surged through and over the waves, taking the occasional breaker over the deck.

Hours later, I was standing in the companionway staring at the towering seas chasing us along, when a breaking wave sent us sideways and into a crash-gybe; then a knockdown. The violence of the throw broke our reinforced aluminium tiller just below where it was attached to the self-steering lines, and the rudder jammed under the hull. I quickly pulled down the rest of the mainsail and managed to free the rudder after a strenuous half-hour in the cockpit and several ice-cold showers from breaking waves. I then discovered that the electric autopilot had "locked" — so now we had no effective self-steering at all.

I hove-to and set to work in the cockpit and stern scoop to jury-rig a new tiller to the stump of what was left and repair the windvane self-steering. It took hours. Working in those conditions was like trying to make a jigsaw puzzle on the back of a galloping horse, and I was being continually soaked by waves over the side filling the cockpit.

That night the wind rose beyond 60 knots, then over 70. We took another huge wave on our side and went crashing over and down its frothing slope. When it passed we were still pinned over on our side. Again, we had no steering. The windvane and water servo-paddle of the self-steering gear had both been sheared off by the weight of the breaking wave.

I was exhausted and scared. I found myself standing in the companionway, clutching its sides with white knuckles. Some great fist was squeezing my stomach with an iron grip so it hurt. I was sweating and breathing in shallow breaths. The seas, which had been huge, were now towering citadels of black ocean marbled with turquoise and foaming white. They had no white-caps; these were being torn off and thrown aside before they could begin to form properly. The noise was deafening – the banshee screech of the wind in the rigging, the thunder of the tumbling ocean.

I stared up at the black, angry sky and closed my eyes. Dear God, save us all from this hell. What had begun as a dream, to sail alone around the world, had become a living nightmare.

BEGINNINGS

The intense heat and humidity of an August afternoon had just about everybody in Charleston, South Carolina, off the streets and out of it. Even the cars seemed to trudge slowly along the roads as if burdened themselves by the oppressive atmosphere.

The BOC Challenge marina adjacent to the passenger ship terminal, and specially built for the event, was no hive of activity either. Most of the skippers and their shore crew were elsewhere. Many had walked down the street to the air-conditioning of Squeaky's bar for a "cold one". A few people sauntered along the waterfront boardwalk, and one or two had managed the extra few yards to look at the fleet in the BOC marina. It was an impressive sight that lifeless afternoon – twenty monohull sailboats of such diverse shapes, sizes and colours, each the product of different theories, imaginations and budgets.

I was standing on the dock wondering whether duty or Squeaky's would win the silent debate in my mind, when I noticed an elderly couple gazing at the boats and not realizing they were within my hearing.

"Lordy, Lordy. Just look at all that, will you," said the old lady, shaking her head slowly from side to side. Her furrowed brow beneath a loose mop of blue-grey hair registered both concern and disapproval. "These fellas must be hound-dog crazy – sailing on their own round the world, indeed. What in heaven's name is the point of that?"

It seemed more like a statement than a question. Her husband, I presumed, by her side joined in the head-shaking. His face had all the qualities of a seasoned prune and its expression echoed her sentiments.

I looked up at them both from the pontoon. I wanted to explain. But her eye caught mine and she pulled him away with a single protective sweep, like a mother with a child unexpectedly confronted by a drunken tramp. They walked away with a purposeful step and their prejudice still intact. They had seen the evidence. We were all guilty as charged. And that was the end of the matter for them.

For me, the adventure that had begun as a dream ten years ago, and that had become such an obsession for the past eighteen months, was about to begin. The summer of 1994 found me in Charleston with my 48-foot sloop *Sky Catcher*. Remarkably, we had just won Class II of The BOC Transatlantic Challenge singlehanded race and we were making final preparations for the main event, The BOC Challenge 1994-95.

The old couple's question was not an uncommon one, of course. Perhaps it was not an unreasonable one either. Here we were, a small gathering of individuals who were about to sail alone around the world. It would take more than a brief dockside conversation with a couple of sceptics to explain how and why!

In fact it was only when I began to sail on my own on a long passage just a few years earlier that the reasons for my comfort with being alone, and wanting to confront myself with a solitary test, began to dawn on me. I undertook my first long solo passage in 1987, in preparation for the singlehanded transatlantic race from Plymouth, England, to Newport, Rhode Island, the following year. It was those ten days alone at sea, more than at any other time before, that gave me the space and opportunity for deep reflection. It was an appalling trip in an unfinished boat, with two days of it hove-to in a gale. But it was one of those times in my life when the "what's it all about?" questions crept out of the woodwork of my subconscious.

I was in my mid-forties, but this was no mid-life crisis. These were not troubled times for me – in fact quite the opposite. Indeed, it was probably the luxury of a settled and hassle-free existence that nagged me to take on a new challenge. By that time in my life, and my career, two things had struck me quite forcibly about humankind. Very few people I knew had a good balance in their lives. All too many were consumed by their work and "stressed out" – to the detriment of not only their health and families, but their work also. The second realization was that as most people became older, the harder they tried to remove risk and challenge from their lives. It seemed to me that removing the risk of failure did little to enhance the possibility of success, if one defined success in this context as a fulfilled life rich in experience rather than simply a long one. Even in business, it seemed to me, avoiding the risk of failure was seldom rewarded with success.

I did not want my life to end with a long list of "if onlys" and "wish I hads".

None of this explains an appetite for solitary challenge, of course. For this I had to dig deeper. As with so many aspects of all of us I found the answer in my early and formative years. Vast swathes of it had been spent alone, both enforced and by choice. I was to discover that being alone had little to do with being lonely. Indeed, aloneness can be a joyful and deeply rewarding state. Although I have spent a great deal of time alone in my life I have seldom felt lonely.

~~~~~~~~~~~

In the Seventies I was working for an American company at its European head-quarters in Brussels. We all worked extremely hard there, and travelled a lot. I was in my early thirties and began to worry about "burning out" too young. I needed a hobby, and I liked the idea of sailing.

I bought a 13-foot dinghy which we car-topped to a lake in Holland most weekends. For the first few weeks my son "Ant" (Anthony), then nine, was content to let me play with the new toy, using him as movable ballast. My Norwegian wife Tove sat on the shore with a book, keeping a close eye on us as we sailed up and down and around the lake. No good would come of it, she was sure of that. She had concluded that I had no idea what I was up to, and the confusion of indecisive orders from me, audible to everyone on shore, was clearly beginning to annoy our son. Ant and I persisted with it, though, and we gradually taught ourselves to sail.

In 1978 the family returned to England, where I had taken a new job. The dinghy came with us, but slowly gathered moss and cobwebs leaning against the outside wall of the garage. Two years later, and dangerously close to being forty when they say life begins, I decided that the time had come for a new adventure.

"How about buying a boat and doing some sailing together?" I asked during one of Ant's infrequent long weekends at home from boarding-school.

"Great!" said Ant, beaming from ear to ear.

"Oh God!" said Tove. "I thought you'd grown out of that. Anyway, you've got a boat already, going green in the garden."

"No, no. I mean a real boat. One we can go cruising in, live on board for holidays, that sort of thing," I explained. "The Brighton Boat Show is on this weekend."

Ant punched the air with excitement. Tove groaned.

The boat show had attracted a large crowd. The sun was shining and there was only a light breeze. Ideal conditions for selling a boat to a first-time buyer! We bought one that afternoon, a Leisure 27 called *Fleur du Cap*. She was 27 feet long, had teak trim throughout, a gleaming dark blue hull, and she seemed to have more space below than her overall length would allow.

Fleur du Cap was assigned a berth in the inner harbour of the marina. The following weekend we went down there to equip ourselves and the boat with all those things one must have to go sailing!

We all bought white foul-weather gear and white boots, thick fishermen's socks and jerseys, quilted gloves, towelling scarves, woollen watch-hats, tide tables, charts of the south coast of England, knives on the end of lanyards, a full set of crockery and cutlery with little anchors on each piece, plastic drinking glasses with different knot motifs on them, saucepans and a plastic bowl to match the colour in the galley. Much of what we had bought could have been had for half the price at a supermarket or department store in town; but buying these things in the chandlery seemed the more nautical thing to do.

We spent two weekends on board without moving from the dock. Tove was quite happy with this arrangement. I really felt I needed some expert help with our first time under sail and I persuaded a very experienced friend to join us.

Dick Kenny raced an OOD34 at that time. He had been sailing most of his life, and had written a book, *Looking at Sails*. He knew what he was up to on a boat.

Dick inspected our boat thoroughly above decks. He pulled at the shrouds and backstay while staring up at the mast, bent down to look at the chainplates and mast step, and finally asked what sails we had. I asked him if this was the sailing equivalent of kicking tyres and asking "What's she got under the bonnet?" but he did not seem to be greatly amused.

Once out of the marina, Dick ran up all the sails one after the other in the gentle breeze and showed me how to trim them. We even had the spinnaker up for a while, and I marvelled at how easily he had got it up and down on his own. The afternoon seemed to be over before it began. I learned many things that day, including one simple truth about all sail boats that I have always remembered when adding "essential" bits and pieces of gear.

"The sails are the only things that make a boat move," Dick explained. "Everything else on board, absolutely everything else, slows it down. So if you want to go fast, make sure you have good sails and don't carry anything or anyone on board you don't actually need for the passage."

Ant and I loved sailing. The more experience we had the more we enjoyed it. Tove, despite her best efforts to fight off chronic seasickness, disliked it and hoped it would be a short-lived fad. The fact that it was to become an increasingly important facet of my life no doubt contributed something to the collapse of our marriage a few years later.

A solo trip around the Isle of Wight was followed by a more ambitious voyage to France, across the Bay of Biscay, with Ant. By now we had a new boat, a 32-footer which we called *Sea Troll*. It was on the return passage from France that Ant and I began to discuss future sailing adventures. We felt ready to take on the two-handed Round Britain and Ireland Race the following year, and we began to nourish fantasies of crossing the Atlantic together the year after.

~~~~~~~~~

While *Sea Troll* might have been suitable for the Round Britain race she was not a boat in which I would have wanted to cross the North Atlantic. With that dream in mind, I sold her soon after our return to England and began looking for something larger and more suitable. Ant and I visited the Southampton Boat Show in the autumn and began negotiations for the construction of a customized Diva 39. In her standard form she was a fairly comfortable crusing boat. Built in Sweden, she had the classic Scandinavian narrow beam and was just over 38 feet long.

I wanted a boat that was going to be both quick and strong. After a visit to the builders outside Stockholm I contracted to have one built with a lot of carbon fibre and Kevlar in the hull, and to have her length extended to 40 feet with a "sugar scoop" moulded to her stern. It was an exciting project for me, and I visited Stockholm several times while she was being put together. She was shipped to the east coast of England the following spring and we launched her there. I had the name *Tsunami* (a tidal wave created by a sub-sea earthquake, typically in the Pacific, that travels at a deceptively fast speed) painted in large red letters on her sleek grey hull.

Ant and I sailed her as much as we had time for in the few weeks before the start of the Round Britain race, and our passage from the River Orwell on the east coast of England to Plymouth in Devon served as our qualifying sail.

It was a tough race; five legs and four stopover ports where we all had an enforced forty-eight hours lay-over. Each leg was two or three days of rough weather and tricky navigation, followed by two days of intensive hospitality ashore. We were exhausted by the time we returned to Plymouth, a respectable fourth in our class, changed by the experience and with our ambitions fired up.

The real turning point in our sailing came halfway through the race. We both felt a bit seedy as we rolled along the waves towards the island of St Kilda, off the western isles of Scotland. We had been drinking heavily in Barra the night before and missed the shipping forecast that morning. If we had heard the promise of

Storm Force 11 we would have done the sensible thing and postponed our departure. But by the time we knew what we were in for we were well out to sea.

By afternoon the wind was up to 40 knots and it continued to build into
the night. Everything around us was a shade of grey, as dark as it ever is at 60°
north in mid-summer. The sea was a boiling confusion of marbled breaking
waves, their tops blown off and carried away by the storm-force winds screeching through the rigging. Thick angry clouds raced across the sky. It was the tail
end of a hurricane, someone told us afterwards, with winds over 60 knots much
of the time.

We were screaming along with too much sail up; but *Tsunami* was moving
well, and it would have been difficult to reduce sail in those conditions. In less
than three hours we had covered nearly forty nautical miles, surfing off breaking waves almost continuously – often at speeds beyond the speedmeter's limit
of 15 knots.

After surfing off one wave we would settle briefly into a trough, feel our
stern being lifted by the next wave, then take off again. The speed would build:
nine, 10, 11 knots . . . a great rooster tail of water fanning up from our stern with
a low roar . . . 12, 13, 15 knots, a curtain of foaming sea rising high and along the
full length of both sides of the boat. The tiller required finger-tip control and
total concentration to keep her on track. Occasionally she would shear off and
attempt to round up into the wind, with green and white water crashing across
her decks. It happened a few times before the inevitable drama.

This was the third leg of the race and we were heading for Lerwick in the
Shetland Isles, mid-point of the two-thousand-mile course. With the wind
showing no sign of abating, Ant went forward to the mast to put the last reef in
the mainsail while I stayed in the cockpit to steer. A moment's inattention, just
one brief moment as I fussed with the reefing lines, and we were in trouble.

A wave caught us side-on and swung the back of the boat round. The boom
slammed across with incredible force. As *Tsunami* rolled over on her side,
another wave broke over the wave we were on, driving us sideways down the
steeply angled wall of water. The mast was horizontal. Ant was clinging on to it,
tethered by his safety harness, waist-deep in frothing sea water. I was hanging on
to a winch in the cockpit and could only watch the sea pour into the boat
through the open main hatch. My brain was working so fast it all seemed to be
happening in slow motion, and I felt strangely more a spectator than a participant in what was happening.

We bounced back up again before fear had a chance to grip us. There was no time to think about anything now but dropping the mainsail altogether and putting her back on course. Ant crawled back to the cockpit, shaking his head slowly, a broad grin on his face. Words were not necessary. We both knew whose fault it had been. I pumped out and cleaned up the boat myself.

It was at the end of the race that we both resolved to enter the two-handed transatlantic race the following year, and the singlehanded transatlantic race two years after that. It was then also that my thoughts of competing some day in The BOC Challenge singlehanded round-the-world race made the transformation from ambition to a kind of personal commitment.

We spent almost a week in Plymouth at the end of the Round Britain race in "decompression" and in cementing some new friendships, some of which have lasted to this day. We tended to see the same people during the mandatory forty-eight hours in each of the four ports of call in the race. One was Margaret Thomas who was following her husband round. Alan Thomas was sailing in his 40-foot monohull with a New Zealand sailor he had rescued from a sinking catamaran during the previous year's singlehanded transatlantic race. We were to become good friends of the Thomases in the years to come and Alan, who ran his own computer software and services company, gave Ant his first job after university. He also owned a 26-foot boat called *Dream Weaver* that looked like a small submarine and which was to play an important part in Ant's sailing career a few years later.

Ant and I spent the winter planning for the following year's two-handed transatlantic race. *Tsunami* was ashore in Lymington, one of the Solent ports on the south coast of England. We went down at Easter to begin preparing her for the coming season, and were horrified to see her condition. Virtually the whole hull was a mass of blisters. I asked the foreman at the yard to look at her and give me an opinion. He ran an eye over her, shook his head, and said I needed a surveyor. The surveyor came the following week and said he wouldn't cross the English Channel in her, let alone the Atlantic. He said I needed a lawyer!

It took almost a year of litigation to extract a little over half of my investment from a reluctant agent and builder, and the opportunity for Ant and me to race together across the Atlantic had passed. However, during that summer in the middle of it all, we decided that if we could not race together, we would hold to our commitment to race against each other in the singlehanded transatlantic race two years hence.

Ant found himself a job in Saudi Arabia, as a sales engineer for a medical equipment company, to earn some "heavy bread" to fund his campaign. Early in 1987 I bought a 39-foot boat that had been raced by a crew of nine, and had her converted for singlehanded sailing. It was another of those decisions that was a triumph of ambition over experience.

The blue-hulled *Spartan of Wight* was sailed round to Shotley near the mouth of the River Orwell. There she was put in a shed and began her transformation to become the yellow-hulled *Piper Rising* – new keel, new mast, rigging and sails, new cockpit and deck layout, water ballast tanks and watertight bulkheads down below. The boat cost me £22,000 and I thought from the estimates I had been given that about that much again would take care of the conversion. It became a needlessly expensive folly which could have been avoided so easily with more experience or advice, and less dreaming.

The boat should have been completed in time for me to undertake my qualifying sail that summer; but the project needed three times as much time, as well as that much more money than originally budgeted, and I left the Orwell with the boat uncomfortably incomplete. I sailed her north to Lerwick, through the desolate and dirty North Sea, in mostly apalling weather for almost ten days. I spent the thick end of two days hove-to in a gale. I was exhausted by the time I reached my destination, twenty pounds lighter and several inches thinner, bruised, minor scratches going sceptic, and my feet and hands waterlogged, white and shedding their skin. It was a brutal lesson, but one that left me both wiser and more confident in both the boat and myself.

I had made several mistakes. Leaving for such a passage with an incomplete boat was the first. The deck hatches were unfinished and let in great bucketsful of water when the decks were awash. Because the engine did not work I had a diesel generator strapped in the middle of the boat, and filling its small tank from a jerrican in a lurching sea meant that much of the fuel ended up in the bilges. The bilge pump did not work so I had to use a bucket and cup to bail out, and the foul mixture sloshing around in the bottom of the boat poisoned every little nick and scratch on my hands and arms. My feet were soaked in my boots the first day out, and stayed that way till I reached Lerwick. They had a dreadful stench when I removed my boots and thick woollen socks on the dock.

I had decided that I would not be ruled by routine, and that I would eat and sleep when I felt like it. That was probably my worst mistake. When the gale hit I was already tired, and I then faced two days with almost no sleep at all. And not eating enough left me weak at the end of it. The problem of diet was exacerbated by the fact that my only box of matches ended up in the bilges on the second day out, and despite every attempt to dry them in lavatory paper next to the hot cylinder head of the generator, I had no means of lighting the stove. The match heads, once dry, simply crumbled when I tried to strike them. I ate cold beans, fruit, bread, nuts and chocolate for the rest of the passage, and drank only cold water.

That Christmas Ant returned to England with less money than he had originally anticipated, but still determined to find a boat in which to sail the race. Alan Thomas had offered him the use of *Dream Weaver*, and we went to Plymouth to see her.

She was propped up in a cradle at Alec Blagdon's yard by the Mayflower Marina. She had been there more or less unattended for eighteen months. She was, in essence, a 26-foot cigar tube, five feet wide and four feet six inches high. She had a crude and temporary patch on a long gash in her battleship-grey hull. Her cockpit was the size and shape of a dining room chair. We pushed back the small deck hatch and went inside. It was all damp, musty and covered in mildew, and some of her woodwork was rotting. It looked an unlikely, even dangerous proposition.

The boat had been designed and built by American naval architect Jim Kyle. Alan had acquired her to do the previous singlehanded transatlantic race; but had then thought better of the idea and sailed in his 40-footer instead. Jim still had an affection for the little boat, and Alan had decided to give her to him and his wife as a wedding present. The deal for Ant was that he could do the delivery to Newport, Rhode Island, in the race so long as he fixed her up first.

It was, as they say, the best offer in town. After a brief deliberation and discussion with Alec Blagdon about the work that needed to be done, Ant made the commitment, commissioned the work including a new bright orange paint job, ordered new sails, and returned to Saudi Arabia to work out his notice. When he returned, he qualified for the race by sailing down to Portugal and back, and we completed our final preparations for the race together.

~~~~~~~~~

We moored alongside each other in Queen Anne's Battery just over a week before the start of the race. The fleet that had assembled for the event was an odd collection, from small production boats to the colourful and heavily sponsored 60-foot monohulls and multihulls being sailed by the international "rock stars".

Plymouth Sound would have been as still as a mirror if it had not been for the hundreds of boats, competitors and spectators disturbing its surface on the morning of the start. A light, inconsistent breeze took us slowly past the break-water into an almost windless area behind the start line, restricted to competitors and official boats only. The multihulls were striding through the fleet at three or four times the speed of the wind itself, kings of their jungle who could go anywhere they wanted and be sure everyone else would get out of their way. Their gaudy hulls and huge expanses of Kevlar sails were alive. They were flexing their muscles and preening themselves in a kind of ritual dance before the start, like arrogant peacocks strutting through a chicken yard. That suited me fine. For me, as for most of the smaller monohulls, this was a private endeav-our, a personal challenge, that needed no limelight.

Ant and I sailed past each other a few times as we waited for the noon start. We smiled and waved to one another, and shouted words of encouragement and wishes of good luck. It was not until the gun was fired and we had crossed the line that I began to relax a little. I had been plagued by two anxieties for several months. The first was knowing that Ant would be out there crossing the Atlantic, alone and out of touch with anyone because he could carry only a short-distance VHF radio. If he found himself in difficulties he would be very much on his own. His only concession to my anxiety was to agree to carry a satellite tracking device so others ashore could follow his progress if not actually be in contact with him. My other anxiety was simply making it to the start. For everyone who would cross the line there would be dozens who had dreamed of doing so, and some would have made serious plans for it. Some would have to pull out just weeks or even days before the event because of some last-minute crisis with their boats or personal lives.

I remember when Ant and I first discussed doing the race with Robin Knox-Johnston, who had become a friend since his involvement in the first BOC Challenge as race director. He had said that such an event would present two problems for us. "The first is the decision, the personal commitment, to do the race," he had told us. "The second is the persistence and stamina to overcome all the obstacles and difficulties you'll encounter in getting your boats and your-selves to the start. After that it's just sailing!"

Ant and *Dream Weaver* were a hundred yards behind *Piper Rising* and me as the start gun fired. It was not long before the whole fleet had stretched out, the big multihulls over the horizon and out of sight, and the smaller boats disap-pearing behind me. I turned round several times to search for a glimpse of *Dream Weaver* – an orange dot with a white sail above it, like some diminutive excla-mation mark, dwarfed by the colourful clutter of other boats and the ever widening horizon with its dull smudge of land disturbing the symmetry of its smooth arc. Finally I turned round for a last glimpse and he was nowhere to be seen. I wondered and worried when I would see him next.

We had a pre-arranged time late that afternoon to talk over the VHF radio while we were still likely to be within range of each other. I could hear him very clearly. We talked excitedly about the experience of the start, and agreed that the light wind and sunshine was the best we could have hoped for. It enabled us to become used to our boats and relax before having to face whatever was out there in the weeks ahead, and without having to contend with any misery on the first day. We exchanged positions and arranged to talk again in the morning. By then we were further apart and could barely hear one another. We wished each other fair winds and good sailing, and that was the last I would hear from him for several weeks.

For me the race was a mixture of frustration, fear, calm reflection, and intense elation. The thing that distinguishes long-distance passage-making alone from almost any other undertaking is its capacity to deliver such extremes in emotional experience.

There were wonderful days when the wind was steady and the sailing easy, when the sun rose and set in a blaze of colour, when the dolphins played around the boat, when I could lay in the cockpit naked listening to music or reading a book, days when I would literally tingle with the joy of it, the sense of real freedom. And there were days when it was not like that at all.

A little over a week into the race we had one day when there was not a breath of wind for almost a full twenty-four hours. By then I was thinking and talking about "we", *Piper Rising* and me, not "I". We had become as one in my mind, utterly dependent upon each other like Siamese twins. We had seen nothing at all for a couple of days – not a ship, bird or fish. It was as if we had dropped into a hole, and I soon developed the conviction that we were the only ones in it. Everyone else, I was certain, had good wind and was making good progress. There was a long swell running which meant we were rocking from side to side and sometimes being slapped under our transom by the rising water. Whether the sails were up or down, it all made a lot of noise and my frustration built to an unbearable and irrational intensity. In the late afternoon I grabbed one of the winch handles and thrashed the cockpit seat with it, swearing at my ill fortune, and then threw it as far as I could out to sea. I stood in the cockpit panting and screaming before collapsing into a corner, crying and laughing. Much more of this and I would go mad, I thought.

There were two occasions during the passage when I experienced a strange and almost mystical sensation that I had never had before.

One of these was during the worst night of the passage. Visibility had been poor all afternoon and it became worse as the black of night fell over us. Although we had seen nothing for several days I decided to put the radar on stand-by, and turned it on every hour to see if there was anything around us. Sometime after midnight I became conscious of lightning in the distance. It was not close, because the muffled and barely audible thunder followed some time after each dull flash.

I turned on the radar for a routine check – and there, suddenly, was a target several miles ahead of us. It disappeared for a few seconds, then reappeared as a larger blob on the screen, slightly to one side. On the next sweep there were two blobs. I watched the radar screen, fascinated and a little alarmed. The blobs merged and grew into a great crescent two miles wide, and the end of its tail moved towards us. Then three new blobs appeared in quick succession, close to the crescent which grew into a large oval shape.

A new and larger blob appeared less than two miles directly ahead of us, followed by a loud clap of thunder. I suddenly realized I was watching an electrical storm, and it was about to engulf us! I went into the cockpit. It had begun to rain heavily and the wind was building. I reefed the mainsail right down and furled the headsail to a small triangle. Down below watching the radar had been like playing one of those amusement arcade war games. Up in the cockpit it was real.

The rain was heavy, but not in the ordinary sense of "heavy rain": I could feel the weight of it pressing me into the cockpit, and it was flattening the sea and bouncing off it. The thunder was at times continuous and the lightning came down in brilliant, angry, jagged bolts that struck the sea sometimes less than a hundred yards from the boat. My breathing became shallow, I was mumbling aloud a prayer for help, cold and clammy sweat mingled with the rain down the back of my neck, I felt knots of pain between my shoulder blades, and I was scared. How long would it be before one of those bolts of lightning would find our tall mast and its steel rigging?

Then I suddenly felt this sensation of being detached from where I was and what I was doing. I was watching myself with the curiosity of an uninvolved observer. I was reminding myself of things I had to do and little details I might otherwise forget. I went below and brought up my "Oh Shit!" bag into the cockpit. I put on my life jacket and slung the bag over my back – a rucksack containing a little food, water, emergency position beacon, flares, hand-held VHF radio, and other supplies. I also untied the liferaft and made it ready for launching. Soon the wind was gusting around 50 knots, and we were skidding across the flattened black sea; it was like riding a bike over cobblestones. I had worked out an orderly plan for abandoning ship if the need arose and I sat there, calmly wondering if my escape plan would work. I saw no reason why it should not; but I had absolutely no experience on which to base such an assumption.

Eventually the storm rumbled off behind us, and as it did so my "other self" seemed to rejoin me again. Things were back to normal. I said a prayer of thanks and made a cup of tea.

There was another occasion when this happened to me, and that was when I had to climb the mast. I was, and still am, terrified of heights. The thought of ever having to climb the mast appalled me, even though I had had steps bolted to it to make the task easier. On this occasion the shackle holding the top of the mainsail to its halyard had become snagged in a mast-fitting two-thirds of the way up, and nothing I could do would shake it free. I had to go up there and do it myself.

After a moment of panic in the cockpit I went to the mast, put on the bosun's chair, tied it with shaking hands to another halyard, took a deep breath, and began to climb. The higher I went, the greater the force with which the swaying mast was trying to throw me off. I had not gone far before I was again apart from myself, observing what I was doing, offering gentle advice and encouragement. It was only after the line had been freed and I was back down in the cockpit that I began to shake again and feel "normal".

Life aboard *Piper Rising* was good. With the experience of my qualifying passage, I had provisioned the boat generously for the crossing with tinned meat, vegetables, fruit, butter, cheeses and pâté, as well as fresh vegetables, fruit and eggs. The bulk of the provisioning had been done at Harrods in London and I had invited Ant to do the same at my expense. "Take whatever you think you'd like," I had told him, and that was what he did. As he unpacked his Harrods boxes at Queen Anne's Battery, our neighbours watched with some amazement as jars of Californian asparagus, quails' eggs, and even a few small pots of caviar, began to pile up on the pontoon. We both took a small amount of drink on board, a couple of boxes of wine and a few half-bottles of champagne, for the high spots.

I drank my last half-bottle as *Piper Rising* and I sailed through dense fog over the Grand Banks off Nova Scotia, before the final run down the coast of North America to Newport, Rhode Island. Fishing boats, other coastal traffic, bad weather and a torn headsail meant I had no sleep during the last fifty hours or so; but I was well pumped up with adrenalin when we reached the finish line. Friends were there to greet us with ill-deserved congratulations: we had taken twenty-seven days to do what should have been accomplished in three weeks. Pete Dunning threw us a bottle of champagne from the committee boat.

All that remained now was to await Ant's arrival. Despite the fact that his boat was only two-thirds the length of *Piper Rising*, I did not have to wait long! He was less than two days behind me – the youngest skipper in the smallest boat in the race, and the new record holder for the passage in a monohull of her size.

He arrived unannounced in thick fog early in the morning. The wind had died, he could not raise race headquarters on his radio, so he skulled his little boat across the finish line, down Naragansett Bay and into Newport. The first I knew of his arrival was waking with a start in my bunk with his nose a few inches from mine and a fat grin across his weather-beaten face. I hugged him and cried.

I hurriedly put on some clothes and we sat in the cockpit of *Piper Rising*, drinking coffee and babbling away to each other. I was eager to swap "war stories" with him. I told him about the electrical storm and about having to climb the mast, and I asked him what had been his worst moment. He sat there for a while with a cheeky grin on his face. "I don't know really," he said, running a hand through his long damp hair. "I think it was probably that afternoon about five days ago."

"Yes, yes," I said impatiently. "So what happened?"

"Well," he continued, "it was like this. It'd been a cloudless day. I'd been reading a book in the morning and I fell asleep in the cockpit. I woke up halfway through the afternoon with the side of my face and chest red with sunburn – yes, I think that was my worst moment!" Ant had a well-developed talent for keeping his feet on the ground, and for making me feel about an inch tall!

Two years later was the third running of The BOC Challenge and, during it, what had once been a fantasy became a serious intent. By the time the fleet reached Punta del Este my ambitions were firming into a plan. Somehow or other, I was determined I would be in the next race myself, if at all possible.

CLASSIC

The BOC Challenge was first run in 1982-83 and quickly became established as a "classic" event in the international yacht racing and adventure sports calendar. It had certainly achieved this status by the third running of the event in 1990-91. From its very beginning, the race has involved many of the best and bravest sailors in the world, and some of the most fascinating and romantic personalities of any sport. Singlehanded sailors, perhaps by definition, are more individual in personality and diverse in background than those who compete in most other sports. And those who compete in an event like The BOC Challenge are driven by much more than the desire to participate in a sailboat race. They seek adventure and self-fulfilment – even the heavily sponsored "rock stars" in the maxi boats. Perhaps this is why it has been the subject of so many books and television programmes, and several hundred thousand newspaper and magazine stories around the world.

As an event, The BOC Challenge had a curious conception and birth, and a company like BOC was not perhaps an obvious candidate to give it life.

BOC began life itself as the Brins Oxygen Company in 1886. It became the British Oxygen Company and then, in the 1960s, changed its name to BOC. By then most of the company's operations were outside Britain and its businesses were involved with far more than the production of oxygen. In the early 1980s BOC was, as it is now, a multinational company whose principal business interests in industrial and speciality gases, health care and vacuum technology, were global. When I joined the company in 1980 (as chief executive – corporate relations), its largest markets outside the UK were the US, Australia and South Africa. Since then its development has been principally in the Pacific region and the third largest of the sixty or so markets in which it operates today is Japan.

In the early Eighties, too, BOC was a very decentralized company and its subsidiary operations abroad traded under a variety of names, none of them BOC. I had been hired into the company by the charismatic Dick Giordano, who had been brought over from America to run the whole group after BOC acquired Airco Inc, of which he had been president. My job, in essence, was to make sure the company had the reputation it deserved with all those who could influence its fortunes – from those who invested in it to those who worked for it.

Dick was one of those larger-than-life personalities who achieved instant notoriety in Britain by being the country's highest paid business executive. He brought an entirely new culture and style to the company, as well as an ambitious strategy to grow the business. He had an instinctive style of management and he wanted BOC to matter, both inside the company's worldwide operations and in the external marketplace. We developed a number of new communications programmes to help achieve this. We also developed a good working relationship. It probably helped that he sailed too.

It was while we were casting round for something a bit out of the ordinary to provide creative linkage between the company's main businesses around the world that I was approached by a British adventurer and sailor, Richard Broadhead, then twenty-nine years old. He was looking for sponsorship to compete in a race called "Around Alone": a singlehanded round-the-world race being organized out of Newport, Rhode Island, in the US.

I was intrigued, particularly since I read every sailing magazine I could lay my hands on and had never heard of the race. I asked my friend Dick Kenny to visit Newport as a potential entrant, for a quick and covert assessment of what scope there might be for BOC to become involved in the event itself. The race was being organized by a small group of enthusiasts with no money and little experience, and they knew they needed help. They had planned a course from Newport to Cape Town, to Hobart in Tasmania, to Buenos Aires, and back to Newport.

The race could do a lot for BOC, I thought. In Britain, our principal business of industrial gases was seen as a dull commodity in which we were assumed to have a near monopoly in a predominantly home market. Yet in fact we were an exciting business in a very competitive global marketplace. Linkage with an event that by its very nature was global and competitive was a natural choice. Add to this its inherent qualities of courage, stamina, the need for attention to detail and the ability to distinguish between a gamble and a calculated risk – qualities that in a different context were essential to success in business – and the analogy was fairly complete. Then add to all of that the opportunities for customer and VIP entertainment at a "world class" event in some of our principal business markets, and surely this was a winner. Not everyone in the company felt that way of course – especially the golfers, who outnumbered the sailors by several-to-one, and who thought we should be sponsoring golf. I figured that when a golfer took my job the company would probably sponsor golf. I felt no embarrassment in this. I knew that if we sponsored something in sailing it would get my full and enthusiastic attention, evenings and weekends as well. I'd make sure the company had a full measure of value from it.

I asked Dick Kenny to introduce me to Robin (now Sir Robin, having been awarded a knighthood in the 1995 Queen's Birthday Honours List, for services to yachting) Knox-Johnston, with whom he had been at sea when they were both merchant navy cadets. With Dick Giordano's endorsement for the project in principle I discussed it with Robin and, having struck a deal with the Newport group, set up a new race committee under Robin's chairmanship. We altered the course to include Sydney and Rio de Janeiro which better served BOC's business interests, we changed the title of the event to The BOC Challenge, we published a new set of rules, and then we set about promoting it. The race was scheduled to start in August the following year, 1982.

Robin was very instrumental in establishing the character of the event, and I was pleased I had had the wit to put someone with his background and experience in charge of it. All too many boat races are organized by people with little experience of sailing in the kind of event they are running. The result is frequently decisions that make no sense to the competitors, and a gulf of both understanding and attitude between sailors and organizing committee.

There were some wonderful characters in that first race, and it brought me into close contact with a new world of adventure that I had only read and dreamed about in the past. Robin himself was a legend, having been the first person ever to sail around the world alone and non-stop, back in 1969 – and I wanted someone to run the race who would have instant credibility with both competitors and the media. The race captured the imagination of everyone who had anything to do with it, and the competitors were all great ambassadors for the sport and their countries. We had seventeen entrants from the UK, US, France, South Africa, Australia, New Zealand, Czechoslovakia and Japan. Ten finished. Two boats were sunk and two others ran aground – one off Australia, the other on the Falkland Islands. There was no loss of life; but there were several stories of great seamanship and heroism, including an extraordinary rescue of Frenchman Jacques de Roux from his sinking boat in the Southern Ocean by Richard Broadhead who, in the end, never found sponsorship and sailed the race with his own and borrowed money. In fact that was true for almost everyone in that first event.

These pioneers of The BOC Challenge included professional naval seamen like South Africa's Bertie Reed and France's Jacques de Roux; men who had taken a leave of absence from their businesses to compete like Australia's Neville Gosson, America's Francis Stokes and Britain's Desmond Hampton; former newspaper editors like Dan Byrne from Los Angeles and Paul Rodgers of London; the Tokyo taxi driver Yukoh Tada; Tom Lindholm who had been a Los Angeles vice squad detective and at fifty-seven was the oldest competitor in the race; a former sled-dog driver and photographer from New Zealand called Dick McBride; and Richard Konkolski, a stateless refugee from Czechoslovakia.

Virtually every one of those in the first Challenge had made some considerable sacrifice to be in it, and others were to make sacrifices along the way. Frenchman Guy Bernadin sold his restaurant to be there in the smallest boat, the 38-foot *RATSO*. Tom Lindholm withdrew from the race only a few hours after the start with equipment failure. David White, who was one of the principal originators of the event, had put everything he owned into his new boat and withdrew in Cape Town with significant hull damage. Dick McBride, who had taken five years to build his steel staysail schooner in his spare time, accidentally beached his boat on the Falkland Islands and was dragged off by the British Navy to complete the race. Neville Gosson completed the course too, but returned to a collapsed business empire at the end of it. Desmond Hampton brought his campaign to an abrupt halt by running aground on Gabo Island off southern Australia in the famous *Gypsy Moth IV*, which he had chartered for the race. Francis Stokes rescued fellow American competitor Tony Lush from his sinking boat in the Southern Ocean after it had been thrown head-over-heels by a freak wave. The race was cluttered with great tales of glory and disaster.

Three things above all others in that first great BOC Challenge made a lasting impression on me.

When Desmond ran aground we sent a camera crew in a plane to find him. Having just come through the treacherous Bass Strait, fatigue had been his downfall and a wind shift had taken him onto the rocks while he was asleep. Our cameraman found him dispirited and dishevelled and desperately tired as he struggled to clear the boat of anything worth salvaging. With a microphone shoved in his face at such a moment in his life he could not have been blamed if he had pleaded for time to think, found some excuse for his predicament, or told the camera crew simply to leave him alone. But Desmond stopped what he was doing, gave the crew five minutes of his time, and said: "I can blame no one but myself for this. When you sail on your own you are responsible for everything that happens. This is the essence of singlehanding. The sea is a harsh element – and I got it wrong." With that he went back to work. It took great courage to say what he had said, and Desmond maintained an exceptional dignity. It contrasted markedly with one or two competitors in subsequent races who blamed faulty equipment and the incompetence of others for the difficulties or disasters they encountered.

Frenchman Philippe Jeantot also impressed me throughout the race. He arrived in Newport with the best sponsored boat, a purpose-built racing thoroughbred, *Credit Agricole* – the first of the "new generation" of long-distance singlehanded racers that became known as "BOC boats". He was the favourite to win, and no one was surprised when he arrived at the first stop in Cape Town almost two weeks ahead of his nearest rival. He was a former paratrooper in the French Army and a diver by profession. In fact he held the world record for the deepest dive at that time. No doubt his experience as a deep sea diver had taught him the importance of attention to detail, but he was mature far beyond his twenty-nine years. He remained unchanged by the success of winning the race and all the media and public attention lavished on him during the event. He lacked the arrogance and unpredictable selfishness that so often attends outstanding performance and notoriety in sport. He was the real progenitor of modern singlehanded passage racing, with his then unique combination of technical skills, personality, effective sponsorship and public relations, and a boat that was a significant breakthrough in both concept and design. He changed the face of such events as The BOC Challenge for ever, and had many seeking to emulate his approach in subsequent races.

Aside from these individual examples of outstanding character, the overriding memory I have of the first BOC was the bond that existed between the racers and the sense of "family" that built up among them and with those organizing the event. It was an extraordinary experience for everyone involved and many lasting friendships were forged. While the character and influence of the sailors had been largely responsible for this, it probably would not have happened if it had not been for Robin Knox-Johnston's own individual style and personality in running the race. It was Robin who declared in advance that "this race is so tough, everyone who finishes the course must be considered a winner." I liked that thought and it has been a recurring theme of the race ever since.

The BOC Challenge had been a great success by almost any measure, and it had attracted considerable media attention around the world. Everything about it and those who competed in it inspired me. We all wondered how this success would cause it to change the next time round.

In the best book ever written about any of The BOC Challenge races, *Out There*, published soon after the first event, its authors Herb McCormick and George Day wrote: "The first BOC Challenge was conceived and raced by enthusiastic adventurers, whose seamanship and personal integrity made the race a success. The ranks of professionals may crowd out the amateurs in future races, diluting the camaraderie of the fleet with a competitiveness born as much by their will to win as from the corporate sponsors that will make future races possible. Never will there be another round-the-world race like this premier edition. But the traditions established in this first race will continue to nourish racers, offshore sailors and adventurers everywhere for years to come."

~~~~~~~~~

Four years later we had twenty-five starters, most were sponsored, and about half the fleet had been built for the event. Seventeen finished. It had its share of drama and tragedy too. Not far short of Sydney, American Warren Luhrs was dismasted on board *Thursday's Child* and he sailed into port under jury rig. On the third leg of the race Englishman Harry Mitchell ran aground in New Zealand and was forced to withdraw. On the same leg, twenty-eight-year-old Canadian John Hughes capsized, lost his mast, and then sailed a staggering four thousand miles under jury rig around Cape Horn to the Falkland Islands.

Worst of all was the tragic and still unexplained loss of Frenchman Jacques de Roux. A submarine captain by profession, he was one of the most competitive yet prudent of seamen, with huge reserves of experience to draw on. The satellite tracking system showed him following an uncharacteristically erratic course a few days out from Sydney. Eventually a plane and power boat were dispatched to check. There was no one on board. There was a half-eaten meal in the galley of his neatly kept yacht and no sign of either panic or disaster. She was sailed to the nearest port and hauled out. There was a deep gash in her keel. No one had a good idea how it got there. It was hard to believe Jacques had been lost in what we must presume to have been a freak accident. Not only was he an accomplished and experienced singlehanded sailor, he was also a gentle man with much humility and wit, and a wide circle of admirers – especially after his heroic persistence in the previous race when he was rescued by Richard Broadhead after bailing his boat continuously for three days in the icy Southern Ocean.

By the end of this second BOC Challenge, Robin had tired of the administrative chores involved in running the race and had developed a powerful thirst to compete in it himself. It was sheer providence that, the day after he and I discussed this at the prize-giving, Mark Schrader approached me with a proposition. Mark, the first American to sail around the world alone south of all five Capes, and one of the successful competitors in The BOC Challenge just finished, was a Sixties psychology graduate from the University of California, Berkeley, and with his wife Michele had run a residential school for delinquent, maladjusted and educationally subnormal children in Seattle. We agreed this was a fine background for someone wanting to run a race for singlehanders!

"Look," he said to me earnestly. "I don't think you realize what a great event this is, and how much greater it could be in the future. I want to help you realize its potential."

Mark's ambitions for the race were in line with my own. I wanted to see it grow, I wanted it to achieve more in terms of publicity and international notoriety, I wanted it to be more professional, but I also wanted it to retain its unique personality and "family" spirit. So did he. We made a few amendments to the rules, changed the third stopover from Rio, where almost everyone had had a bad time, to Punta del Este in Uruguay, and talked to some sports marketing agencies about finding new sponsors to help share the financial burden of funding the race.

Six feet tall and stocky, with a greying beard, rich sense of humour and a naughty schoolboy's twinkle in his eye, Mark was a good team leader as well as an accomplished solo circumnavigator. He had a short fuse for idleness and incompetence but a generous heart for those with dreams and grit. This probably came from a childhood helping his family farm in Nebraska – "a dirt farm that suffered enough droughts, pests, and storms to finally drive us off the land. It taught me lots about life, and how to fix diesel engines!"

By the time the next race was on the horizon, Mark was a partner in a yacht brokerage and charter business. He took a leave of absence from this and his wife Michele turned their horse farm over to a caretaker for a year while the next race was on. He managed the race well and coped admirably with its increasing complexities. We were expecting more from the stopover ports and they were demanding more of the event. Competitors and their sponsors were becoming more demanding too. We had imposed tighter budgetary controls, but sharpened our own expectations of the event in terms of media publicity, customer and VIP entertainment, and the need to attract other people's money into the race. The sports marketing agency we had hired said they expected to raise two million dollars. They raised just a few hundred thousand and we fell out over it. They helped us to land IBM as the "presenting sponsor" of the race, but the race management team managed to bring in Champagne Mumm and AT&T. Mark and I resolved to do this job too on our own next time round.

Once again the event was deemed a success. And once again it had its share of drama and tragedy. Frenchwoman Isabelle Autissier was dismasted in the Southern Ocean and sailed into Sydney under jury rig. Josh Hall, at twenty-eight the youngest skipper in the race, was forced to have an operation on his left knee in Sydney after a bad fall on board, and he finished the race in a surgical brace. South African John Martin thinks he must have hit a "growler", a chunk of ice, on the third leg and had to be rescued from the holed and sinking *Allied Bank* by fellow countryman Bertie Reed. But the greatest and seemingly most pointless tragedy was the suicide of one of the most popular men in the fleet, Yukoh Tada of Japan. He withdrew from the race in Sydney, having decided that the boat he had designed and built with funding from many supporters in Japan was dangerously unsuitable for the passage. To those of us outside his culture it was assumed that this "loss of face" was more than he could bear. Yukoh was a fine man, with great humour and humanity, and he had many more friends and admirers than he ever knew.

Mark and I began planning the fourth edition of the race as soon as the third was over. BOC had a new chairman, Patrick Rich, and there had been some anxiety about whether or not he would support it in future. We kept the suspense going until the night of the prize-giving, when Pat announced there would indeed be another BOC Challenge.

~~~~~~~~~

Mark and I decided the time had come for a step change in several aspects of the event – to encourage its further growth, and to make up for some of the mistakes we had made in the past.

We held a detailed review meeting with Pete Dunning, who had been race coordinator from the beginning. In fact Pete had spent most of the past twenty years managing the Goat Island Marina in Newport which had been "home" to singlehanded sailing in North America. His experience, quiet common sense and sound judgement had been a key factor in the style and character of The

BOC Challenge since its inception. Now retired, he was able to give us more of his time, which proved invaluable as we developed our thinking on how we might better use the rapidly emerging technology for communications, tracking the fleet, and for providing competitors with a good weather service (having decided to ban private routing and other assistance not generally available to all contestants).

In fact, this whole area became a focus of attention in our search for other sponsors to join BOC in the event. IBM equipment and technology acquired a new status of importance for the race, their new and powerful laptop computer, the ThinkPad, becoming an essential piece of on-board equipment which we gave to each competitor. IBM computers were also key to the race management operation. We struck a deal with Trimble Navigation, enabling us to provide each competitor with a Trimble Galaxy unit which combines the Global Positioning System with Inmarsat-C satellite data communications capabilities when linked to the IBM ThinkPads. With these essential pieces of hardware in place, we concluded negotiations with COMSAT to furnish some dazzling new technology that would enable race management to track the fleet, communicate with each boat individually or collectively, and provide each skipper with a customized weather service and some ingenious new routing software to help plot a course on board. Other global sponsorships negotiated for the race all added value to the event in one way or another – Helly-Hansen's new line of sailing clothing, Hertz rent-a-car; travel discounts through the Rosenbluth Group and The Travel Company; CompuServe on-line information systems; Medical SeaPak on-board first-aid kits and Maritime Health Services medical advice; Omega watches; and a large supply of Champagne Mumm!

Media coverage had been good in previous races; but we knew the event deserved even better. We hired Dan McConnell to help us, attracted by his experience of promoting great adventures like Everest climbs and the Iditarod sled-dog race across Alaska. He brought in Lazlo Pal, a producer of adventure movies, to help with the television package which we knew to be essential to our ambitions. He hired Herb McCormick for in-port media relations, on a leave of absence from his job as executive editor of *Cruising World*.

We also decided to upgrade significantly our demands on the host ports. We had an event that brought international attention to wherever it went, so we laid down some clear requirements for its in-port infrastructure. Dave Abromowitz, our local organizing committee chairman in Cape Town, helped keep the event there by rounding up support from local businesses as well as the tourism authority and the Royal Cape Yacht Club. We were glad not to have to move from this most hospitable of ports. Sydney too came close to losing the event to Hobart; but our local organizing committee there, under the chairmanship of Ian Kiernan (who competed in the second BOC Challenge) pulled local business and political support together to ensure Sydney could meet our new port brief. Mark and I visited several ports on the east coast of the US before deciding on a change from Newport to Charleston. The event had outgrown Newport and the handful of committed enthusiasts could not pull the local community behind it. It was a pity, and we knew we were entering uncharted waters in Charleston. But what the team in Charleston lacked in experience of such an event they made up for with commitment and enthusiasm and the very strong desire to have the race. They saw it as a focal point for their new multi-million-dollar waterfront development, and as a vehicle for putting Charleston on the map as a place to visit. They saw how they could use the event for their own purposes, and that was the key to it. We knew that the more good they could see our race doing for their community, the more they would put into it.

We had toyed with the idea of starting and/or finishing the race in Britain. Mark and I reviewed proposals from five ports in the southwest of England and in Wales. Even though we had finally decided to start and finish the race in Charleston, we still wanted to find a way of tying Europe into the event. We were so impressed with the presentation from the tiny Cornish town of Falmouth that we decided to run a transatlantic race from there in advance of the round-the-world event.

During the first BOC Challenge a school administrator in Newport called Mame Reynolds developed a teaching programme that used the race to help kids in her schools learn maths, science, geography, and "life skills". She and I talked about her programme often, and finally we put in some seed-money to help develop it for schools elsewhere in the US. It was a successful educational programme that fed largely from Mame's drive and commitment to it. She called it the Student Ocean Challenge, and by the second race, hundreds of thousands of school children across America had access to it. We helped Mame to take it to other countries in the third race, and gradually added an "environ-mental" element to the programme.

Concern for the world's marine environment had become a strong feature of The BOC Challenge. BOC was inclined to have the race support this effort, but the momentum for action really came from a handful of competitors.

Ian Kiernan from Australia, for example, says it was his participation in The

BOC Challenge 1986-87 that awakened him to the issue. When he returned to his home in Sydney he worked diligently on a project he called "Clean-Up Sydney Harbour". He, along with the public relations "queen" of Sydney, Kim McKay, who has helped to publicize every BOC Challenge in Australia, put the project together in 1988. Several thousand Sydney-siders helped collect many tons of plastic and other rubbish, three thousand syringes, four cars and a bus from in and around Sydney Harbour one day in March 1989. "Clean-Up Australia" followed, and now the two are working with UN agencies to "Clean-Up The World". It was for this work that Kiernan was named "Australian of the Year" on Australia Day 1994.

When Mark Schrader went round the world first he did so to support the Marine Conservation Society of America. In The BOC Challenge 1986-87 he was one of the competitors leading the parade in encouraging others to "keep your plastic crap on board till you reach port." When he became race director we created BOC Oceanwatch, a combined environmental and educational programme incorporating the Student Ocean Challenge and the ambition of new initiatives in marine environmental protection and conservation. Pat Rich had this high on his agenda of expectations of the event too.

In Britain we gave this some muscle by funding a project through The BOC Foundation for the Environment of which I was also a director. It would use local schools in Falmouth, Eastbourne, Swansea and Humberside, to spend a year "profiling" the local coastal environment, determining the sources of pollution and recommending remedial action. A similar programme was put in place in Charleston, and several hundred schools across the country agreed to participate again in the Student Ocean Challenge education programme. BOC businesses in South Africa and Australia undertook to support the education programme in their countries too.

Knowing that I would be taking part in The BOC Challenge this time rather than simply fussing about it from the sidelines, I appointed one of our US staff members, Kent Martin, as event director. He knew nothing about sailing and had no history with the race. But he knew about event management and understood BOC's agenda, and would add this insight to the team.

The BOC Challenge had come a long way from those first days in the early Eighties. I felt I had put everything and everyone in place to ensure its success in 1994-95.

PREPARATIONS

Preparing my "campaign" for the Challenge was not a simple task. For a start, I had to decide what I was preparing for. The answer to this was not as obvious as it may seem. One simple lesson, from life and business: first define the task, only then is it possible to develop a plan that can succeed. If you don't know where you're going, any road will take you there!

The task in this case was not simply to prepare a boat and myself to participate in The BOC Challenge. How I chose to define my ambition or objectives as a competitor would determine the extent and nature of the preparations. The requirements in terms of boat, budget, skills and physical fitness necessary to win either Class would be quite different to those needed for just a safe passage around the course.

It did not take long to analyze the key factors in this. A boat that could win would require a budget I could not afford without massive sponsorship. Sponsorship on that scale introduced a level of commitment to others and attendant pressures I did not want. Besides, it would also require me to have a level of sailing skill and seamanship that would make winning a credible proposition – and at my age, with my relative lack of experience, and in the time available, that simply was not remotely possible. Ergo, my project would have to be closer to the other end of the scale. Yet, I did not want to scrape by in the smallest boat allowed by the rules, take forever, and have no time to enjoy the festivities (and some rest) in the stopover ports.

To me, the line between success and failure was clear, and it was crossing the finish line back at Charleston. There could be varying degrees of success, like doing well against the competition – and degrees of failure I did not want to contemplate. I decided, therefore, that I wanted to complete the circumnavigation, in some comfort, and in a respectable time. It seemed to me that this was the most I should reasonably expect. That then became the task.

Preparations alone were a marathon undertaking, requiring a heavy investment of time, money and emotion. It was not entirely without pain and frustration, and it required planning, persistence and patience. With the number of others volunteered, press-ganged or paid into various kinds of involvement in the project over time, it was a process that also underscored the reality that mine was far from being a "singlehanded" challenge. Yet it was all, for the most part, hugely enjoyable, even therapeutic. For me the preparations became a deeply rewarding element of the whole enterprise. How this must have contrasted with the professional racers for many of whom the preparations were a tedious necessity, a means to an end, along with all the attendant agonies of big-time sponsors with their accountants and insatiable publicity machines. For them, being at sea was mostly what mattered, and a real shot at winning was what most of them had promised their backers. Yet, how envious I was of their sailing skills, seamanship, and self-confidence in this arena.

But the professionals in the fleet knew that painstaking preparations could make all the difference in the world to success or failure. Isabelle Autissier and Giovanni Soldini were not alone in the lengths to which they went to ready themselves for the race. Isabelle had her new 60-footer designed and built a couple of years before the race so she could undergo exhaustive sea trials well in advance. In fact her successful attack on the New York to San Francisco record around Cape Horn was a planned part of her preparations for the BOC. Giovanni bought the 50-foot Class II winner from the previous BOC Challenge to practise on and learn all he could before designing and building a new boat for the 1994-95 event.

My preparations began with the purchase of a suitable boat in September 1991. Mark Schrader and I had arranged an eight-day tour of five ports on the east coast of the US to help us decide where we should start the 1994-95 event. We had a Sunday free while we were in Newport and I had picked up some details on a couple of boats that interested me. At that time, I was far from certain I could organize my life to do "the BOC", but I had decided to buy a boat that would be suitable for it . . . just in case!

Sky Catcher (then *Retrac*) was moored in Gloucester, Massachusetts, a couple of hours north of Newport. Mark and I decided to look her over. To my eye, she was a pretty boat, with a proud countenance, tall and slender Bergstrom rig with swept-back spreaders, a clean deck and compact cockpit, but perhaps too much freeboard and just a bit "stubby" at the stern. Out of sight was a thin blade keel with a winged bulb at the end of it, almost ten feet below the waterline. She was champing and pulling at her mooring, like a restless horse at its bit.

She could take pride in her brief past — as *Mariko*, and with Courtney

Hazelton as skipper, she had won her Class in the 1988 singlehanded transatlantic race (for which she had been built that year). I had met Courtney when he
was working on a boat in the 1986-87 BOC race, and we had met again in
Plymouth at the start of the transatlantic event. He was short and stocky, with
long blondish hair tied in a ponytail and piercing blue eyes. He looked like he
ought to be on a Harley-Davidson with a full set of Hell's Angels studded leather
gear, but he was as mild-mannered a man as you will ever meet; he knew how to
sail hard, and he knew how to fix most things. He had been a boat builder and
inspector at Hunter Marine.

Mariko had been built in 1988 as a development project by Hunter Marine in
Florida. They had taken the mould for a Hunter 45 off-site and put a construction team at work to build a boat that would be light yet strong enough for
serious blue-water racing. After the 1988 race, she was sold to a businessman
who owned a cruising boat and wanted to try singlehanding. I was told he tried
it once in her and was scared half to death. She had been hanging on her mooring more or less ever since. She was clean but very open above decks, and empty
below except for a couple of bunks and a primitive galley. She looked uncared
for and in need of exercise, but she looked sound and I quickly built up a picture
in my mind of what changes would improve her for my purposes.

I telephoned Courtney in Florida for an opinion on the boat, and a view on
what some of the modifications I had in mind might cost. I put in a low-ball offer
on the boat and told the broker that if the deal was not done by the time I left the
US eight days later, it would be withdrawn. We had several conversations in
the following days, and the deal was struck over the phone from the airport
lounge twenty minutes before my departure for London.

Mark's advice was invaluable as I fine-tuned my thinking on what basic
changes to make. He and a friend sailed her for me to Jacksonville, Florida,
where I had arranged for Courtney to do some of the work on her. Courtney
introduced me to a young marine architect, Skip Miller, from nearby St
Augustine. A gangling, laid-back man around thirty, Skip's passion was surfing
and I hardly ever saw him in anything but shorts and sneakers. He was perfect
for the project. He had a quiet intelligence, a sense of aesthetics that matched
mine, and considerable imagination and ingenuity in translating concepts from
the back of an envelope into practical solutions. We spent hours discussing modifications and new ideas on the boat and over the phone. Sketches and new
thoughts were exchanged through the mail and over the fax machines in his
Florida office and my home in England. This was fun, and Skip was wonderful

to work with. He had a lot of ideas of his own to contribute, but he knew how to listen.

Gradually *Sky Catcher* began to take shape. And once work began on the refit, new ideas became imperatives too – like modifying the layout of the water-ballast system, re-ordering the stowage space and seating arrangement, and adding a "venturi slot" to the hull (about which, more later). Most of the big items were completed in Jacksonville, and Courtney's workmanship was both painstaking and expert; but we moved her to St Augustine halfway through so Skip could have the project more tightly under his control. This was a good move for a number of reasons, not least because it meant he ended up knowing every bolt, fitting and idiosyncrasy of the boat, which made him invaluable as shore-side crew organizing *Sky Catcher* for the whole venture. He would be my key contact when anything needed fixing at sea, and he had agreed to be in each port during the race to help fix whatever needed fixing there too.

We added a little over three feet to her stern which improved her looks considerably, and her performance. We removed the bridge-deck, improved access to the companionway, and added a fixed cuddy over the forward end of the cockpit for foul-weather protection. We also added a radar/antenna arch at the stern to accommodate an array of equipment including cameras and powerful waterproof stereo speakers. Down below we added watertight bulkheads fore and aft to comply with the BOC rules; a sail bin (that converted to a queen-size berth) in the new forward cabin; a bosunry, clothing lockers, storage bins, settee/pipe-berths and shelving either side in the main saloon; a fully equipped galley, and decent heads with a hot freshwater shower. Everything about it was practical and looked right. But Skip's absolute triumph was the gimballed navigation station. There was hardly a feature on it he had not designed, built, modified and fine-tuned himself. With an after-market BMW fully reclining car seat, the whole assembly including the nav' table was built to rotate through an angle of forty-five degrees – making it possible to be upright and comfortable at almost any angle of the boat's heel. A full range of navigation and communications electronics was added, along with a CD and tape system for good music.

I wanted lots of "redundancy" in essential on-board systems that related to good seamanship, ease of passage-making, and peace of mind. A full inventory of safety equipment was installed, including three Emergency Position Indicator Radio Beacons. We put in two wind generators, four large solar panels, a 150amp/hr alternator on the engine, and a separate small diesel generator. We installed a water desalinator, and carried a separate emergency hand-operated machine as well. We had four ways to steer the boat, even before I had to touch the tiller myself: the Monitor windvane, an Autohelm 2000 driving the trim-tab on the rudder, and both 4000 and 7000 Autohelm models driving the tiller direct. Below in the navigation station we had two back-up Global Position Systems from Magellan, and two IBM ThinkPad computers. For communications with the outside world we had installed a fixed and a hand-held Icom VHF radio, an Icom IC-M700 single side-band radio, the Trimble Galaxy satellite communications unit for data – and to all this we added a leased Scientific Atlanta Inmarsat-M Mari-Star satellite telephone. In addition to the two-burner gimballed stove in the galley, we fitted a separate Balmar Sea-swing single-burner. Separate CD and tape players fed the powerful saloon and cockpit speakers, and we also had portable CD and tape systems as back-up.

We had two suits of sails made, almost all of Sobstad's Genesis cloth. We had a mainsail and staysail built to try out in the 1993 Bermuda One-Two Race and other sea trials. Keith Lorence, a partner in Sobstad's Seattle loft, sailed with us in late 1993 and then built the rest of the inventory: a new fully battened mainsail, new staysail and two headsails, and a large "drifter" on a separate furler. Keith gave us a lot of attention, but the choice of sail material proved to be a bad one. I came to wish I had gone a more conventional route with Dacron or one of the more robust materials.

I was reminded often of the time when, during the first sail I ever had on a keel boat of my own, Dick Kenny told me that everything on a boat, except the sails being used, slowed it down. Our modifications must have added a thousand pounds to our overall weight, but I classed them all as essential to my safety, comfort, or peace of mind. But I was increasingly conscious of the mounting cost of the project as well.

New ideas came from many sources. I never tired of asking questions of people who had a lot of singlehanded experience, those who had sailed around the world before, or those who knew about boat design and equipment. One such source was Lars Bergstrom, the closest thing to genius I've ever met. "Lars from Mars" is what some called him. His mind seemed to operate at a different level to the rest of mankind, but he never made you feel dumb. Six-foot-something and with a shock of white hair, he was an engineering wizard with many inventions to his name. He was closely involved in the original design of the rig and keel on *Sky Catcher* and had done most of the design work on both *Hunter's Child* and *Thursday's Child* – both entries in The BOC Challenge 1994-95, the latter being a true breakthrough boat in the early 1980s.

Lars and I talked about my boat a couple of times soon after I had bought her, and he came sailing on her as well in the summer of 1993. He had many thoughts to contribute; more than I could handle. But one in particular intrigued me.

"You know, you could think of putting a 'venturi slot' in the hull," he said thoughtfully, in his thick lilting Swedish accent. "What we always try to do is reduce the wetted surface of a boat because that only produces drag and slows the boat down. That's particularly true of the back of the boat where the hull rises because it is not only wetted surface, but it creates a kind of vacuum which tends to hold the boat back even more. So, if we can introduce a flow of air particularly over the back part of the hull we should be reducing drag and increasing speed."

He'd probably had the idea in the bath one day, and it seemed to make sense the way he described it. I wondered why no one had thought of it before, and I knew that any other engineer would have blinded me with science in describing it to me. But Lars knew how to communicate.

Skip took the idea and made it work. Thirty ¾-inch holes were drilled in a line around the hull about twelve feet from the stern and just behind the aft watertight bulkhead. An open tube was glassed over the holes inside the boat, ending in a single wide opening in the cockpit to provide a free flow of air. A lip was glassed into the outside of the hull just forward of the holes to create a water flow that would suck the air out and over the last quarter of the hull. This was the last major modification to the boat, completed when she was out of the water in the spring of 1994 before her passage to England for The BOC Transatlantic Challenge.

Lars also persuaded Steve Pettengill, and Hunter Marine President Warren Luhrs, to build in a venturi slot on *Hunter's Child* while she was undergoing extensive modifications at the Hunter Marine yard in St Augustine. Steve later confirmed the effectiveness of the system . . . he said it whistled and hummed loudly at high speeds.

〜〜〜〜〜〜〜〜〜

Preparing myself for the Challenge was less demanding and less expensive than preparing the boat. Indeed, it was not until I had the boat in a state that I could seriously contemplate doing the race that I began tackling this aspect of the project. There were four parts to it: organizing my life so I could have the time to do the race, my physical fitness, my state of mind, and "provisioning" for my bodily and psychological needs.

In November 1992 I had a long conversation with Pat Rich, the then chairman and chief executive of BOC, reminding him that it had long been my plan to retire at fifty-five (in December 1995) and that I desperately wanted to compete in the next BOC Challenge. I asked him to agree to me having a leave of absence to do so; but undertook to continue to be responsible for the successful outcome of the race for BOC.

"There's just one proviso," Pat told me, agreeing to my request. "I don't want anyone else to know about this until January 1994 when you have to lodge your entry – I don't want you being a lame duck around here." It was a generous decision on his part, but he sailed himself and he had some empathy for my scheme!

Keeping it a secret was tough. As 1993 rolled on I had to bring a few people into the plan, particularly those involved with the boat. What had begun as a project to upgrade her had become a complex and expensive enterprise, and funding all this work was giving me a problem. If I was not to end the race in debt, I would have to raise funds from elsewhere.

In the summer of 1993 I worked out a detailed budget that would see me through to the finish line and secured an overdraft facility at the bank to cover it. That became my "worst case". Reducing this exposure would be tough, I knew that, and I was handicapped in two ways in seeking other people's support. The first was that I did not stand a cat in hell's chance of winning anything. The second, a self-inflicted but necessary handicap, was that I was not prepared to promise anything to a potential sponsor that I was not entirely confident I could deliver. I had seen too many others in the past fall into this trap – promise anything to secure the money and be in the race! Pressure, misery, and sometimes the threat of worse lay down that path. It could not possibly be worth it.

I knew the president of Hunter Marine, Warren Luhrs, and he put me in touch with his marketing people. I did not ask for money, but I did want to know if they could help in other ways – berthing at their yard in St Augustine, technical help while I was there, and some back-up during the race. Since they had already decided to enter their 60-footer *Hunter's Child* in the BOC and would have a full technical crew with a container workshop in each port to support that campaign, maybe they could give me some time and space too? The Hunter people were interested in my project, wanted it to succeed and pledged their support. It would cost them virtually nothing, but be worth a lot to me. It made sense.

I also wrote to a few people I knew in other companies. I had worked out a schedule of commitments I was prepared to make in return for varying levels of funding. I did not want to "sell" the name of the boat to a sponsor, nor did I want any one sponsor to feel they owned the project, the boat, or me. I figured that close to a hundred thousand dollars would cover the major costs associated with actually doing the race, and my "going to heaven" solution would be to have this split between three principal sponsors.

For the most part, I got the replies I expected: "We'd love to help, but we have a policy of not sponsoring individuals"...."My chairman is into golf and I'm afraid that's all we're allowed to get involved with"...."If it was up to me I'd help of course, but we have a sponsorship committee and they don't like dangerous sports..." But it wasn't all like that.

I opened the letter from Jim Baldwin, then chairman and chief executive of the Carbide Graphite Group Inc, with a sense of hope but little expectation. I had known Jim since joining BOC. He had been a director of the company and, in the mid-Eighties, completed a leveraged buy-out of our carbon-graphite business with the division's president, Nick Kaiser. Jim's letter began: "So you're really going to do it – congratulations! You can count on us! We will go for the full package! And enjoy every blooming minute of it!"

I wondered if there were any more like Jim out there – I needed two more like him – and continued the search even after the start of the race.

Towards the end of 1993 a few people in BOC's world headquarters in Windlesham, Surrey, where I had my office, began to wonder what I was up to. The company had a corporate membership at the Foxhills Country Club, ten minutes down the road. I started going there three times a week to use the gym. I had one of the instructors map out a programme for me to improve my aerobic fitness and increase my upper body strength. By early 1994 I was going four or five times a week and I began to feel I was finally getting somewhere with it.

I did fifteen minutes on the rowing machine, five minutes on the tread machine, then about twenty-five minutes of weight training. I wasn't trying to be Superman, but I knew that this kind of programme would help me in several ways. I had always found that when I was fit I felt good, slept better, and was more relaxed about life in general. A reasonable level of general fitness would give me a better attitude and aptitude on board – especially for the long periods of time on my own that I could expect in The BOC Challenge. I knew too that if I had the physical strength to make reasonably light work of sail handling and other tasks operating the boat, I would not only enjoy it more and have a greater sense of self-confidence, I would be less inclined to put off essential chores for lack of energy or inclination. It was so easy to sit in the cockpit with the wind rising, knowing that reefing or a sail change was required, yet doing nothing and telling oneself the wind would probably die down soon enough. These bad decisions almost always led to grief; inevitably the task itself became more strenuous and difficult, but it also often meant straining or breaking equipment.

I knew that many of my fellow competitors would be on a more demanding training regime than mine, and maybe I should have been too. But I had a job that gave me little enough free time and I found the whole process of working out in the gym pretty boring. I could not have done it at all for long if it had not been for the goal I had set myself: to achieve a level of fitness and strength that would make life on board easier. As it was, even my modest programme suffered a significant setback in late March 1994. My left knee had been troubling me, but I put this down to evidence that the programme was working – on the basis of "no pain, no gain". I was wrong. Suddenly one day my knee started to swell, hurt, and click. An MRI scan revealed a lateral tear in the cartilage. After consultations with a surgeon I decided not to have it removed (there was not enough time for a full recovery before my transatlantic crossings in May and July). I'd have to live with it and be careful. The damage had evidently been done many years earlier, and I discovered the worst exercise I could have subjected it to was rowing!

I had thought long and hard about what I could do to prepare my mind for the Challenge. I was not sure what steps one could take in anticipation of an extended period of aloneness and for dealing with trauma in a lone situation. I did not think that one's mental preparedness could be approached in the same way as the physical preparation. I knew competitors who consulted psychiatrists, sleep therapists and others with claims to similar black arts. I heard of one who trained on long-distance passages with electrodes taped permanently to shaved patches on his head for some kind of "scientific" analysis. I had a sneaky feeling there was more mumbo-jumbo and witch-doctoring in this area than I wanted contact with, so I avoided seeking advice I knew I was likely to disdain and disregard.

In any event, I did not believe I would have much of a problem with being alone – I never had before. But I knew that my state of mind would have a significant effect on my enjoyment of the Challenge and my performance in it. There were two dimensions to this.

The first and crucial factor would be to have absolute confidence in the boat and in my own ability to see the project through. That is why I insisted on so much redundancy in essential on-board systems for navigation, steering the boat, and generating power. That is why I also negotiated a leave of absence that allowed me to depart in April, four and a half months before the start of the main event. It would give me ample time to test everything on board fully and to build up an extensive base of experience on the boat with two Atlantic crossings, including The BOC Transatlantic Challenge.

The second would be not to take too many shore-side troubles with me to sea. There would be no running away from them out there and alone at sea they would only fester and grow. Personal worries and emotional baggage would weigh heavier with every passing day in these circumstances. In this, my life had become both complicated and simplified by a relationship that had begun as friendship and developed into love. The complication was two-fold. First, it added an emotional dimension to my life that might become a source of anxiety for me and would, I knew, for her once the race was on. Second, Julia worked in BOC and keeping "us" reasonably secret so long as we both were there was a tough assignment. But this was all a small price to pay for the enduring qualities of the relationship. We became engaged just after Christmas 1993. Julia became increasingly supportive in the administration of the project which simplified things for me considerably. I knew that my doing the race would be very difficult for her; but she was determined not to let this be a burden on our relationship or the project.

There was also the question of provisioning. What would I need to take with me on board to nourish my physical and mental wellbeing for such long periods of time and to accommodate the extremes I would encounter? I would be alone, isolated as if in space, in my little "capsule" on the ocean and with whatever I had furnished as my "life support system". I would have to contend with debilitating tropical heat and endless weeks of sub-zero temperatures; days of balmy sunshine and gentle breezes, and fierce Southern Ocean storms with waves the size of office blocks; days when I would be brimming with inner peace and self-confidence, and times when I would be scared out of my wits, exhausted, demoralized.

Good food and good clothing would go a long way towards taking care of my physical needs. Good music and good books would help to moderate my state of mind, providing entertainment as well as food for thought.

A lot of technology had gone into the design and fabrics for suitable clothing in recent years. What was available today was significantly better than that of even a few years ago. Helly-Hansen, the Norwegian sailing clothing company, provided us all with a few items of worthwhile gear for nothing, and made their entire range available to us at a discount. This supplemented my existing inventory of clothing. I decided to take three sets of everything I might need for really bad weather – heavy duty foul-weather "oilies", a quilted inner layer, thermal underwear, and next to the skin a silk long-sleeved vest and long johns. Three layers of gloves: silk, thermals, and outers. Two layers of socks and balaclava: silk and thermals. The layer of silk was not some personal fetish. It was inherited wisdom from a previous circumnavigator who told me it absorbed and dispersed sweat and made life inside all the other layers infinitely more congenial!

One of the problems with long-distance passage-making is that it tends to be bursts of intense activity as punctuation marks in a narrative of gentle idleness. You clothe yourself for the long periods of modest inactivity, yet must somehow accommodate the frenzied attack on a sail or a winch. Staying dry and warm on a cold day and in bad weather is a neat trick, but one worth getting right. Staying clean would be important, too – and for this the answer was large quantities of baby "wet-wipes", as well as mild liquid soap.

Food would be a dilemma. I liked good food, and I enjoyed cooking. I did not eat fish or fatty meat, and I did not like soggy vegetables. On a long journey on a boat, especially one without a freezer, that was a problem. The only competitor I know to have had a freezer on board was Australian Kanga Birtles in the last BOC Challenge – he said he was not prepared to go so long without a fresh steak, and frequently tormented other competitors over the radio with descriptions of his diet. Most, though, took simple rations of freeze-dried food, rice and tins of tuna – and little or no alcohol. Niah Vaughan was one who ran a "dry" boat but his diet was enlivened by a number of whole home-cured hams!

The eventual answer, on *Sky Catcher*, was a combination of irradiated meals, good tinned meat (hard to find), tinned vegetables, fresh vegetables for the first few days, and enough fresh onions and garlic to last the trip – one of each for every day I expected to be at sea. I have yet to eat a meal at sea that could not benefit from the flavour and texture of freshly fried onion and garlic. This would take care of my basic needs; but what of my "fancies" – those days when one needed something special? I packed a good stock of lightly salted peanuts and dried fruit, Toblerone, Snickers and Mars bars, enough apples and oranges for one each day, tinned fruit and sweet condensed milk, honey, marmalade and black cherry jam, Camembert cheese and butter, real bread for the first couple of weeks and Scandinavian wholewheat crispbread for the rest of each leg.

At least two good meals a day was what my body needed at sea, and in between times it needed titbits and snacks, chocolate and nuts. And tea of course, and coffee too – good fresh-brewed coffee as well as the instant stuff. To this had to be added boxes of wine (one glass with dinner), mini-bottles of Mumm's champagne (for those special moments), and good single malt whisky (to be consumed in moderation, but essential for the best and worst occasions).

Selecting the right diet of music and books was almost more difficult than choosing the food I would take. I knew little about music, but loved to listen to it. Good music to me could be anything from Pink Floyd to Puccini or Pavarotti, and I assembled a library of almost a hundred CDs and tapes within that range. I knew from many past experiences that music could help me hold on to or change a mood.

Books were more of a problem because they took up more space than CDs, and while I knew I would always have time to listen to music, I did not know how much time or "mind" I would be able to devote to reading. So I decided to cheat. On each leg I would take a couple of books to read, and other books on tape to listen to. That seemed to me to be a balanced and fairly undemanding diet.

~~~~~~~~~~

The closing phase of preparations for The BOC Challenge was The BOC Transatlantic Challenge singlehanded race from Falmouth to Charleston, preceded by a west-to-east transatlantic "shakedown" with Skip as crew.

The passage from America to England in May was tough. We had nine days of gale-force winds, and a "knockdown" which wiped some of the equipment from the top of the mast when it dipped into the sea. But *Sky Catcher* handled herself very well with the Monitor windvane at the helm almost all the time. We sailed close to four thousand miles in a creditable twenty-one days. Our best day's run was 240 miles – a high average of 10 knots for a boat of our length, even though it was accomplished with the help of the Gulf Stream. We did better than two hundred miles on another five days, and our top recorded speed was just under 19 knots.

It was the perfect opportunity for Skip and me to put the boat and her equipment through a little torment and stress. We discovered a few leaks through deck fittings, decided on some modifications in the galley to make it more user-friendly, agreed on some small changes to the deck layout and the need to cover all locker spaces and shelves in the main saloon to reduce the havoc of a future knockdown. The sails, headsails in particular, did not stand up to the passage too well and the Sobstad loft in the UK concluded on examining them that they were nothing like strong enough for the kind of sailing I was doing. Keith Lorence agreed to build replacements. Generally, though, the passage confirmed *Sky Catcher*'s suitability for blue-water solo racing and validated all the major decisions we had taken on both the changes we had made to her and the equipment we had added.

My lasting memories of the trip were the knockdown and our final gale in the last three days. We were almost on a dead run with 40-60 knots of wind whistling up from behind us. As we sailed onto the Continental Shelf the seas became shorter and steeper, with the wave height around twenty-five to thirty feet. Because we were being driven by the wind in the same direction as the waves, the seascape lacked dramatic movement. Under the dark and lowering sky, the waves looked more like rolling hills of black anthracite slurry than water, until the tops of them started to break off and cascade down their steep sides in turquoise and frothing white torrents. Up above, the seagulls were actually flying backwards, their through-the-air speed of 20 knots or so no match for the wind speeds they were encountering. It was a very odd sight indeed to see them flying tail first across our stern and over the boat in the direction in which we were sailing.

Sky Catcher was hauled out at the Pendennis Shipyard the day after we arrived in Falmouth for a week to fix the prop shaft, change some through-hull fittings, and have her bottom faired and anti-fouled. The Autohelm 7000 and Balmar diesel generator were then installed, a new fuel tank constructed and fitted, and the deck leaks fixed. But our work list beyond this seemed endless.

On the BOC docks I met the Reverend David Roberts who ran the Falmouth Mission to Seamen. He had vivid memories of Robin Knox-Johnston's departure from and arrival back in Falmouth in 1969, following his unprecedented non-stop solo circumnavigation. He had given Robin a Bible before he left, which Robin returned at the end of his historic passage suitably inscribed. David quite unexpectedly asked me if I would like to take the same Bible on my circumnavigation. He wrote in it the following inscription: "God speed Nigel. I know that the Good Angel that looked after Robin in the past will surely take care of you in the present." I felt I had been entrusted with a precious artefact.

The last couple of weeks in Falmouth were hectic. Julia juggled her duties as event manager with helping me provision *Sky Catcher* and making sure I left nothing behind. We had no quiet time together at all, which we both regretted.

While the passage to England had been tough, it did not compare with the misery and frustration of The BOC Transatlantic Challenge back to Charleston. I was not in a buoyant mood to begin with. Skip and I had not planned the work programme on *Sky Catcher* well and we had three people working on the boat right up to the moment we were towed from the dock for the start. I threw my bags of clothing onto one of the bunks that morning and had no time to stow any of it before the tow-boat arrived.

Several thousand spectators lined the hills around the harbour to see the start at noon as the morning drizzle turned to rain, and just about everything that could float was out there too. Once at sea I began to relax. The Class I boats romped ahead of us, but it soon became clear that Niah Vaughan in the 50-foot racer *Jimroda II* (ex *Airco Distributor* in which the late Mike Plant won Class II of the second BOC Challenge, and as *New Spirit of Ipswich* Josh Hall brought home to third place in Class II in the third BOC race) and I were going to have a tussle at the head of Class II. We were neck and neck and well ahead of our competitors at the end of the afternoon as we approached the Scilly Isles. I went south of them, and he went north under spinnaker. Three days later I came up on deck with my morning cup of coffee to see him a hundred yards to the side of me! We dogged each other for a couple more days before I began to pull out a bit of a lead.

The first ten days of the race were mostly gales, and having found myself unexpectedly in the lead I was unwilling to give it up. But the cost of pushing myself and *Sky Catcher* to maintain and build on it was not insignificant. Within the first few days I had two bad falls in the cockpit – the first brought a bleeding lump the size of an emu egg on my right shin, the second taking a chunk out of my right elbow which left me with a virtually useless arm for the rest of the race. I was probably the only competitor to sail most of the race truly single-handed. Once ashore in Charleston the elbow had to be drained and treated, and its recovery was slow. Damage to the boat began to mount in those first ten days also – torn sails, a broken winch and other deck hardware, failed autopilots . . . neither the boat nor I deserved such punishment.

Niah had his problems too and, during our twice-a-day chats over the SSB radio, we promised each other vast quantities of cold beer in Charleston for making one another work so hard. Friendships began to develop during these sessions on the radio. Niah, from the northwest of England, called me "the fox". He earned his handle, "the professor", after spending several days teaching

Harry Mitchell, a fellow Brit, how to use the on-board computer system. Harry spent huge amounts of time chatting to the luckless South African Neal Petersen and encouraging American Floyd Romack as he struggled to contend with the bad weather.

At the end of the first ten days I had a lead of 125 miles. The Class I boats were well ahead of us, with Britain's Mark Gatehouse on *Queen Anne's Battery* (ex *Credit Agricole III* which won the 1986-87 BOC Challenge) in front and taking the "Mad Max" northern route towards and through the fog, ice and fishing boats off the Grand Banks of Newfoundland. In Class II, Cornishman Robin Davie in his 40-footer *Cornwall* was gaining on Niah and me, twenty-six-year-old Neal in his home-built *Protect Our Sealife* was suffering gear and rigging failures, seventy-year-old Harry in his 40-foot *Henry Hornblower* was keeping pace behind Neal with Floyd in his 50-foot *Cardiac 88*, and Karl Brinkman of Germany was forced back to restart a week late in *Caribbean*.

My lead on Niah was cut from over a hundred to thirty-five miles in one night when I went south and fell into a windless hole for twelve hours about halfway across, while he continued west and enjoyed good wind. Thereafter, the race was a cat-and-mouse game with fickle winds, the Gulf Stream wandering around the western half of the North Atlantic in a drunken stupour, and determined competition. It was endlessly frustrating and we all experienced long hours of no wind at all from time to time, interspersed with savage bursts of 30-40 knots. Niah and I traded places in terms of "distance to go" several times as we played out our respective strategies. Mine was to move south so I could cross the Gulf Stream close to the latitude of Charleston. His was to continue west and hope for a wind shift that would favour a shorter route direct for the finish line. The wind, when it put in an appearance, was persistently out of the prevailing southwest, which eventually forced him to follow me south and my lead was more than two hundred miles when I crossed the line.

In Class I, Frenchman Yves Parlier on the 60-foot *Cacolac D'Aquitaine* (ex *Group Sceta* which won the 1990-91 BOC Challenge) clinched a three-hour victory over Mark Gatehouse who had led most of the way, and third-placed Jean Luc Van den Heede on his 60-foot *Vendée Entreprises* was only hours behind him. It was a thrilling finish.

I crossed the finish line 28 days, 23 hours, 50 minutes and 10 seconds after the start in Falmouth. I had not slept for almost the last three days because of the unpredictable winds and then the constant threat near shore of shipping and fishing boats. I was exhausted, elated, thoroughly drained. Many friends were there to see me cross the finish line, between two buoys flanking the main shipping channel a few miles offshore. Once I crossed the line their little boats bobbed alongside. First to board *Sky Catcher* was Julia. We hugged. I cried.

CHARLESTON

Approaching Charleston from the sea you pass through the narrow channel between Sullivan's Island to the north and Fort Sumter just off James Island to the south. Here it was that some of the first English settlers arrived in April 1670 to create Charles Town, in honour of King Charles II. Here too, in the summer of 1776, the Colonies presented the embryonic nation with one of its earliest victories in the Revolutionary War by dispatching the British fleet and the three thousand soldiers it had brought to quell the rebellious Carolinians. And here the first shots of the American Civil War, still referred to today by diehard Southerners as "the war of Northern aggression" or "that late great unpleasantness", were fired. This is still a place where, to some, Northerners are "Yankees" or "damned Yankees" – the former being those who visit, the latter those who decide to stay!

Downtown Charleston is situated on a peninsula some five miles from the channel, sticking out into the bay and framed by the Ashley river on one side and the Cooper river on the other. To reach it, you sail past Sullivan's Island with its colourful waterfront homes, and Patriots Point where a land-based museum and collection of historic battleships make up what claims to be the largest naval museum in the world. From there you cross the Cooper river to the passenger ship terminal on the peninsula itself. To the left of the terminal is the city's Waterfront Park and walkway that eventually leads past the stretch of meticulously preserved historic waterfront houses to the Battery at the tip of the peninsula and its White Point Gardens. A short way up the Ashley river from there lies the City Marina where The BOC Transatlantic Challenge boats were berthed on their arrival, and where the competing skippers were welcomed into the open hospitality of the Charleston Yacht Club.

It is a proud city with a strong sense of its own character and past maritime and trading importance. Here, it is said, the Cooper river meets the Ashley river to create the Atlantic Ocean.

Having just arrived from England by boat myself, it was not difficult for me to imagine what it must have been like for those first colonists who settled here. Three ships had left England in 1669 and only one, the *Carolina*, arrived the following spring, in the company of an unnamed sloop. The crew and passengers were probably as exhausted as I was on my arrival. Their crossing would have been far more hazardous and uncertain than mine had been, however, and they would have been deeply relieved to have reached "the other side". Chances are it was a hot sunny day for them too, with dolphin and manatees swimming in the harbour and a rich variety of bird life in the swamps and forests around it, just like today.

Like so many others who came to America from England at that time, the settlers of Charles Town sought to create for themselves a place where they could enjoy the trappings and affectations of an aristocracy they so admired and envied back home – large houses, formal gardens, servants, finery, and the respect of those lower down the social order. Much of this has been preserved or restored by several historical and heritage societies in Charleston, helping to make tourism one of the city's key industries.

I soon discovered that traditional Southern hospitality was very much alive and well in Charleston too. As the BOC competitors arrived in town we were each assigned a host family, or offered free accommodation. For my first few weeks I stayed in an apartment owned by a retired army colonel who was taking some holiday in Colorado – "We're just delighted to have the opportunity to help you out . . . " For the last few weeks I stayed in a small carriage house in fashionable Meeting Street down by the Battery, owned by a local businessman who lived in the mansion next to it – "You can't imagine what a pleasure it is for us to have you live in it while you're here . . . just let us know if there is anything else you need."

The Charleston organizing committee for The BOC Challenge had done a good job making sure the town knew about the race and got excited about it. I cannot remember going into a single shop or restaurant with a BOC Challenge shirt on without being drawn into a conversation about the event. Just after Mark and I decided to move the race to Charleston three years earlier, Mayor Joe Riley called a young local businessman, Robbie Freeman, and told him he was looking for "someone bright enough to pull this thing off, and stupid enough to take it on." Robbie assembled a good team around him, among them Steve Steinert, a lawyer and president of the Chamber of Commerce; Walter Erhardt, a realtor and "Mr Fix-it"; Jimmy Huggins who ran the South Eastern Wildlife Festival and had been persuaded to organize a Maritime Festival around the weekend of the start of the Challenge; and Helen Turner, director of the local Visitor and Convention Bureau. Others were co-opted with the passage of time as the scale of the undertaking and their commitment to its success grew. They were going to do their bit to help make The BOC Challenge 1994-95 a world-class event in Charleston, even if it took all their waking hours to do it – and in the few months before the race it did just about that.

The arrival of the Transatlantic Challenge fleet and, slightly in advance of it, most of the race management team, added to the pressure. The new BOC Challenge marina next to the passenger ship terminal was under construction and finished on schedule in the middle of August. It was a fine facility, and in the perfect spot in town for public visibility, off the end of Market Street. In fact it was perched off a piece of boggy landfill that had once been ship dockage in Charleston's halcyon days of sail, with the original wood pilings and ring cleats still sticking out of the marsh. The terminal itself, which was to become race headquarters, exhibition hall and party centre all in one, was recarpeted and refurbished. The BOC Challenge communications centre, which would coordinate all communications with competitors during the event under the direction of race coordinator Pete Dunning, was set up in a comfortable trailer near the terminal. When Pete had his huge radio antennae assembled and mounted on a seventy-foot pole next to the trailer, I christened the place "Langley" (CIA headquarters in Virginia). Banners and posters went up all over town. Armies of volunteers were pressed into action hosting skippers and their shore crew, manning the marina round the clock, towing boats, selling merchandise, helping to organize and steward events . . . the list of tasks was a long one.

While all this was going on, the list of registered BOC Challenge entries began to shrink. American Chris Bernie, who was building a new 50-footer in Charleston, withdrew for lack of funds. Australian Michael Wignall pulled out, due mainly to a "lack of preparation time". Wolfgang Quix of Germany, who had a new 50-footer built for the race, withdrew for the same reason. So too did American Paul Harder Cohen who had entered Class I of the two previous Challenge races as well and still could not make it to the start line. At the end of August two American sailors based in the Pacific northwest announced their withdrawal. Ray Thayer had a new Class I boat, but delays due to technical problems meant he could not meet the deadline to be in Charleston. Andy Upjohn, with a new 50-footer, felt he wanted more experience with the boat before undertaking a circumnavigation. Norwegian Hans Skaar pulled out while on his qualifying trip to Charleston because he had run out of time.

I had seen this happen in all three previous BOC Challenge races. The attrition rate as start day approached was always high. It was a real struggle calling for long-term planning and the ability to overcome a plethora of technical, financial and emotional obstacles. You have to have a real obsession about making it to the start line to be there.

With the BOC Transatlantic Challenge boats already in port by early August, the rest of the round-the-world competitors began to arrive one at a time over the next few weeks. The fleet that gathered was as impressive as it was diverse.

First prize for discomfort and lack of amenities went to Italian Giovanni Soldini's *Kodak*. She was the first of three new 50-foot racing thoroughbreds in Class II to arrive in Charleston. She was low, wide and sleek, with a plumb bow, a broad scoop stern, and minimum deck hardware. The only access to her main cabin was a vertical hatch in the cockpit. It was fun watching the more generously proportioned members of the scrutineering committee squeeze themselves through for their inspection. There wasn't much to see below deck, nor any headroom either. Moving about had to be done on hands and knees, and there was little furniture except a simple navigation table at which Giovanni had to sit cross-legged on the cabin sole (floor). His galley was a small, camping, gas single-burner, suspended from the deckhead by a few pieces of line. A sail bag on the cabin floor was where he sat and slept. Giovanni had bought *Servant IV*, Class II winner of the last BOC Challenge, and gained a lot of experience with her before she sunk after loosing her keel in a race. He then spent two years building his new machine, a development of *Servant IV*, largely with labour from a youth drug rehabilitation centre near his home town in Italy. He was justifiably proud of that achievement alone.

David Adams of Australia arrived a few days before the deadline with his new 50-footer, *True Blue*. She had many of *Kodak*'s design characteristics, except she was not as broad at the stern and had a mast as tall as some of the 60-footers. David had sailed a 60-footer in the last BOC, a converted race boat constrained in design by the IOR rules and normally sailed by a crew of a dozen. She was no match for the one-off open class racers she was up against. Unable to raise the funds for a new 60-footer, David decided to "go for gold" with a new boat in Class II instead.

Fellow Australian Alan Nebauer had a mean-looking 50-footer too, part-sponsored by his home town of Newcastle (New South Wales). He had sailed all the way from Australia, diverted to Tahiti to repair his autopilots, used an outboard motor to negotiate the Panama Canal, had one hundred litres of petrol delivered to him while becalmed off Florida, then lost the engine bracket from the stern of his boat, before arriving in Charleston just a couple of hours ahead of the noon deadline on 7 September for all competitors to be at the BOC marina.

These were definitely the three favourites in Class II before the start, with the shortest odds on David Adams because he was known to be an experienced fighter who knew how to go the distance. The rest of Class II covered the full range from 40-50 feet. In addition to the three hot favourites there were four other 50-footers, *Sky Catcher* at 48 feet, and three at 40 feet. Apart from the three hot boats, all but two of us had sailed in the transatlantic race: Briton Niah Vaughan and American Floyd Romack in the 50-footers *Jimroda II* and *Cardiac 88*; Harry Mitchell and Robin Davie from Britain and South African Neal Petersen in the 40-footers *Henry Hornblower*, *Cornwall*, and *Protect Our Sealife*. Noting the awesome competition as it arrived in Charleston, we decided to form ourselves into an unofficial "Not The Fifty Foot Class"! I had T-shirts made up with this legend on them and gave them to everyone in the transatlantic race at a lunch they all decided I should host for winning our Class.

Class II was completed by the arrival of Simone Bianchetti in the 50-foot *Town of Cervia*, *Adriatic Sea*, and Minoru Saito in the 50-foot *Shuten-Dohji II*. Simone, a swarthy twenty-five-year-old, was the youngest in the fleet. Minoru had completed the last BOC Challenge in *Shuten-Dohji II* and had sailed alone from Japan to be in Charleston for the start of this one.

While the favourites were obvious in Class II, they were more difficult to pick in Class I.

Christophe Auguin of France, winner of the last BOC Challenge, arrived with his radical new *Sceta Calberson*; low, broad and with an immense rig, her primary steering system was a short joystick on either side of the cockpit that controlled the autopilots. Two stubby little tillers on the exposed after-deck were for emergencies only. When I met Christophe in the race office the morning he arrived, I asked him if there was much work to be done on her before the start. "Of course there is," he smiled. "She's a new boat after all!" By the end of the day her mast was out and she had been towed to a nearby boatyard with a long work list.

Frenchman Jean Luc Van den Heede (known as "VDH"), with his very light, narrow and low-budget ketch *Vendée Entreprises*, was also a fancied entrant, although the odds were slightly longer on him because his boat flew in the face of conventional wisdom on what was required for a predominantly off-the-wind race like the BOC. However, his reputation for being able to tough it out in the worst conditions, and to fix most things that might go wrong, was unequalled. He had been around the world alone three times already, finishing the last non-stop Vendée Globe race in second place with his boat flooded to within a few inches of her deck.

The only woman in the race was also a hot favourite. Isabelle Autissier, a veteran of the last BOC, arrived with *Ecureuil Poitou Charentes 2* in which she and a crew had knocked fourteen days off the sailing record from New York to San Francisco earlier that year. A handsome, beamy boat with pretty graphics on her hull and sails, she had a radical and controversial keel that could be swung from side to side to assist the water ballast in reducing her angle of heel while under way.

Two American boats thought to be in contention by the dockside experts were *Coyote* and *Hunter's Child*. *Coyote* had been built by the late Mike Plant for the last Vendée Globe race. Mike was never found after she lost her keel and capsized in mid-Atlantic on their singlehanded passage to France for the start. The boat washed up on the south coast of Ireland and Mike's fiancée Helen Davies had her shipped back to the US and rebuilt. *Coyote* looked beautiful with her broad sleek lines, simple deck layout, elegant "stars and stripes" graphics, and tall mast. Her skipper for the BOC was David Scully, whose past experience had been predominantly with multihulls so he was certainly used to sailing at speed. On his qualifying passage in *Coyote*, just a few weeks before the start, he collided at night with a fishing boat a little over a hundred miles offshore and limped into his home port of Newport, Rhode Island, for hasty repairs. In Charleston there were dark mutterings in the marina about lawsuits, insurance claims, and the boat having a jinx. Another campaign that seemed to have its share of problems was the Hunter Marine-sponsored *Hunter's Child*. Built a few years earlier, her original performance had been disappointing and little had been spared to improve this for the BOC. Her stern had been broadened, the front eight feet of her bow reshaped, and a taller carbon mast built along with a new suit of sails. The project had been blessed with perhaps too many advisors; but she was a handsome boat and had a very experienced skipper in Steve Pettengill.

Class I was completed by four less fancied "dark horses", older 60-footers, but each with a strong pedigree. Britain's Mark Gatehouse was sailing *Queen Anne's Battery* in which Philippe Jeantot had won the 86-87 BOC when she was called *Credit Agricole III*. Mark had done a great job refitting her, adding a mizzen mast and surprising everyone with his dazzling performance in the BOC Transatlantic that summer. Fellow Brit Josh Hall, who sailed in Class II of the last Challenge, was back this time with *Gartmore Investment Managers*, formerly *BBV Expo '92* in the last race. American Arnet (Arnie) Taylor was there with *Thursday's Child*, built by Hunter Marine in the early 1980s and still potentially a very fast boat. South African Jean Jacques ("J-J") Provoyeur arrived with *Ben Vio* in which Bertie Reed sailed to a sixth place in the last BOC as *Grinaker* – but J-J had built the boat and was out to prove she was capable of a far better performance.

All twenty competitors arrived with long work lists to be completed before the start. The Charleston organizing committee had put together a yacht services team with each of its members assigned to act as liaison for four or five boats in the race – lining up discounts with local suppliers, sourcing parts and equipment, and arranging an orderly work schedule for those who wanted their boats hauled out. The earnest and affable Scott Wallis ran the committee and finally had to take six weeks away from his business to cope with his commitment to the BOC fleet.

The work list on *Sky Catcher* was long but did not involve serious structural or technical problems. Autopilots had to be repaired, the SSB radio and other electrical equipment needed work and checking, the diesel generator had to be insulated and boxed in, the headsails had to be repaired for use as spares and replaced by stronger ones, some deck hardware needed to be replaced and the winches stripped and serviced, and I decided to have steps bolted all the way up the mast. In addition to this, everything on board had to be checked – every electrical connection, every bolt and screw, hatch seals, every inch of the standing and running rigging and their various attachments. Skip was fully occupied with all of this for most of our stay in Charleston, with help from Andy Darwent who had joined the *Sky Catcher* team in Falmouth and who decided to visit Charleston to be a part of the main event also. We worked through the list methodically, but there were the inevitable hitches and hang-ups when parts were delivered late or not entirely to our specifications.

Towards the end of August one of our two new headsails arrived by plane from the Sobstad loft in Seattle, three thousand miles across the country. The new sails were to be stronger than the ones which had been built earlier in the year and which had not survived the two transatlantic crossings. The old sails had been recut, repaired and strengthened in Falmouth, but they were not going to be man enough for a circumnavigation. We went sailing that morning to try out the new headsail, and by the evening it was back on a plane to Seattle: its dimensions were slightly wrong and it was missing the all-important foam padding up its leading edge that would enable it to hold its shape when furler-reefed. This was a great frustration for me, and no doubt for the sailmaker too, and I found it hard to understand how these things happened. But my experience paled into insignificance when compared to some of the horror stories being told by fellow competitors about their dealings with other sailmakers.

By early September the passenger terminal had completed its transformation. The media centre was equipped and running, the race management office was a hive of activity, and the various sponsor exhibits and the BOC Challenge Club were almost completed. By then we were having daily race management meetings at eight in the morning to keep track of progress on all fronts – social events, media arrangements, coordination with the Charleston organizing committee, security in the terminal and on the docks, preparations for the start, planning briefing meetings for the skippers. There was a huge amount of detail that had to be tracked if things were not to go wrong, and Mark and I were the only two with any history with the event to draw on.

Work continued on all the boats in the marina as well, adding, replacing or checking equipment and gear. Fund-raising was still on the agenda for some of the skippers. J-J was selling tours of his boat. So was Robin, who also had a full range of *Cornwall* merchandise, from mugs to T-shirts, to sell. Neal was on the road both in and outside South Carolina, following every lead to secure a bit of support here, a bit there. Several of us were roped in to speak at schools, yacht clubs, Rotary and the Chamber of Commerce. Some also became involved in discussions with the "Can-Do" committee of South Carolina educators, who wanted to develop some school-based experiments with the skippers as they had done in the past with astronauts. I agreed to participate in two projects – one a study of the effects of the race on "body composition", and the other a "sampling" of the oceans of the world to determine the constitution of the sea in different places.

The second of these studies would require me to fill and collect six small plastic phials with sea water about every thousand miles around the world. These would then be analyzed in the schools at the end of the race for mineral and other content. With each sampling I had to note the latitude and longitude, depth, sea temperature, and general weather conditions. The first involved keeping a log of my daily food and drink consumption and weekly measurements of waist and hips. It also involved a body scan to determine bone mass, fat, muscle et cetera, before I left. The day before the start of the race I was handed my scan results and a cover letter making a special note of my remarkable fitness!

This work with the "Can-Do" committee was a good example of how the race had fired the imagination of people who had little or no interest in sailing, and demonstrated the value of the race beyond its obvious boundaries. In the week before the start three thousand schoolchildren from in and around Charleston visited the marina and the passenger terminal exhibits. Neal Petersen reckoned he himself lectured to nearly a thousand school children in the State. And beyond this local activity, there was Mame Reynolds' "Student Ocean Challenge", which, under the umbrella of BOC Oceanwatch, used the race as a live teaching tool in thousands of classrooms around the world. For me, as for most of the other competitors, this all added enormously to the experience of being a participant in the race.

Julia, who had had to return home a week after my arrival to attend to work and family commitments, arrived back from England two weeks before the start to help me with final preparations — sorting out my clothes, buying my provisions, keeping a check on my daily schedule of commitments, assembling everything that had to be shipped to Cape Town for the second leg. It was great to have her back and to put a little more order into an increasingly hectic period. Every day, I had meetings to do with race management and briefings as a competitor. Scrutineering had to be completed, there were events to host for our race management team and the Charleston organizing committee, social engagements with my main sponsors the Carbide Graphite Group, a few parties with all the competitors, a host of people who wanted to look over *Sky Catcher* and have their picture taken with her skipper, and several media interviews.

All the competitors and their boats were the subject of a great deal of attention. Even people who knew nothing about sailing visited the marina to see what we were all about. The questioning was endless – "What does it cost to do this? . . . What do you eat? . . . What happens to the boat when you're sleeping? . . . Isn't your family worried? . . . How long will it take? . . . Why are you doing this?" On more than one occasion, having explained what the race was about, where we would stop and when we expected to be back in Charleston, I was asked, "OK, but when you're actually sailing, how many people will you have with you?"

I had more than two hundred people look over the boat while she was in the marina, friends and strangers. One old lady asked if she could have a look and I gave her the guided tour. She inspected everything very closely, like a mother would her son's first apartment, and as she left she said: "Look, I don't want you to think I'm being nosey, but I don't think you've got nearly enough toilet paper with you. Take a hint from me, young man, and get a lot more; you can't imagine what it's like to be without it!" She was serious, and I thanked her for the advice.

Ant arrived a week before the start, after three and a half months journeying in Russia, Mongolia and China, and after two and a half days travelling on buses, trains and planes from Tibet. He helped Skip with the boat, servicing the winches and other gear. He was having some trouble with Western reality and the time difference, and we had too little time together for me to have a full appreciation of his own adventures. But it was great for me to have him around.

In the last couple of days before the start, countless friends and acquaintances showed up on the dock from all over the world, including a number of past BOC competitors who simply could not stay away from the event. To these had to be added the Board of Directors and senior management of The BOC Group, and several hundred BOC customers from throughout the US.

The pressure was building for all of us and, just as we were wondering who might not make it to the start line, Floyd Romack announced he would be a late starter. It had nothing to do with his preparedness or that of his boat. His only daughter was to be married the following Saturday and he said he would never forgive himself for missing it.

While we were all intensely busy getting ourselves and our boats ready, there were several social events to distract us when the need arose. The pace and tone was set by the welcome party at the Hob Caw Yacht Club, the night of the first official skippers' briefing meeting. We were taken there by members in their small boats and had a cook-out by the club pool. Our media director Dan McConnell and COMSAT's Paul Hunter were the first to jump in fully clothed. Others followed, with a great roar of approval going up when Harry Mitchell stripped all his clothes off and jumped in. His wife Diana looked amused but embarrassed, while it came as no surprise to the rest of us. Harry was the fleet jester and, as he put it, he was extremely pleased with the effect on his seventy-year-old frame of having spent the last two weeks of the transatlantic race naked in his cockpit.

Other social engagements, like opening night of the Charleston Maritime Festival of art and crafts, were more sober affairs; but Charleston had been like one long party that none of us wanted to end, or have to leave. The night before the start, however, had to be the final formal farewell – a *bon voyage* party for the competitors with two thousand guests in the terminal and an outdoor concert by the Charleston Symphony Orchestra for several thousand more, culminating in a spectacular fireworks display over the harbour. Before the concert there were speeches, then each competitor was introduced to the crowds. There were people in the streets as far as one could see, and a small gathering on top of the nearby multi-storey car park. As we were each introduced, we were escorted onto the stage by a Citadel Military Academy cadet carrying our national flag, and were greeted by a line of dignitaries including BOC's CEO and deputy chairman Pat Dyer, and Dick Giordano – back again as chairman of BOC – who the next day, as for all previous BOC Challenge races, would fire the start canon. As we each walked up, a huge wave of applause engulfed us. Everyone there wanted to wish us well; but I had this curious sense that it must have been a bit like that for the early Christians as they entered the amphitheatres of ancient Rome to meet the lions!

I had a late dinner that evening with Julia, Ant and Rid Bullerjahn, an old friend who had flown in from Boston to see me off. We drank more champagne and reminisced. I had a few hours sleep, and woke to discover the streets were wet; it was cloudy, but there was wind! I was down on the boat at seven. Julia followed, then Rid, Ant, Andy, Skip and his father. Andy was dispatched to buy more bottled gas and diesel fuel. Julia fetched breakfast of doughnuts and coffee. We readied the boat, and awaited our tow out.

At nine-thirty we slipped our dock lines and were pulled out to our towboat, the 40-foot motor vessel *Fish-Tails Four*. The crowds lining the dock and the walkway in front of the terminal gave us a great cheer. On the long trip out to the start line, all seven of us on board drank yet more champagne, dodged the rain showers and waved at every passing spectator boat. There were hundreds of them. Small sail and motor boats up to the huge *Provincetown* which accommodated the BOC party of nearly a thousand people. The *Spirit of Charleston* motored alongside us for a while, with her eighty Carbide Graphite Group guests lining the rail and giving us several rousing cheers.

We slipped our tow and tacked through the spectator fleet. Suddenly I noticed Skip was climbing the mast. I stared up and could see him inspecting the headboard of our alternate mainsail, which we had put on the boat the day before, and the halyard lead into the mast. When he came down to the cockpit he did not tell me what I wanted to hear. The way it was set up, there was obviously a potential for halyard chafe with the mainsail over on the port side. This

Sky Catcher *inside and out. Key among the external modifications we made to the original boat were the antenna arch, fixed cuddy over the companionway and front of the cockpit, and sugar scoop extension to the back of the boat. Below decks, we added watertight bulkheads fore and aft, a galley and heads, storage and locker space, and designer Skip Miller's* pièce de résistance — *the gimballed navigation station. The BMW reclining car seat and chart table are secured to a frame that moves through a total of 45° so I can sit upright at whatever angle of heel the boat is.*

(ARTIST: JOHN MOXHAM)

Left Sky Catcher *is winched out for a bottom scrub and anti-fouling, and some work on the rudder, at Pendennis Ship Yard, Falmouth, before the start of The BOC Transatlantic Challenge. No doubt this helped us to win Class II.*

(PHOTOGRAPH: NIGEL ROWE)

Above *School children participating in the Student Ocean Challenge, learning about navigation from Steve Pettengill aboard* Hunter's Child.

(BILLY BLACK)

Left *Some of the transatlantic boats at the BOC marina in Falmouth, specially built for the event, viewed from the mast-top of Yves Parlier's* Cacolac D'Aquitaine *which subsequently won Class I.*

(TOM BENN/PPL)

Right *Telling a Charleston TV station how to get to Cape Town by sailboat. We were all the subject of much media attention.*

(KYLE HENCE)

Top Crowds visited the specially constructed BOC marina at Charleston every day in the build up to the start of the race. (BILLY BLACK)

Bottom The eve-of-start festivities concluded with a spectacular fireworks display over the harbour. (BILLY BLACK)

Top *A rare line-up of all the BOC Challenge starters. Left to right:* (back row) *Arnie Taylor, NR, Floyd Romack, Neal Petersen, Alan Nebauer, J-J Provoyeur, David Adams, David Scully, Isabelle Autissier, Steve Pettengill, Niah Vaughan, Mark Gatehouse, Jean Luc Van den Heede;* (front) *Robin Davie, Simone Bianchetti, Minoru Saito, Harry Mitchell, Giovanni Soldini, Christophe Auguin, Josh Hall.* (BILLY BLACK)
Bottom *The start from Charleston. The grey day and drizzle did not deter the spectator fleet.*
(JACQUES VAPILLON)

Above *The ever-smiling Minoru Saito on* Shuten-Dohji II.
(JACQUES VAPILLON)

Left *Lars Bergstrom demonstrating an ingenious use for a fender to climb* Sky Catcher's *mast.*
(JULIA HUMBERSTONE)

Opposite Sky Catcher *under sail on one of those special days of sunshine and balmy breezes.*
(NATHAN WILLIAMS)

The activity I loathe most when sailing alone — climbing the mast. The retractable steps help me get up quickly, but do nothing to untie the knot in my stomach. The smile reflects nervous terror! (JACQUES VAPILLON)

meant that, to be safe, I would have to put a reef in the main when on starboard tack. I told Skip that if it looked like a real problem we should go back to the dock and fix it. He said it should be okay, and that if it was a problem I'd know pretty soon! Not a great piece of news with which to start such a long passage.

Now it was just under half an hour to the gun, and the rules required me to be sailing alone by twenty minutes to. It all happened so quickly, which was probably just as well. There was no time for prolonged farewells, no time to say all the things that came to mind. I gave Skip, Ant and Julia a big hug each and helped my party of six off *Sky Catcher* onto the little chase craft sent to pick them up. It looked to me as if Julia had tears in her eyes but she kept her head well down and didn't look up. I watched the little boat disappear into the spectator fleet, then turned *Sky Catcher* towards the large safety zone behind the start line, kept clear of all but a few official boats to give competitors plenty of room for manoeuvre. At one end of the line was the Coast Guard vessel *Northland*, at the other was the minesweeper, the USS *Osprey*.

Tacking around the safety zone, I passed and exchanged waves with Mark Gatehouse, Jean Luc, Neal and J-J. About a minute before noon I headed on an oblique course for the line. Immediately ahead of me was Neal, and in front of him was David Adams. David was short-tacking down the line, just staying the right side of it. His six-foot-four-inch, broad frame made *True Blue* look small and he was throwing the boat around as if she was a dinghy. It was an impressive sight. Crowding in behind me were *Queen Anne's Battery* and *Ben Vio*. Further down the line were *Sceta Calberson* and *Ecureuil Poitou Charentes 2*. Then there was a puff of smoke from the cannon on the USS *Osprey,* and the sound of ships' hooters all around us.

CHARLESTON

TO THE

EQUATOR

EAST

It looked to me as if David Adams in *True Blue* was over the line first. Neal Petersen in *Protect Our Sealife* was behind him at our end of the line. Crowding in behind him were *Sky Catcher*, Mark Gatehouse in *Queen Anne's Battery* and J-J Provoyeur in *Ben Vio*. Further down the line, and over at roughly the same time, were Isabelle Autissier in *Ecureuil Poitou Charentes 2* and Christophe Auguin in *Sceta Calberson*. We were a bit tight for water at our end, but it was a long enough line for there to be plenty of room for everyone. Soon though we were engulfed by the spectator fleet, "dirtying" the wind, making the sea choppy, and adding to the general air of excitement.

The wind was about 15 knots out of the south, perfect for reaching to the east and this is exactly the direction in which the whole fleet began to head. On *Sky Catcher*, we were making 10-12 knots of boat speed and the spectator fleet soon began to thin out. For a while we sailed alongside the huge *Provincetown*, which BOC had hired for the day to entertain almost a thousand customers and other guests. The guardrails of her three decks were thick with people. I could see Pat and Shirley Dyer up on the bridge deck and I think I could recognize a few other people as well. I wondered what they must be thinking of what I was up to now they could see me alone in my little boat. I could hear snatches over the ship's public address system, "...*Sky Catcher*... Nigel Rowe...BOC..." I stood up in the cockpit and waved. They all gave me a rousing cheer and waved back. It made me laugh.

A few speed boats visited us, with video- and stills-cameramen being soaked and thrown about in the chop like olives in a drunk's martini. Two or three helicopters buzzed us as well, with legs and cameras hanging out of their sides.

Within a few hours, Niah Vaughan in *Jimroda II* was alongside and slightly ahead of us to the north. Beyond him was Josh Hall in *Gartmore Investment Managers*. To the south, I could see another boat I took to be Giovanni Soldini's *Kodak*. I could see three boats ahead on the horizon and half a dozen behind us. Then, as dusk was upon us, *Sky Catcher* and I were alone.

I lay back in the cockpit with a rum and coke in the tin cup Julia had given to me. It had "Guz", her nickname for me, painted on the side. From the sailing point of view it could hardly have been a more perfect evening. The sea, without the spectator fleet to disturb it, was easy to plough through. We were leaving a hissing trail of bubbles in our wake, and the wind generators were humming as they pumped power into our batteries. The sun disappeared behind a wide salmon pink cloud to leave a full moon in a clear sky which rendered most of the stars invisible. It was almost like daylight, with the moon making the sea glisten and sparkle. A few hours after dark, a school of dolphin visited us, swam alongside and criss-crossed playfully at our bow. They seemed to be saying, "Isn't this the greatest evening . . . isn't this fun!"

Somehow I was not in a mood to enjoy it. For one thing I felt physically and mentally exhausted by the last few hectic days in Charleston. I was sad that the "Charleston experience" was over. Most of all I felt a heaviness about not seeing any of my friends and loved-ones for so long. It would be two months before I would see Julia in Cape Town, and next spring before I would see Ant or my mother again, and I hadn't seen her since the beginning of July. I felt strange and unsettled. I loaded the CD player. "Paris Texas" first up, then Leonard Cohen's "Songs From A Room"; then others like it that were in harmony with the melancholy I felt. These feelings needed some freedom to express themselves and be felt. This mood needed to play itself out. I was disappointed not to feel elation at this point, but it was part of the experience.

Part of it also, I think, was a new recognition of the magnitude of the undertaking ahead of me, and the fact that despite all the time, money and effort that had gone into the project over the past couple of years, this was still only the beginning. It had cost a lot just to get to this point, but now the planning, the preparations, the talking, had come to an abrupt halt and the job itself had to be done. I had put so much at risk to do it – at a minimum an uninsured boat that had soaked up all my savings – and the anguish I was putting others through ashore while I was at sea alone was something I could not ignore.

The size of the job that now had to be done was brought home to me even more forcibly the next morning. Over a cup of coffee, I pulled out the handful of cards and letters which had been thrust into my hands just before the start, and which I had not had time to read. They were mostly from schoolchildren in Mame Reynolds' Student Ocean Challenge programme. They asked a lot of questions: "Do you ever get scared when you sail in the night-time?...Why are you taking part in this race?...Does it get cold, if so I'm sorry to remind you?...I love your boat's name, why do you call it that?...Do you ever get lonely? ..." They all wished me luck and said they would be following me all the way round. One said, "Don't give up even when it gets tough", and another put a PS on her letter, "Don't drop out, PLEASE!". One sent me a paper inflatable globe, about six inches across.

I blew it up, and sat at the navigation desk turning it round and round in my hand, my eye following the course we had all set out to take – Charleston to Cape Town, to Sydney, to Punta del Este, back to Charleston. I don't know why, but this more than anything forced me to acknowledge anew the scope of what I had embarked upon. It was not as if I had not stared at a globe before, or studied the charts for the whole course, or thought deeply about doing the race for at least a couple of years. It was simply that here I was, alone, at sea, and just a few miles into the twenty-seven thousand I would have to sail before I could say the job was done. I shivered as a chill ran down my spine. I was going to have to apply one of the maxims of "Rowe's philosophy for life" to get through this: almost any task can be accomplished if you break it down into easy manageable bites. I was going to have to take this race one leg at a time. And for the first leg, I was going to have to break it into two manageable bites – Charleston to the equator, then the equator to Cape Town. The first "bite" was therefore no more than a transatlantic crossing, and I'd done that a few times before...so what's the big deal!

That first morning a line squall passed through with a lot of rain and 30 knots of wind. It left behind a sunny day and 15-20 knots of wind still from the south. We powered into and across the Gulf Stream, averaging 10 knots of boat speed and sometimes hitting 16. That evening on the radio "chat-hour" with other competitors I learned that the leading 60-footers were *averaging* 16 knots. This was truly great sailing.

I still had not slept much. I never do the first two or three days out – not so much because I can't, but because I don't like to. The first couple of days one is too close to land, with its attendant coastal shipping and fishing boats, and this was particularly the case around the Gulf Stream. I had little appetite, but I forced myself to eat. Lunchtime that day I fried three eggs with potatoes and a thick slice from the ham Julia had bought for me the day before the start. The ham was so salty I could not eat it all, and I spent the afternoon sucking on a bottle of mineral water. On the evening chat-hour I mentioned this to Niah, the acknowledged fleet expert on hams, and he suggested cutting a piece a day in advance and soaking it in water overnight. I said I'd give it a try.

Niah was in buoyant mood, as was Robin Davie in *Cornwall*. Neal Petersen, on the other hand, was in a deeper melancholy than even I had been. It will pass, I assured him, just give it a little time. I think he too was missing the "Charleston experience" where he had been entertained and helped by a large number of people, and he was missing his girlfriend Gwen a great deal.

Whilst in the Gulf Stream I filled my first sample phials with sea water for one of the "Can Do" projects I had undertaken, and began the log of my daily intake of food and drink for the other. Whilst rummaging through the paperwork on this, I read the cover letter from the doctor in Charleston who was running the programme and had supervised my initial examination and body scan. I was somewhat surprised to read in it: "Your body composition shows that you are very fit and have a good bone density. Body composition is three kilograms bone, fifteen kilograms fat, and sixteen kilograms muscle with nineteen per cent fat. Normal percentage fat is about twenty-five to thirty per cent . . ." The statistics meant little to me, except to recognize that there were another forty-four kilograms of something else in my body, presumably mostly water! But I was extremely surprised, and comforted, to be deemed "very fit".

The days soon began to develop a rhythm, with a few elements of routine which I tried to keep to a minimum. Sleep could have no routine; I had to take that when I could and when I needed it – although I found I was catching more during the night than during the day. I deliberately had no routine times for eating. I usually had a cup of fresh-brewed coffee at sun-up, and always had a "happy hour" with a rum and coke at sundown; but breakfast could be any time between sun-up and six hours later, lunch may or may not happen, and dinner could be at dusk or hours into the night. It just depended on how hungry I felt and what else had to be done on board. The only certainty about dinner was that it would include a fried onion and half a garlic!

The other certainty was that whether the sun shone or not, it would be stiflingly hot down below and, if the sun was shining, blisteringly hot in the cockpit too. In fact, I spent almost all my time in the cockpit, naked during the day and with shorts and a T-shirt at night. The heat was such that the plastic wind direction arm in one of my cockpit instruments melted and stuck against the instrument's face.

There was a routine to the radio schedules with other competitors. I enjoyed these conversations and recognized their value as a "safety net" for us all. There was a routine also about the two daily "broadcasts" via COMSAT to the fleet that we all looked forward to with some eagerness. Around 13.00 hours each day, race headquarters sent us a list of fleet positions so we could see where everyone else was. A few hours later, Meteo Consult in France sent us weather information – narrative describing where the high and low pressure systems were, and a weather forecast in "picture" format showing predicted wind directions and strengths for the following four days over an area of at least 30° by 30°. The fleet positions and weather forecasts were key pieces of data for us all in determining which course we would choose to sail.

It was clear within a few days that there was no single view on this. Within the first three days the fleet had fanned out, a few going dead east or slightly north of it, several going well south of east, and the rest of us sailing a bit south of east.

There had been a lot of discussion in Charleston about strategy for the first leg. Indeed, it was the only leg in which strategy was likely to play a major role in the outcome. To reach Cape Town from Charleston one has to sail about 60° south and 100° east. There are several obstacles and other factors to be considered in picking a course. The main physical obstacle is the northeast hump of Brazil, about 35° south and 45° east of Charleston. Between the two lie the "horse latitudes" of little and unpredictable wind, and the doldrums. The prevailing wind north of the horse latitudes is westerly, and south of them easterly or southeasterly. There are currents and counter-currents around the hump of Brazil also, which meant we would all want to give it good clearance. The risk in going south too early is that the prevailing winds could make it difficult to clear Brazil. From there to Cape Town the principal consideration is the South Atlantic high, often a large area in the middle of the ocean with little or no wind in it that one needs to sail around anti-clockwise. The prevailing winds for the first 30° south of the equator are also southeasterly or easterly, with unpredictable winds often between 20° and 30° south. Then, below 30°, they usually come in with a vengeance from the west.

Conventional wisdom, therefore, was to sail to the east as much as one could at the beginning of the leg, to give one a straighter shot at the hump of Brazil in the easterly and southeasterly winds lower down.

As the first week of the race unfolded, it became very clear what choices each of us had made. Isabelle Autissier and Giovanni Soldini chose to go east, to pick up the westerly winds that would take them quickly to a position from which they could move south with comfort and speed. Much of the rest of the fleet scuttled off to the southeast, using to full advantage the unusual southerly and southwesterly winds with which we began the race. The choice that Isabelle and Giovanni had taken was the subject of much discussion on the chat-net. "You know, I reckon Giovanni's homesick and he's going to Cape Town via Italy," joked one of his Class II competitors. "Yeah. That, or he's just following the only woman in the fleet — you know these Italians," came back another.

Meantime, I and a few others were reaching slightly south of east. As the weather picture unfolded it became clear we were heading into a stretch of high pressure and little wind. I decided to move north of it. It was a bad decision. As I moved north it slid north too, and smothered me in its embrace. Stubbornness and, it has to be said, a continuing weather forecast that predicted I would clear it in a couple of days, kept me in it. One day when I covered fifty miles, Giovanni further north sailed close to three hundred, and those to the south were knocking off daily runs close to two hundred. On another day I had the spinnaker up and down four times and the big light drifter up and down twice, tacking six or seven times, to claw another few miserable miles to the east.

I'd done it again. Just as I had seemed to find every windless hole coming across in the transatlantic race, I'd managed to find the first available one in this race too. It reminded me of when my father was teaching me to drive a car some thirty-six years earlier. He told me then I had an uncanny knack of finding every pothole in the road and driving into every one of them. This was clearly a skill I had transferred to my sailing!

There were good days and bad in these early stages of the race. One day we had company in the form of a beautiful little bird, smaller than a sparrow, with brown-grey wings and a pale yellow body. He looked alert and in good shape, if a little tired, and did not seem at all frightened. He followed me everywhere. I called him "Titch". When I was in the cabin, he was down there with me. When I was up on the foredeck fussing with the furling gear on the light drifter, he was there right beside me with his little head cocked to one side and following my every move. He didn't seem to want to eat or drink anything, and I found him dead the next morning in the cabin by the mast. He looked so pathetic and lifeless and weighed absolutely nothing. I wrapped him in a white paper shroud, asked God to bless his soul, and cast him to the deep. He must have wanted somewhere warm and friendly to go to die. It was a sad day, and prompted some discussion over the radio about how little wildlife there was in evidence. I had seen a few tiny fish lurking under a patch of Sargasso weed one day when we were crawling across a glassy sea at about one knot. I saw a few of those white birds with long forked tails that are a native of Bermuda, when we were a few hundred miles from there. I saw dolphin, and several mornings found flying fish on the deck or in the cockpit. But I had seen nothing else at all. Others remarked on the lack of wildlife as well, including Harry who reported one dead-calm day being overtaken by a large turtle – about the only thing he'd seen at all with any life in it.

If there were bad days, there were certainly good days also. Days when the sun shone in every sense of the word. A couple of days after the sad demise of Titch, we unexpectedly picked up a little wind and began to make some serious progress once more. In my diary for 26 September I noted: "Yesterday evening was the best yet – steady wind driving us at a comfortable eight to nine knots in a calm sea . . . warm, and a couple of hours of opera with a rum and coke in the cockpit – 'Pavarotti In Hyde Park', some Puccini, and 'A Night At The Opera'. A magical experience!" But at this stage of the race the good days were rare.

If there was a race in this for me, it was against Niah in *Jimroda II*, who I beat into second place in the transatlantic race. We had a bet on it – whichever of us reached Cape Town second would buy dinner for four at the famous Mount Nelson Hotel. He had decided to go south, and within a week or so was a few hundred miles ahead of me in terms of distance to go to Cape Town. Minoru Saito in *Shuten-Dohji II* was another 50-footer I thought I could beat, but he too was now well ahead of me to the south also. At first I was philosophical about my plight, and we joked about it over the radio. At one point, a week or so into this nightmare, I and a few other competitors agreed we should petition the Admiralty to mark the area from 69° to perhaps 50° west, below Bermuda and somewhat to the north of Nares Abyssal Plain, as "Nigel's Windless Plain" – after all, I was the first to discover it and I spent far more time than anyone else exploring it! One day, I sent a message to race headquarters via COMSAT: "Little wind. Little sleep. Little fun. Can we please come back and start again."

Several entries in my diary record the misery of it: "The wind has been fickle or mostly non-existent for hours . . . Weather still horribly fickle – sun then rain, wind strength and direction all over the place . . . We're well and truly stuck in a high pressure ridge, continued slow progress with puffs of one-to-five knots . . . Really not a good day at all, we've been crawling along at two or three knots . . . Dreadful night, virtually no wind and this has been going on for several days now . . . Another dreadful night of no wind, sails flapping, gear clanking . . . Another dazzling sixty miles noon to noon! . . . We've drifted all night with little vespers of wind every now and then to crack the mainsail . . ."

Finally, *I* cracked. I noted in my diary the morning of 29 September: "This morning was a real low point. After another bad night and little prospect of improvement in the next couple of days, I realize that making up the ground now lost is virtually impossible. I shall also be much later in Cape Town than I had planned, which will constrain the time for all that will have to be done to the boat, and on other things to which I am committed." After all the time, preparations, expense and other sacrifices, I'd managed to blow the race in the first couple of weeks! I couldn't believe it. It was no one's fault but mine – I'd read it all wrong and taken a very bad decision on the weather – and the price was too much to bear. That afternoon I stood in the cockpit, clenched fists in the air, and screamed at the top of my voice, "GIIIIIIVE MEEEEE MOOOOOOORE WIIIIIIIND!" I stamped my feet. I thumped the dodger with my fist till it hurt. Then I did it all over again, before slumping in the cockpit feeling both better and worse. Better because I had given vent to these pent-up feelings. Worse for the same reason. It had been a childish tantrum. I gave myself a severe talking to: It was a wonderful sunny day, wasn't it? . . . There was nothing broken on the boat, was there? . . . Had I not said at the outset that my goal was simply to finish? . . . Being in the wrong place at the wrong time was my own damned fault, wasn't it? . . . So pull yourself together, man!

That night I had cheese and crackers for dinner, and for several hours through the late afternoon and evening, I nursed a bottle from the crate of champagne that my friend Jim Baldwin had put on board the day before the start. We each have different ways of punishing ourselves!

Of course, my problems were insignificant compared to some. Simone Bianchetti had returned to Charleston soon after starting, with autopilot problems, and it was a couple more days before he restarted. Arnie Taylor had autopilot problems also, but decided to try to fix them at sea rather than give up the time involved in returning to Charleston or diverting elsewhere. Floyd Romack was late starting anyway so he could attend his daughter's wedding, but he was off within hours of arriving back in Charleston, a week after the rest of us had left. Neal Petersen decided to divert to Bermuda just a few days into the race with a broken headstay. Worst of all, though, was the withdrawal of Mark Gatehouse in *Queen Anne's Battery*. Having nearly won the transatlantic race, he was once again up with the fleet leaders and well to the south when he decided to return home to England to deal with business and personal matters that were praying on his mind.

Mark's withdrawal came a couple of days after I had confessed to my tantrum in the cockpit, and both incidents gave rise to some lengthy discussions on the radio about the psychology of singlehanding. None of it was very profound perhaps, but a good theme to kick around when you're out there on your own. The consensus was that you can't take troubles to sea with you, and enjoying sailing alone was all about "attitude". After the conversation Niah sent me a note via COMSAT. It included the text of a letter written by an eighty-year-old man who had just learned he was dying, and Niah said he had made its theme his life's philosophy. The letter said: "If I had my life to live over again, I'd try to make more mistakes. I wouldn't try to be so perfect. I would relax more. I'd be sillier than I've been. In fact I know very few things I would take so seriously. I'd take more chances, I'd take more trips, I'd climb more mountains, I'd swim more rivers, I'd watch more sunsets, I'd go more places I'd never been to. I'd have actual troubles and fewer imagined ones. If I had to do it over again I'd start barefoot earlier in the spring and stay that way later in the fall. I'd ride more merry-go-rounds and I'd play with more children. I'd sail more seas. If I had my life to live over again. But, you see, I don't. Life is God's gift my friend – make the most of it."

I copied this into my diary and noted: "It flies in the face of everything I had been taught, growing up and going to school in England of the 1940s and 50s, but it has much to commend it. I don't think I shall ever scale its dizzy heights but I have spent some time reaching and struggling up its foothills. It is all about balance, isn't it? Even that old man knew there was more to life than swimming in rivers, climbing mountains and going barefoot in the spring – but he knew there had not been enough of that in his life. The balance had been wrong, for him at least. And that is also true, I think, of everyone I know, including of course myself."

I am not sure how all of this, and the thinking I did about it afterwards, contributed to the next day, but it definitely had a touch of Camelot about it. In the morning, sunny and not a cloud in the sky but with enough wind to keep us moving at a few knots, we had about thirty dolphin with us for an hour, playing about the boat and doing what they seem to like best of all – criss-crossing in our bow-wave. It was a lazy day of steady if unspectacular progress. In the late afternoon I became concerned about the apparent power draw from our batteries or, perhaps, a lack of power input from the solar panels (the wind generators were producing nothing in such little breeze). I turned everything off except the Trimble Galaxy Unit. Surely it could not be drawing three and a half amps! Then

I discovered I still had the inverter switched on, feeding the fridge with about three amps. Well, that meant that inadvertently I had a chilled bottle of Mumm. What a waste it would be to let it warm up again!

I drank much of it through the evening, having spilled about a quarter of it in the cockpit when I opened it, leaving a sticky trail across to the drain holes. As night fell I began to feel I should stir myself and wash out the cockpit with a bucket of sea water. But, just as the wind came up at night to blow away the leaves in Camelot, a light shower of rain swept over us and did the job for me.

The next day at noon I decided enough was enough and we were going to head south. Niah was now five hundred miles closer than me to Cape Town, according to the previous day's position report. Minoru was not all that far behind him. Isabelle was a thousand miles in front of everyone else, and Giovanni had a stranglehold of several hundred miles on the lead in Class II. Yes, it was time for a change.

SOUTH

It felt good to be moving south. It *was* good to be moving south. At last we were beginning to take longer strides across the chart. We turned south at about 25° north, 45° west. After the first couple of days the wind began to move round to the east and we crossed 10° north just under a week later at 35° west. I still wanted to be east of 30° by the time I reached the equator, and that was looking well within our gift now unless the wind pulled too far south.

That first week of southing we covered about twelve hundred miles. The wind gradually built in strength – two to 10 knots in the first couple of days, then a stretch of 10-20 knots for several days, with a light patch at the end of it which was an absolute gift from heaven in view of what needed to be done on *Sky Catcher*.

My troubles began four days into our march south. From my diary for 7 October: "Around 03.00 today woken by a tremendous noise and shaking. Blades off both wind generators – presumably hit by something! Broke more off trying to lash down starboard side (swollen and lacerated forearm to prove it!), then lashed port side. By then the radar alarm was shaken off its fittings. I just hope I can fix one of the generators – five blades missing from starboard, one from port, and I certainly don't have six spare blades. It'll be a real problem for me to remove and replace the equipment up on the arch in these lumpy seas; but with 25 knots over the deck that's what I need to do for charging! One at least will have to be fixed because I certainly don't have enough fuel (for the diesel generator) to last us to Cape Town."

It was lucky I was in the cockpit already and could wrestle the generators to a standstill quickly. Once a blade goes on them they are completely out of balance, and it was as if some giant hand was trying to shake the whole "antenna arch" off the back of the boat.

There is a wonderful line in Oscar Wilde's *The Importance Of Being Earnest* where, Ernest having explained that he had lost both parents as a child, Lady Bracknell comments, "To lose one parent may be regarded as a misfortune; to lose both looks like carelessness." Losing both wind generators had not been due to any carelessness on my part, but losing six blades had. The four gashes in my left forearm told me I had probably knocked out four blades myself, and despite searching everywhere in the boat, I could find no spare blades at all. This meant that, unless I could remove the hubs to which the blades were attached, I would have to remove both units completely and cannibalize one to fix the other.

What caused the damage in the first place is still a mystery to me. In talking about it over the radio, the best explanation seemed to be a direct hit from a school (or is it a flock?) of kamikaze flying fish. "If you'd been there with a pan you'd have had a lovely breakfast of diced fish, you know," joked Harry. I had never seen flying fish that high out of the water. They usually seemed to fly, often for a hundred yards or more, quite close to the surface of the sea. But I had found one in the foot of the mainsail one morning, and a couple of days after having the generators knocked out I noticed fish scales and other debris right at the top of the Monitor windvane – so flying fish sounded like reasonable suspects. And there were certainly flying fish around that night because one had landed on me in the cockpit a few hours earlier. I remember making a mental note at the time to try not to sleep with my mouth open!

What had knocked out the generators was of academic interest to me at the time. The problem now was how and when to fix one of them. For someone whose electrical expertise was tested at home by having to change a fuse or a light bulb, this was going to be a real challenge. And it was one which was going to have to be postponed until the sea was sufficiently calm for me to stand even a fighting chance of grappling with the units up on the antenna arch. In the meantime we were going to have to use as little electricity as possible. This meant no fridge, no electric autopilots, no satellite phone, minimal use of the radio, no lights, and almost worst of all, no music.

A couple of days later I noted in my diary: "I'm beginning to think we might manage without a wind generator if we have to – if we get a fair bit of sun (for the solar panels). With everything off except absolute essentials, we're using a base load of about two amps. The SSB (radio) and "C" (satellite data communications) give us some healthy peaks, but I can use them sparingly. So that's twelve hours at night of two amp hours (twenty-four total) and twelve hours at one amp hours (twelve total, assuming one amp hour only average from the solar panels) and six amp hours for the SSB and "C" – grand total of forty-two amp hours per day. This is about an hour of diesel generating time and I have enough fuel for at least forty hours. It should take me less than another forty days to reach Cape Town. But there's no margin for error."

They say there is no better cure for a headache than a good kick in the shins. That day I noticed a couple of potentially more serious problems that took my mind away from dealing with the generators. The boom vang had come detached from its fitting at the base of the mast, and the lower tab on the goose-neck fitting holding the boom to the mast had been half chewed through by the cotter pin securing in place the vertical bolt through the upper and lower tabs. Both were the product of bad engineering, and I should have spotted these problems in Charleston.

The problem with the gooseneck was caused by the absence of a good stout washer between the cotter pin and the tab, to protect it from the upwards pull of the mainsail. The only solution I could think of at the time was to sail the rest of the leg with one reef in the mainsail, and thus remove the upwards pull altogether.

The fault with the vang was more complicated to put right, and I managed to make matters worse myself before engineering a decent "fix". The nut on the bolt holding the base of the vang to the mast fitting had unthreaded itself. The top of the bolt had a ring on it, to which were tied all three reefing lines; so it too was being pulled upwards. The answer would have been a split pin through a hole drilled into the nut and the bolt. I did not have a drill bit on board capable of going through that much steel, so I would just have to watch it and probably tighten it every day or so. However, in putting the bolt back, I managed to twist off the ring at the top of it (probably a bad weld in the first place) and had to put the bolt through with the nut at the top and a mole-grip wrench permanently attached to the stub of bolt at the bottom, to stop it coming apart again. I also drilled a hole either side of the nut in the upper tab and bolted a plate over it for added security. It took me the best part of an afternoon to deal with the vang. It was another of those jobs on a boat that would have been done in a tenth of the time with an extra pair of hands. The main problem was to lift the boom just enough to suspend the vang in exactly the right spot for putting the bolt through it and the mast fitting. In the end, I managed to do this by tightening the second reefing line at the back of the sail (to pull the boom up) and then tightening the main sheet (to hold the boom steady). For me, this whole exercise was a major achievement!

Finally the wind died to a whisper, the sea calmed, and there was no excuse for putting off repairs to the wind generators. I climbed up onto the arch with a bag of tools, hoping more than anything else that I could remove the hubs and remaining blades from the generators. As I feared, however, the aluminium hubs had fused themselves to their steel shafts and the quick solution was out of the question. There was nothing else for it, both generators would have to be removed and dealt with down below. With a hammer and large screwdriver, I managed to prize open each of the generators' clamps and remove them. In both cases, the wiring inside their stand-pipes was tight and I had only an inch to play with. Both had to be cut, and I would have to find another way to wire them again; but that was something I need only think about if I could put together one complete unit.

Much to my surprise that turned out to be the easiest part of the whole operation, with the right tools and just enough patience to refit six blades at their correct angle in one unit. So far so good. Now to remount and rewire it. I could think of only one solution, and that was to drill a couple of holes in the stand-pipe, pull the existing wiring out of the lower hole, attach new cable to link it with the generator and thread that through the upper hole with a mouse line. The whole job was done by lunchtime the following day; but there was not enough wind to test for success or failure. It was enough of an achievement for me, however, to warrant a celebration, and I broke into another bottle of Mumm for the evening. The next day there was sufficient wind briefly to confirm the success of the operation.

The achievement was marred only by some physical damage to my left shoulder. My right arm was still weak from the injury incurred during the transatlantic race, which meant I was having to compensate for it by using my left arm. In man-handling the generators up on the arch I somehow managed to strain my left shoulder and upper arm, something that was to continue to plague me for months ahead.

We were now around 10° north and about to enter doldrum territory. Apparently the doldrums are usually found between 5° and 8° north, at the longitude we were and at that time of year. Not for us, though! We ran into a patch of really light and fickle weather around 9° north, and then hit real doldrum weather between 4° and 2° north. I had imagined the doldrums to be sunny days and calm seas, chasing little puffs of wind under each passing cloud. In fact the sky was totally grey, and big heavy rain clouds moved about with a wanton aimlessness. Under these clouds was torrential rain and up to 30 knots of wind. Between them was little wind at all, and what there was came at us from all directions. We were forever reefing and unreefing, and tacking this way and that. It was exhausting and unrewarding sailing.

It was a sunny day as we approached the doldrums, though, and one without much wind either – a steady two or three knots out of the east. I noted in my diary: "This morning has a 'beginning of time' feel about it. As the grey horizon filled in with pink, and as the darker grey ocean became blue, small fat silver fish flopped on the surface of the sea, which was almost glassy still." That morning also, the radar detector alerted me to a passing ship. I called her on the VHF. She was the *Bergeland*, a Norwegian tanker bound from Europe to Brazil. I had a long conversation with her Indian captain who was fascinated by the race and what it involved. We talked about England and India which I had visited on business. It transpired that he was a shareholder in BOC's Indian company, and quite a satisfied one at that. It may have been this that prompted him to offer me a tow across the doldrums! No one will know, he said. I would, I replied. He said he was joking, of course, and we both laughed.

I did not laugh so much, however, when I had my next encounter with a ship a couple of days later. I spotted her by chance coming over the horizon and kept a close eye on her as she approached. Her bearing from us remained fairly constant – we were on a collision course. I called her on the VHF. "Ship on my starboard side, ship on my starboard side, this is the sailboat *Sky Catcher* about three miles ahead of you to your port." No reply. I repeated the broadcast several times as we approached each other. As it happened, she passed ahead of us without either of us having to alter course. I still kept calling her though, ending my broadcast with "Dammit, is there nobody there!" Five minutes later the VHF clicked and a voice with a Polish accent asked if he could help.

"Yes," I replied. "I've been calling you for half an hour. I thought we were on a collision course and you passed just a little ahead of me."

"Ah," he said. "I hope there was no chance of a collision . . . "

I asked if he had his radar on, as my radar detector had not picked up a signal at all. He said his radar was on, but I didn't believe him. I don't know if he was the captain or the only person on board they could find who spoke English. I suppose I should have asked and pursued this apparent lack of a good lookout on board. But I noted in my diary: "I hope whoever was meant to be on watch got a bollocking!"

We finally cleared the doldrums the following day, our thirtieth at sea. About 1° north, they began a fight with the southeasterly trade winds. They slapped us around a bit with 30-knot squalls before giving up the struggle and letting the southeasterlies pull us from their grip and over the equator. By then another drama was in its final stages of being played out.

The day before my wind generators lost their fight with the kamikaze flying fish, I had a rare conversation with Minoru Saito on *Shuten-Dohji II*.

"How is everything going?" I asked.

"Oh, not so well," he replied. "I have very bad leak. Pumping much water every two hours."

"Every two hours!" I exclaimed. "Are you in any danger, are you in any danger?" (Why is it that when we speak to someone whose language is not English we shout and repeat everything?)

"No, I don't think so," he replied. "Anyway, I go to Cape Town. Talk to you next sked maybe."

He did not sound concerned, but I was worried for him and relayed the substance of our conversation to race headquarters. I had a message back saying that he had had a leak sailing from the Panama Canal to Charleston before the race but had elected not to have it fixed there. However, would I please keep race headquarters informed of any developments.

In the days that followed, my concern, and that of others except Minoru, grew. Diary entries over the next few days recall my growing anxiety: "Minoru on the radio – said he was still pumping every two hours, 200 litres! He thinks it is coming in several places but mostly headstay chainplate and centreboard of his keel. He says he is not worried and confirmed his intention to go to Cape Town... He is pumping twenty gallons every hour. Says he wants to continue to Cape Town. I've advised against it and asked race headquarters for advice. No one can do that for thirty or more days, and he has a heart problem!... Minoru sounds tired. I'm really quite worried about him... Minoru reports he has now measured exactly what he is pumping out – thirty-eight six-litre buckets every two hours. Frightening!... Today Minoru is only thirty miles or so from me. In these headwinds, he is taking on more water – 250 litres every two hours."

I kept a regular schedule of radio contact with Minoru three times a day. Robin Davie talked with him once or twice a day too. We made sure one of us was on the radio and available to talk with him every four hours if he wanted to, and mostly he did. Gradually he acknowledged that proceeding to Cape Town may not be possible and we discussed his options with race headquarters and others in the fleet. At first the island of Fernando de Noronha was considered, but it transpired that although there were divers there, it had no harbour and nowhere he could go to get at the bottom of the hull. Other ports on mainland Brazil were considered, including Recife and Fortaleza. Finally, through persistent phone calls and conversations through the Ham net, Pete Dunning at race headquarters made contact with a boatyard in the port of Cabadelo, not marked on any of the larger scale charts. It was run by an Englishman and, as luck would have it, a cruising sailor from Cape Town who knew Minoru from the last BOC Challenge was there.

"I go to Cabadelo," Minoru said, when all the options had been put to him. He and I kept our regular radio schedules until just a few hours before he reached the port, where a tow was waiting for him. He sounded exhausted but as unflustered as he had been throughout the previous eleven days since he first told me of his leak. All that time he had pumped his boat out every two hours, and at times when the seas were rough and he was taking more in, every hour. During the day he used the high-volume Edson hand pump we had all been given just before the start, and at night his electric pump. And all the time he kept his boat sailing at a good speed. It was a remarkable performance.

As I crossed the equator, Minoru was well on his way to Cabadelo. I had clawed back a few miles from Niah's lead over me, Giovanni was holding on to his lead of Class II by a wide margin, Isabelle was maintaining her staggering lead over everyone else two thousand miles ahead of me, and Floyd Romack was bringing up the rear of the fleet two thousand miles behind. Thirty days had gone, and I prayed the second half of this leg would be quicker.

The bulk of the fleet was now well to the south of us with Isabelle leading the way and leaving a scatter of mixed fortunes in her wake. Herb McCormick watched it all from race headquarters:

Forty-eight hours into Leg One, the compass needle aboard Isabelle Autissier's 60-foot Ecureuil Poitou Charentes 2 remained pinned to the same course heading it had registered since the boat took leave of the Charleston starting line. Zero-nine-zero. Due east. It might as well have been frozen in place, for it was as rigid as the skipper's resolve. Not that Autissier didn't have small moments of discomfort regarding her tactical decision. She was, after all, alone in more ways than one — the only woman competitor in the field, and the lone Class I sailor to pursue so doggedly an easterly route. Yes, prior to departing most skippers had said they would head east in the early going to quickly cross the northerly-flowing Gulf Stream, then bear away and aim for their ultimate destination of Cape Town. But the breeze had swung southerly almost immediately, and the temptation to dip south with it proved to be too strong.

Autissier, who had made the study of weather a top priority since sailing to a seventh-place finish in the 1990-91 BOC, was ultimately unswayed from the correctness of her conviction. The sun topped the horizon on day three and Ecureuil's bow was still pointed straight for it, clipping along nattily at better than nine knots.

To the south and west of Autissier, the situation was not as rosy. Americans David Scully (Coyote) and Steve Pettengill (Hunter's Child) were among Autissier's Class I rivals who had chomped at the tempting bait, and they were now suffering the hangover from the opening night party. For the fast, favourable breeze that had enabled them to burst from the starting gate and rapidly put several hundred miles between them and Charleston was in reality a ruse. It led to nowhere: a dead-end, windless high pressure system. Class II favourite David Adams from Australia (True Blue), parked in the same neighbourhood as Pettengill and Scully, described the situation succinctly in a Standard-C message to race headquarters: "Very hot and more wind in an empty balloon."

Adams had cause to be doubly frustrated. Among the few who were following in Autissier's wake was Italian competitor Giovanni Soldini (Kodak). Like Adams, Soldini had one of the three brand-new Class II 50-footers designed and built expressly for this edition of the BOC (Alan Nebauer's Newcastle Australia was the third). Unlike Adams, Soldini was creaming along at nearly nine knots while the veteran Aussie struggled to make four.

From that point forward, the rich got richer. A week into the race, Autissier had extended her lead over countryman and defending BOC champion Christophe Auguin (Sceta Calberson) to 151 miles. For Auguin, remarkably, it would be one of the high points of the leg. Days later he would descend to a distant sixth place in Class I, and the armchair admirals following the event had plenty to ponder regarding the bow-wow potential of Auguin's freshly built, fourth-generation Open 60 design. "All's okay on board," sighed the skipper in a shoreside missive, "except my place in the race."

But Autissier's lead, though impressive, was absolutely nothing compared to the numbers established by Class II upstart Soldini. Two weeks into the leg he had opened his advantage over Adams in the small-boat division to a staggering 430 miles! Incredibly, he trailed only Autissier in the overall standings as well. His early easterly heading and the uncanny speed of his close-reaching machine had moved his "Fifty" past every 60-footer save Ecureuil.

And if Adams had been uncertain as to whether Soldini would provide him with a fair bit of competition, the subject was no longer open to debate. "Giovanni is going like a train," he said in a note to race headquarters. "He's reaching, while I'm hard on the breeze, so he'll be a couple of knots faster. He picked the weather right at the outset. He and Autissier went right around the high pressure system the rest of us were in. So I've got some catching up to do."

At the front of the pack, Autissier's next tactical hurdle would be where to negotiate the doldrums, a wedge-shaped band of light and contrary winds that stretch across the Atlantic north of the equator at a mean latitude of roughly 4° north. The trick in ensuring a successful voyage through the doldrums is twofold: one must find the narrowest band possible, so as to move quickly through the maddening calms, squalls and windshifts, yet at the same time be mindful not to wander too far west and face an early beat to weather when entering the southeast tradewinds in the South Atlantic.

Autissier, of course, was spot on. Following a course line due south along longitude 29° west, she and Ecureuil Poitou Charentes 2 continued to sail a tactically flawless race. Autissier slowed to a daily run of under one hundred miles just once, then bounded over the equator and into the fresh trades, where she was soon recording 200-mile-plus days with steady regularity.

"She really did get the weather right at the doldrums," marvelled fellow Class I sailor J.J. Provoyeur (Ben Vio). "She only had one day of slow going while everyone else had four or five." Provoyeur, a surprising third in one of the fleet's older, heavier Open 60s, and veteran Jean Luc Van den Heede (Vendée Entreprises), holding onto second in the midst of his fourth solo race around the world, were among a small platoon of competitors who wisely jockeyed to follow Autissier's proven course line.

Yet another trio, willing to gamble on the high risk/high reward theory, set themselves up with quite different strategies for manoeuvring past the doldrums and back into contention. To the extreme west stood Adams (still second in his class) and Pettengill (fifth in Class I); far to the east, on a radically different tack, sailed Scully.

"I am way to the east of the fleet, and desperately looking for the trades," explained the latter. "If they come in soon, things could be looking good. But being out here is like being lost in the country. There are no signs, no one to ask, and even the features that are supposed to be easily indentifiable, like the doldrums or the trades, are a lot less obvious than one would like. There is just no frame of reference . . ."

Adams, Pettengill, Scully, Soldini and Van den Heede all had surprises — some good, some bad — lying just ahead.

And in front of them all, Isabelle Autissier had one more trick up her sleeve.

EQUATOR

TO

CAPE TOWN

FURTHER SOUTH

By tradition, every sailor who crosses the equator for the first time is subjected to a humiliating ritual. It usually involves having some hideous brew of slops poured over him, then some offering has to be made to King Neptune. Fortunately on *Sky Catcher* there was no one on board to administer this foul and barbaric practice, so we decided on a more civilized way in which to mark the occasion. We celebrated our crossing with a champagne brunch — scrambled eggs, ham, fried potatoes with a little onion, crispbread with marmalade. My only concession to tradition was to cast into the sea for King Neptune's enjoyment the three foods I would least like to be without on a long passage: an onion, a garlic, and some champagne.

I had been asleep when we actually crossed the equator in the small hours of the morning, and our celebration was in the middle of that day, with sunshine and a strengthening southeasterly breeze. For the next week or so we stayed on the same tack, down 30° longitude (or "Route Thirty" as I came to call it) with winds that settled into a 15-25 knot range out of the southeast and coming more easterly as the days went by. It was as if the equator had been the top of a hill we had struggled up in the northern hemisphere. Now we were tumbling down the other side at an average of close to two hundred miles a day. It was great sailing and it went some way to make up for all the crap we had had to put up with during the weeks before.

Our first night below the equator, however, was one of truly high drama and deep anxiety that left me and others in the fleet feeling very unsettled for a while. Out of idle curiosity I tuned into the 16Mhz frequency used by some of the competitors to communicate with race headquarters at 20.00 hours each day. Pete and Larry were urgently seeking to make contact with Alan Nebauer on *Newcastle Australia*, to have him divert to Josh Hall on *Gartmore Investment Managers*. There was no mention of the nature of the emergency. I used the satellite phone to call Pete Dunning in Charleston. He told me Josh's boat had hit something, was holed and taking in water, and Josh needed to be taken off as quickly as possible. Josh had called his wife in England on the satellite phone and his plight was national news the next day – a full-page story in one of the tabloids headlined "Hello, darling, I'm sinking!"

I went back to the SSB radio and tuned into the 4Mhz frequency we all used to communicate with each other over a range of a few hundred miles. Josh and Alan had only a nodding acquaintance in Charleston, but subsequently spent a lot of time chatting to each other over the radio. They were roughly the same age, and both had young children. That evening, Alan had come up on the radio at 20.00 hours for his usual chat with Josh, and was already on his way. They were about a hundred miles apart. Alan was making better than 10 knots on a reciprocal course to Josh, who was limping along at two or three.

"I'm well on my way, mate, just hold on there a bit . . . How's it going?" called Alan.

"Oh, not so good. Be as quick as you can, eh," replied Josh. "We hit something up forward of the bulkhead. There's a hell of a lot of groaning up there and water's coming into the main cabin. I just don't know how long the bulkhead will hold, that's my main worry."

"Is it comin' in faster than you can get it out?" asked Alan, with more than an edge of concern in his voice.

"No, not at the moment. I'm keeping pace with it right now and trying to get some gear together for when you arrive. When do you think that'll be?"

"Ninety miles or so, we're doin' 12 or 13 [knots] between us . . . seven-eight hours if we're lucky. You just hold on there. We'll have you off, no worries."

"Yeah, OK mate. Be as quick as you can though, won't you."

"Sure will. Call you again in a bit."

The radio crackled and several of us sat alone in our own vulnerable little craft, waiting for the drama to unfold and praying for a successful outcome. I sent a message to race headquarters reporting the substance of Alan and Josh's conversation, their reported positions, headings and speeds. I brewed a cup of coffee and sat in my companionway seat, an ear to the radio and an eye scanning the sea for anything that might be in our way! It was hard to grasp the apparent randomness with which fate could beckon you out of the crowd and punch you squarely in the face. Poor Josh. Like most of the rest of us his boat was uninsured, all he had saved and could borrow was in it, and a few days earlier his wife had told him they were expecting their second child. Of all the people in the fleet to pick. A little under an hour later the radio crackled to life again.

"*Gartmore, Gartmore. Newcastle, Newcastle.*"

The radio just crackled.

"*Gartmore, Gartmore, Gartmore. Newcastle, Newcastle.* Come on, Josh, come back to me!"

The radio just crackled. I didn't know I could hold my breath for so long and I could sense the anxiety in Alan's voice as he repeated his request. Then, finally:

"Yeah, hello Alan. Sorry mate, I was in the middle of pumping."

They exchanged positions, headings and speeds for Alan to check his calculations. I sent another message to race headquarters.

When Alan and Josh were off the air, I called up everyone else I thought might be listening on that frequency. I found Niah, who could hear both well. Arnie Taylor on *Thursday's Child* could hear both also. Robin, like me, could hear Josh well but Alan only faintly. I suggested we pair off, Arnie with me, Niah with Robin, and stand a close radio watch two hours on, two hours off. We should each send a message to race headquarters whenever there was anything relevant to report, and probably not bother to talk to each other except when changing watches. We'd feed whatever we could to Charleston and leave them to put together the complete picture with whatever other sources they had. We could also provide some communications linkage between Alan, Josh and race headquarters if required. It was agreed and I messaged Charleston with what we had set up. As it transpired, the greatest benefit of this was probably to make the rest of us feel we were doing something that might be helpful. The truth is that we provided a communications safety net that was rendered unnecessary by the skill and character of both Alan and Josh. It was a textbook rescue. A few days after the ordeal, aboard *Newcastle*, Josh wrote the following – partly to record the detail of the event while it was fresh in his mind, and partly I suspect to help exorcize the experience:

The calms of the infamous doldrums were an increasingly distant memory, replaced by the equally dubious pleasures of beating into strong headwinds and lumpy, awkward seas. The discomforts of this point of sail were being more than compensated for by our rapid progress to the south and Gartmore *was in her element as we at last began to catch up those in front and gap those astern.*

Bands of current were occasionally creating some quite nasty cross seas and this was indeed the case as dusk fell on the evening of 17 October, so I was on deck, hand-steering to nurse Gartmore along. Flying down the back of a wave at over 10 knots, I was expecting a soft landing but instead Gartmore smashed into something, bringing her to a shuddering halt. Thrown up hard against the wheel, I immediately knew something very bad had happened. Gartmore gathered herself and got under way again and I rushed below, punching the pilot on as I went. To my horror, I found a huge gash in the yacht's underbody that straddled the forward watertight bulkhead, and water was simply gushing in. We had a situation here. I found myself rushing back and forward through the cabin, trying to decide what to do, trying to prioritize actions but, more importantly, attempting to quell the almost overwhelming sense of panic that was gripping me. An effective mayday was easily sent to race headquarters by pushing the two red buttons on the Standard-C modem, and then I set to trying to stem the influx of water.

Floorboards, sail bags and the jockey pole helped to shore up the area, but already the yacht forward of what had been the watertight bulkhead was full. The bulkhead itself was cracked severely and groaned alarmingly. It was quite clear that the damage was terminal to Gartmore, and that at best she would serve me as an island with a suspect life-expectancy.

ITT JABSCO had been one of my many product sponsors, and I was blessed with some seriously powerful pumps on board. In particular, the mechanical pump, which normally filled my water ballast tanks, had a bilge pump take off and this, coupled with two large capacity electric pumps, shipped around 19,000 litres of water out of the yacht every hour.

Despite this, the water level down below still rose at a disturbing rate throughout the remaining period that I was on board. A priority was to try and keep the diesel engine and sumps batteries from becoming submerged, because these supplied the power for the pumps.

I had been fortunate to be sponsored by COMSAT Mobile Communications with a Standard-M satphone with which I had been keeping in close contact with my wife, sponsors and the media during the race. It now became my primary mode of communications with race headquarters in Charleston, the UK and Brazilian coastguards, and Laura my wife. My first call, about a half hour after the collision I guess, was to my dear friend Peter Dunning, BOC race coordinator. They had received my mayday and I now filled him in on the details. We agreed that Newcastle Australia was the nearest and most easily diverted competitor to come to my aid. Race headquarters would contact Alan Nebauer, her skipper, and I would leave my SSB radio on a 4Mhz frequency to await his call. Time for me was a fast running thing as I tried to deal with issues that would have stretched a full crew, and though Alan and I agreed to speak every half hour, on one occasion one and a half *hours slipped by without my noticing. Alan later told me this had been an extremely concerning period for him.*

Once I knew Alan was heading for me I was greatly relieved, and headed Gartmore *on a course to meet him. With so much flooding up forward, the foredeck was pretty much underwater as we surged downwind with just the staysail set.*

I think that the outstanding memory I will have of the hours it took Alan to reach me will be the sound of tons of water sloshing around in the cabin. It was a simply terrifying cacophony of noise and one which kept my anxiety level far higher than I would have liked.

With my SART hoisted to the lower mast spreader, Alan picked me up on radar at ten miles distance, and to confirm that it was indeed me I sent up a red parachute flare. It was around 03.00 hours when Newcastle Australia *hove into sight — truly an angel in the moonlight; and with nearly three feet of water through the cabin I was ready, to say the least, to get off.*

My concern about the bulkhead collapsing had been such that for over four hours the life raft had been inflated and tied alongside, ready for a quick exodus. We had agreed that a raft transfer was the safest means of evacuating Gartmore, *so as Alan gybed around I clambered into the raft, togged up in Musto survival suit and life jacket. As I drifted clear I was shocked to see* Gartmore's *stricken attitude — bow down, hull down — and despite the whistling wind and breaking seas, everything seemed stilled in sadness for a while. This trance was terminated abruptly by a sea swamping into the raft. Alan brought* Newcastle Australia *to a halt just yards away and heaved me a line which I hastily tied to the raft. Within minutes I had scrambled aboard with Alan, and at last the exertions and traumas were over. I was safe.*

For the rest of us, our joy and relief once the rescue had been completed was overlaid with the heavy thought, "what if it had been me?". I rearranged my own safety and emergency gear on board into what I thought were places that would make it easier to lay my hands on. The big Edson pump, for example, I had left next to the sail bin in the forward compartment. I brought it into the main compartment and stowed it by the mast. I took out some flares from the watertight box in which they all were and stuck them on a shelf where I could grab them in an instant. I put my "grab bag" with its emergency supplies in a place where I could more easily grab it! Later, on the radio, I discovered others had gone through a similar drill. I think we were all very unsettled by *Gartmore's* misfortune for a few days.

But the magic carpet ride south down "Route Thirty" continued. The skies were mostly clear, the days were spent naked in the cockpit, the flying fish continued to fly, the wind continued to blow, and we continued to plough our way through the dark blue sea with comfort and ease.

As we moved south the temperature began to drop slowly. The sea temperature, which had not been below 28C since Charleston, and had been as high as 31C, dropped to 24C by the time we were at 20° south. By then I was wearing trousers and a sweater at night, and I slept below in my bunk rather than in the cockpit.

I don't know if it was because the weather was so routinely the same, or because we had been at sea for so long, but I found my days developing more of a routine as well. Coffee and breakfast were now always at sun-up and before the 08.00 hours radio schedule. I always took a nap in the cockpit in the afternoon. Dinner was always before sundown and the 20.00 hours radio schedule. I was sleeping on and off throughout the night, far more than I had ever done before sailing on my own. About every hour, and never more than two, I would check our speed and direction and spend a few minutes in the cockpit scanning the boat and the horizon. My routine safety precautions were to use lights at night always, leave the radar alarm on day and night, and have the VHF radio permanently on Channel 16.

Minoru was back in the race within a few days of being in Cabadelo, with very favourable reports of his treatment there. Most of his leaks had been repaired and, although he was still taking in enough water to have to pump out every four or five hours, this did not bother him and he was anxious to reach Cape Town as soon as possible. Not long after he left Cabadelo, Simone Bianchetti diverted there as well. He had reported serious delamination of his hull and a related intake of water. The people of Cabadelo must have wondered what sort of race this BOC Challenge was!

Our problems were not over on *Sky Catcher* either. About the time we were beginning to curve round to the southeast to make a better course for Cape Town, the starboard compression strut that helps to hold up the mast, parted from it! I had noticed on one of my earlier inspections that its end fitting was loose in the strut, but it never occurred to me it might fail altogether. I had no idea how serious this was. The struts, stout aluminium tubes attached to the mast at one end and the deck chainplates at the other, were there to take both compression and tension loads. I hastily added a Kevlar rope strap with a block-and-tackle to replace the strut, and put another strap line from the mast fitting forward to the port-side toe-rail. I phoned my friend Lars Bergstrom to seek his advice. "Well, that should hold," he said. "There is so much redundancy in that rig it should be fine."

"Should" was not as good as "will", but it would have to do. I would have to be more cautious and try not to put too much stress on the mast till we had a chance to check it out thoroughly in Cape Town.

A few days later, bad luck struck again. We were now in the southern hemisphere's equivalent of the doldrums, between 20° and 30° south and between the easterlies to the north and westerlies to the south. The wind died one day to less than 10 knots, so I furled up the staysail and unfurled the No 2 headsail, which was now in pretty poor shape through wear and delamination. I opened a can of beer and laid back in the cockpit to enjoy a gentle afternoon.

Bang, flap, slither, splash. The damned sail had parted company with its halyard, slipped easily down the stay, and was now over the side in the sea doing its best to crawl under the boat. It took me an hour to heave it back on board and stow it, by which time the wind was up into the teens again and I had to give up any thought of trying to rehoist it, or the new sail with which I would probably replace it.

I felt like I was crawling across some battlefield, having bits of my armour and jeep shot from under and around me. I wondered how much would still be intact by Cape Town. Meanwhile Isabelle was making history, and the front-runners in the fleet trailed into Cape Town behind her. Herb McCormick was there:

Out from the dark sea, drifting in the lee of forbidding Table Mountain and the seeming whole of Africa beyond, Isabelle Autissier coaxed and trimmed and tweaked Ecureuil Poitou Charentes 2 *with such effortless efficiency that she might well have been a part of the boat herself. The waters around her teemed with the erratic gestures of a huge spectator fleet, all mindless to the impending midnight hour. Autissier paid them no bother. It was as if she were to allow herself the luxury of acknowledging their presence, her goal of winning Leg One of the BOC race would vanish like a dream upon waking.*

Then, just beyond the mountain's lee, Ecureuil *found the fresh breeze and burst forth in a roar of noise and spray and power. Instantly, it was apparent for all to see how this driven Frenchwoman — and her radical 60-footer with its hydraulically-controlled swinging pendulum keel — had managed such a devastating victory over a fleet of the world's best singlehanded sailors.*

And then it was over, the finish gun popped and Autissier could finally allow herself a long sip from the magnum of victory. Boatloads of schoolgirls, clad in matching uniforms and arms laden with bouquets, jostled alongside Ecureuil *for a nod from their heroine. The walls of the Cape city's downtown Victoria & Alfred waterfront complex were lined three-*

and four-deep with a huge throng craning for a glimpse of sailing's newest superstar.

Someone with a sense of theatre had rigged a sound system and the French national anthem wafted over the scene. For her part, Autissier played the crowd like a diva on opening night. She lit a flare, climbed the bow pulpit, and thrust the light into the night, a statue of liberty to the now shattered idea that a woman could not compete in this most "macho" sporting adventure.

The fact that her closest pursuer was hundreds of miles astern rendered her nearly speechless. "I am just astonished," she managed. "I did not think such a lead was possible."

She had completed the course in just under thirty-five days, nine hours, better than two days faster than Alain Gautier's record for the leg in the 1990-91 BOC. But Gautier's mark was posted on the shorter, 6,691-mile voyage from the former host port of Newport, Rhode Island, to Cape Town. Charleston's position further to the west had increased the length of the journey to 6,818 n.m. — another 127 miles.

Autissier was coolly analytical about the strategic decisions she'd made to open her early lead. "First of all, I went very north and east from Charleston at the start of the race," she said. "It was not easy, we started in a strong wind. For me, it was evident that we had to go north, but only two or three other guys went in my direction. I was right, but for one week I was very distressed about that."

She never, however, second-guessed her path through the doldrums. "I knew before the start I wanted to cross between 28° and 30° west longitude," she stated. "It was a very good place."

But it was a move deep in the South Atlantic that changed the voyage from a straightforward exercise in winning to a full-on, unmistakable rout — what sailors call a "hojo", the ultimate "horizon job".

Conventional BOC wisdom says you negotiate the large, breezeless South Atlantic high by giving it an extremely wide berth. The idea is to stay well west and away from it until reaching a latitude consistent with the arrival of the prevailing westerlies, from which you can finally set an easterly course on a straight shot to Cape Town.

Autissier, poring over her weather charts and charting the slow meander of the high on a daily basis, saw a better, once-in-a-blue-moon route. Several hundred miles north of the accepted waypoint for turning east on the home stretch — a waypoint almost universally employed in the three previous BOCs — Autissier bore away to the southeast on a rhumbline heading for Cape Town. From a competitive viewpoint the plan appeared suicidal, for it strayed dangerously close to the centre of the high.

It was, instead, a stroke of inspired genius. Autissier could easily have followed the accepted strategy, "covered" the competition, and held on to her safe lead. But she saw an avenue to accelerate the attack, and she jumped at the opportunity. "Sometimes you have to take risks when you're racing," explained Autissier. "On the weather maps I saw a small front, and I was able to just catch the edge of it. From there, I just kept going east to keep ahead of it as much as possible." For the rest of the fleet it was checkmate, as Autissier began a string of five consecutive 200-mile-days and opened up a lead that at times extended to over 1,300 miles.

Thus it became a race for second. And the next sailor to cross the line – five days and seven hours after Autissier's stunning midnight appearance – was none other than Steve Pettengill (Hunter's Child), he of the sixth-place standing and a seeming lost cause a few short weeks before. But Pettengill, who like David Adams (True Blue) had set off on what might have been argued was a crazy flyer when they opted to cross the doldrums west of the fleet and hug the coast of Brazil in their plunge south, proved there was method to the madness.

Both were the first in their respective classes to reach the prevailing westerlies – while far to the north and east, Jean Luc Van den Heede (Vendée Entreprises) and Giovanni Soldini (Kodak) wallowed in the South Atlantic high after an ill-advised bid to ride Autissier's course, coat tails, and success into Cape Town.

Pettengill's dramatic rush saw him overtake a trio of competitors in a week and a half, and his second in Class I was the best ever American big-boat BOC finish. "After crossing the equator I saw a major high pressure system in the South Atlantic that wasn't moving," he said. "I made a plan to go way west of it, along the coastline of Brazil, and I stuck to it. I knew the other guys were going to be parked. I was just biding my time."

Adams's end run around Soldini was even more unlikely. He'd clawed his way back into the lead by almost willing himself to catch his Italian rival. It set the stage for what would be the closest racing of the Challenge. But upon arriving some two days after Pettengill he could only marvel at the accomplishment of his friend and overall winner Autissier. "Isabelle hit every waypoint spot on and switched off the lights and turned off the fan as she went by," he said.

Christophe Auguin (Sceta Calberson) arrived about five hours before Adams (and almost seven full days after Autissier!) in an entrance that was far from triumphant. The pre-race favourite had been soundly thumped, but he did not make excuses. "One week after the start I knew it might be impossible to catch her, so I had thirty days to get used to the idea that she might be a week ahead of me," he said. Auguin had also been victimized by constant breakdowns, the result of rushing to the starting line with a high-tech composite boat that was late coming from the builder, and which did not enjoy the luxury of a proper shakedown. As Adams and Auguin rafted together, the former could not resist cracking, "Mate, is the glue dry yet?" But Auguin's race was far from over.

Regarding Autissier, in the days and weeks after her conquest she had to deal with *many pointed questions, the leading one being, "What's it like being the first woman to ever win a leg in the BOC?" Her stock answer was always the same: "Maybe that's important for other people, but not for me." As for her chances in the legs ahead, she might as well have been a seer. She said, "Anything can happen with so many miles still to go."*

EAST AGAIN

We stayed just to the west of the island of Trinidade, close to where 30° west crosses 20° south. As the wind began to back easterly, then northeasterly, we started a long sweeping curve towards the east, crossing 30° south at 20° west and just below 35° south at zero degrees, the Greenwich Meridian. But this stretch of the passage was not overly blessed with good fortune either.

Everyone in the fleet looked forward to being below 30° south. At least we would then be in some westerly current and the strong westerly winds would sweep us across into Cape Town. This is the way it almost always is and, indeed, had been for those a week or more ahead of us. By the time we reached there, however, the reliable westerlies had become an extraordinary procession of high pressure systems. On the four-day weather picture from Meteo Consult it looked like catherine wheels of wind spinning across the ocean from left to right. For us, this meant 20-30 knots out of the northeast would move round to the west and die to nothing. Half a day later it would pick up out of the south and start moving round the clock again. In between there was little or no wind at all.

The first windless hole did give me a chance to raise the new No 2 headsail on its furler, however. It took a couple of hours of painstaking work. Two could have done it in a quarter of the time, because one could be helping to feed the sail into the luff groove of the headstay while the other was back in the cockpit grinding the halyard winch. Being a new sail, it was pretty stiff in the groove anyway and it required several trips to the foredeck to ensure the sail had a fair lead into its track. I was glad to have it up though. With just the staysail, we were always sailing a knot or two below what we should have been doing in anything less than 20 knots of wind. Besides, it was good to have solved another problem on board, however small.

The following day we had another burst of 25-35 knots of wind, west of north and just aft of the beam. The mainsail was reefed right down and we had the staysail out, driving us along with a following sea giving us a little 15-knot surf-ride every now and then. The magic carpet down "Route Thirty" had become a rollercoaster and there was not much rest to be had. From my diary for 29 October: "The passage continues to take its toll on the boat and my nerves! Yesterday the diesel generator spluttered to a halt, diesel fuel in the galley, bit of a mess. Close inspection revealed a fractured fuel line right by the intake – the plastic hose had a kink in it which had gone hard and split. Used bits of the desalinator repair kit to fix it. What next, I wondered. Well, it happened today – the furling extrusion on the inner stay has parted from its base. I've no idea how, or if it is a serious problem. A fix is not obvious."

The drum at the base was now at an angle, leaning and banging against the naked rod stay itself. The aluminium extrusion was riding an inch above it, having presumably sheared the set-screws that should have held it in place.

I searched my brain and the bosunry for an idea on how to at least stop the drum banging into the stay. Finally, it came to me! I cut a length from the spare engine fan belt and fashioned a collar which I forced into the neck of the drum. It was not a fun job on a heaving foredeck taking the occasional wave – and getting my finger nipped by the extrusion riding up and down the stay as I prodded the collar into the drum. But it was another problem dealt with, albeit a bit of a "chewing gum and string" fix this time.

I noted in my diary: "This passage has become like Chinese water torture – just waiting for the next thing to go wrong or break. God, I hope and pray we'll stay together till Cape Town. But it's going to be nerve-racking either way!"

That night we had a real pasting with up to 40 knots of wind as it clocked round from the north to the southwest, delivering some pretty confused seas into the bargain. We were swiped a few times by breaking waves, knocking us sideways. I was lying in my bunk on all but one of these occasions and waited anxiously for the clatter of pots in the galley, tools in the bosunry, and banging on deck to stop to find out if we were still in one piece. On the only occasion when I was not in my bunk I was standing by the nav station, holding onto the grab rail above it. My feet were swept from under me and I hung there for a few seconds, waiting for the noise to stop and for the boat to right herself again.

There was always a strange silence after each of these thumpings. Every time the boat came bolt upright and proceeded for a while as if in an absolutely calm sea, before we started to be buffeted again. I would check on deck, look at the windvane, heave a sigh of relief – and wait for the next one.

But the next day we were back to virtually no wind again. From my diary of 31 October: "Light wind. Fickle direction. Poor progress. Meteo Consult project a real bag of worms for the next few days – absolutely everything from zero to 45 knots of wind out of every damned direction. So much for being swept into Cape Town by steady strong westerlies once you're below 30° south!" Then, a few days later: "Yesterday was not a good day at all. With no wind and a swell running, we continue to bob and roll. Dropped all sail in the afternoon because I couldn't stand the noise or the thought of what it was doing to the rig. I checked the sail and cars (attaching the sail to the mast track). The sail is showing signs of wear and the batten cars are horribly worn in the mast track. I'm wondering if they'll all make it to Cape Town, let alone any further. We'll have to have some bronze ones made in Cape Town to replace the aluminium slugs unless the manufacturer has anything better to offer."

But that morning brought company which was to stay with us most of the rest of the way. Three gulls were sweeping from side to side across the horizon behind us, a few hundred yards off. By afternoon there were eleven of them, and three different kinds. There were big grey gulls with a four- or five-foot wing span, pale undersides and dark topsides; slightly smaller birds of an even black-brown all over; and then some smaller grey ones with white patches on the upper surface of their wings. The black-brown ones stayed with us the longest and seemed always to be there. They were fascinating to watch. They spent a whole day flying in circles behind the boat, coming a little closer to us with each circuit. Finally, they were just a few feet from our stern. Then they flew in figures of eight – down one side of the boat, taking a wide sweep around our stern to circle back down the other side. They seemed to be staring impassively right at me as they flew by. We were getting a really close inspection.

Flying is not quite the right word for it either. They hardly ever flapped their wings, which drooped on either side of their bodies. They were gliding mostly, just above the surface of the sea. Their wing tips seemed to brush the water sometimes as they turned. They were not pretty birds. In fact their size, colour and cold stare would have made them seem quite menacing in other circumstances. But they were the most graceful birds I had yet seen at sea.

I talked over the telephone about these and many other things one night with more than sixty school children in a hotel conference room in Newport, Rhode Island. I was the "star attraction" for the evening (20.00 hours in Newport, 01.00 on *Sky Catcher*) as part of the BOC Oceanwatch/Student Ocean Challenge programme. It took forty-five minutes to exhaust their questions – "Skipper Rowe, what's the most scary thing that's happened to you on this passage?... What do you do with the boat at night?... What do you eat and are you fed up with it yet?... What will be your next adventure?... What wildlife have you seen?... What do you do on the boat when you are not sailing?... What do you do about sleeping?" They were gracious enough to give me a big round of applause at the end of it and asked if I would do it again sometime. "Of course, of course," I told them. "With mostly only myself to talk with, this has been the most interesting conversation I have had in almost two months."

For me, the days were now beginning to drag. They seemed suddenly to have forty-eight hours in them. The calendar had changed from October to November, but I reckoned we must still have the thick end of two weeks to Cape Town, given the uncertainties of the wind. I was not feeling lonely, but I longed for the sight and company of other people. Conversation, over the radio or phone, was not enough. In fact conversation, with Julia in particular, lacked that important element of human intercourse – the ability to "see" what people are actually saying as well as hearing the words, which are only a part of the communication process. We agreed to drink a toast to each other at 19.00 hours every evening till I got in – a therapeutic ritual for me – but I couldn't wait to see her in Cape Town. There was so much I wanted to tell her and to hear about.

I had brought some books and plays on tape but had not yet listened to any of them. I decided to break the pace of the day by having an afternoon matinée three or four times a week, with tea and a bar of chocolate. I listened to Tim Piggott-Smith reading Jules Verne's *Around The World In Eighty Days*, Daniel Massey narrating Daphne du Maurier's *Frenchman's Creek*, recordings by Gerard Hoffnung, Bernard Hepton as Smiley in John Le Carré's *Tinker, Tailor, Soldier, Spy*, and Sir John Gielgud and Dame Edith Evans in *The Importance Of Being Earnest*. I found the sudden exposure to everyday sounds of life ashore – walking on gravel, a London taxi, the clatter and conversation in a restaurant, the crackling of a fire in a grate – a little disturbing. I had forgotten all about them. How familiar, comforting, yet wholly inaccessible they seemed. I wanted, even needed, them in real life – and soon!

Fortunately for me, the weather forecast for the last four days was hopelessly wrong. Instead of light and variable winds we had a steady 15-25 knots slightly west of north. This allowed us to steer a course straight for Cape Town and make about two hundred miles a day. It was in many ways the best sailing of the whole trip, in large part I am sure because these were the last four days of the passage.

I did not sleep for the last forty-eight hours. I spent much of our final night at sea in the cockpit, drinking mugs of tea. I also sat at the nav' desk writing a list of everything that would have to be done to the boat while we were in port. I was disturbed several times during the last twenty-four hours by our radar

Previous page *Arriving in Cape Town after nearly 53 days alone at sea. The clouds enshrouding Table Mountain and Lion's Head were mystical and enchanting.* (BILLY BLACK)

Left *Julia doing a spot of "spring cleaning" in Cape Town, scrubbing Sky Catcher's deck.* (BILLY BLACK)

Right *The lead boats tightly bunched as they cross the start line at Cape Town.* (JACQUES VAPILLON)

Below *Hors d'oeuvres, ice cream and champagne were waiting for me on my arrival in Cape Town. My shore crew Skip Miller couldn't wait to get stuck into it all as well.* (CEDRIC ROBERTSON)

Top *A cheery wave from Isabelle Autissier from the deck of* Ecureuil Poitou Charentes 2.
(JACQUES VAPILLON)

Bottom *Steve Pettengill in the cockpit of* Hunter's Child, *arriving in Cape Town.* (JACQUES VAPILLON)

Top *J-J Provoyeur was happy to change the name of his boat to* Novell South Africa *when he finally found a sponsor in Cape Town.* (JACQUES VAPILLON)

Bottom *Happy to be alive. Josh Hall (in the hat) with Alan Nebauer on* Newcastle Australia, *after the latter had rescued him at sea during Leg One.* (BILLY BLACK)

Right *Also happy to be alive,*
Isabelle Autissier on board her
stricken Ecureuil Poitou
Charentes 2 *moments before*
being winched to safety by the
Australian Air Force. She had
been rolled, dismasted and left
with a gaping hole in her deck.
(AUSTRALIAN AIR FORCE/PPL)
It was a textbook rescue by the
Australian defence forces, but poor
Isabelle could not have known it
would become such a sad political
football once she was ashore and
safe. (ADELAIDE ADVERTISER/PPL)

Above Fatigue leads the immensely experienced Jean Luc Van den Heede and his Vendée Entreprises into difficulties and an impromptu Christmas Eve beach party just hours before he would have finished Leg Two in Sydney. (DAVID TEASE/PPL)

Left Several knockdowns in 70-knot winds left Sky Catcher with no self-steering and a broken tiller which I jury-rigged with bits of pipe, a wrench and some Kevlar line. Heath Robinson would have been proud! (NIGEL ROWE)

A fishing boat tows Sky Catcher *into Hobart for repairs. We were followed by* Thursday's Child *and* Shuten-Dohji II. *All three of us had been caught in the same storm that rolled and disabled* Ecureuil Poitou Charentes 2. (DAVIES BROTHERS)

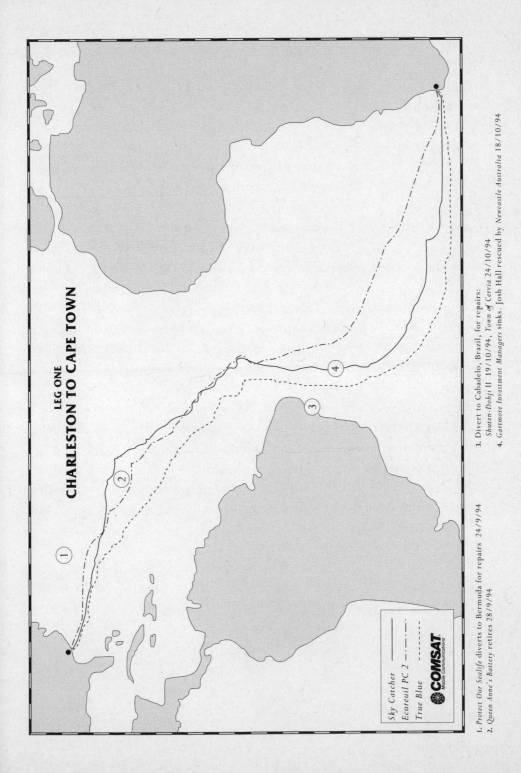

LEG ONE

CHARLESTON TO CAPE TOWN

Sky Catcher ————
Ecureuil PC 2 —·—·—·—
True Blue ————————

COMSAT
Mobile Communications

1. *Protect Our Sealife diverts to Bermuda for repairs 24/9/94*
2. *Queen Anne's Battery retires 28/9/94*
3. Divert to Cabadelo, Brazil, for repairs:
   Shuten-Dohji II 19/10/94, *Town of Cervia* 24/10/94
4. *Gartmore Investment Managers sinks. Josh Hall rescued by Newcastle Australia 18/10/94*

alarm telling me there was a ship somewhere near, and by occasional traffic with Cape Town radio on Channel 16 – both having been silent for several weeks.

About twenty miles out I had my first sight of Table Mountain, shrouded in cloud. Land ho! My God, I was nearly there. More than eight thousand miles of ocean had passed under our keel and I had not seen land for nearly fifty-three days. I could not stop tears of excitement and relief from welling in my eyes.

We were romping along at eight knots. As we got closer to land, dozens of sea birds circled in our wake to escort us in. We passed through a colony of basking seals, lying on their backs and clapping their flippers as if to applaud our arrival.

The grey smudge of Table Mountain acquired some colour as we came closer. I could see the houses and apartment blocks along the coastline, then the movement of cars and people. The wind began to die and a couple of miles from the finish line two National Sea Rescue Institute boats came out to greet us. I could see Mark, Skip, Andy and a dozen others on one of them. Herb McCormick and a couple of photographers were on the smaller one.

"How does it feel now you've reached Cape Town?" someone called.

"Just fantastic," I replied. "But I wish it was Charleston!" They all laughed, probably not realizing that I meant it.

I was standing in the bow of the boat as we crossed the finish line between a sea buoy and a tower on shore. I closed my eyes and thanked God for my safe arrival. I was drained. I was feeling a great sense of deprivation because I had had almost two months at sea, in solitary confinement, with a tedious diet, not enough music to listen to, and on a boat that I felt had had too much break on it. I would now have seventeen days in port – sufficient time, just, to fix the boat. But I was wondering if it would be enough to rehabilitate my mind for the next leg in the Southern Ocean.

CAPE TOWN

TO

KERGUELEN

CAPE TOWN

The welcome on the dock at the Victoria and Alfred waterfront complex, where we all berthed on arrival before being towed to the Royal Cape Yacht Club, was the traditional crowd of friends, fellow competitors, and the simply curious. As we tied up, the owner and manager of the waterfront's Peers restaurant arrived with a plate of fresh hors d'oeuvres, a large bowl of strawberries and ice cream, and a bottle of champagne! My reputation and tastes had preceded me, thank goodness. Each skipper had been "adopted" by a waterfront restaurant for the duration of our stay, and the Breakwater Hotel offered us all a couple of free nights on our arrival. This part of Cape Town at least turned on a special welcome, and it was wonderful to be with people again.

But that evening my thoughts were only on the boat and the Southern Ocean. Skip, Andy and I had dinner and talked beyond midnight about what needed to be done. We concluded that the work list I had written during the previous evening at sea was manageable, so long as we got stuck into it right away. Everything that had broken or had been damaged had to be fixed, there were one or two bits of gear I wanted to have strengthened or replaced, the diesel generator had to be serviced and its exhaust sealed inside the boat; but above all we needed to remove and thoroughly check the mast and rigging. I needed to face the Southern Ocean with my confidence in the rig renewed.

It took me only a few days to find my shore legs and begin to get a good stretch of sleep. Although I had not slept for a couple of days before my arrival, I could manage only four hours the first night. Even then I woke up three times with a start and was halfway out of bed before realizing where I was – "Dammit, we're not moving. The wind's died on us again!" The next morning I went to the race office for a few hours with my "race management team" hat on.

I discovered that Cape Town was having some difficulty with The BOC Challenge in the context of the "new South Africa", despite our initial welcome at the dock and exceptional media coverage for the race.

The problem seemed fairly obvious. Sailing was perceived by many as an elitist sport for whites; South Africans had been generously sponsored in previous events in the old South Africa, and Cape Town had hosted the three earlier BOC Challenge races during the extended period of sanctions and sporting boycotts. Having promised much a couple of years ago to keep the race this time as well, there seemed to be some second thoughts about how "politically correct" it might now be to support it; and, indeed, the two South African entries had already come up empty after trawling corporate South Africa for sponsorship.

Fortunately, by the time the fleet left town on the second leg it was all smiles again, the Challenge loved Cape Town and the city loved the race – even though most of the material help promised by the local tourism authority to keep the event was never forthcoming. Three things helped to change attitudes. First, Isabelle Autissier's arrival, taking line honours by almost a week from her all-male competition, fired people's imaginations. Surely, they concluded, this was no ordinary yacht race. Second, Neal Petersen, a non-white South African who had long been written off by many in Cape Town's sailing establishment as a young dreamer who probably wouldn't even make it to the start in Charleston, was showing his mettle and real determination despite the many handicaps his campaign had suffered. Third, and perhaps decisively, the new Minister for Sport visited the Royal Cape Yacht Club to find out more about the Challenge, lunched there with anxious club officials overlooking Robben Island where he had spent much of the two previous decades as a political prisoner, and afterwards appealed to South African business to support the event and its South African entries. There was a sigh of relief all round and, within days, Neal Petersen had enough support to continue the race and buy new equipment, and J-J Provoyeur – whose wife's persistent campaigning finally paid off – changed the name of his boat to *Novell South Africa*, after the South African software house.

These political manoeuvrings were in mid play when I arrived. While I shared the race management team's frustration with it, I found it faintly amusing and not a great distraction from the task of preparing for the next leg of the race. So far as I was concerned as a competitor, the traditional support for the event from the Royal Cape Yacht Club membership and staff, and the National Sea Rescue Institute whose members were so essential to both the finish of each boat and the fleet restart, was undiminished. Becoming enmeshed in the knitting of yacht club politics, let alone the more complicated *realpolitik* of the new South Africa, was something to be avoided as a competitor and kept in proportion as a member of the race management team. In the past I would have been up to my neck in it all, but my new persona as a competitor gave me a different perspective on its relative worth.

I arrived on a Wednesday and Julia flew in the following Monday. It was great to be with her again. We had a wonderful couple of days at the Sabi Sabi Game Reserve to get right away from the boat and the race for a short while. This was organized for us by Bill O'Reilly, an old acquaintance and the South African dealer for Hunter Marine, and it was an important part of my personal "recovery" plan. Julia and I also had some time to ourselves in our rented Cape Town apartment overlooking the ocean at Green Point, and we managed the occasional meal alone together. Otherwise it was a busy schedule of preparations for the 26 November restart.

As I had begun to loathe the "sameness" of my diet towards the end of the first leg, Julia and I worked together to research food options in Cape Town. We scoured all the supermarkets but were disappointed to find only a very limited selection of tinned food. Finally we discovered a supply of irradiated food in foil vacuum packs at the little store in the Yacht Club, assembled a sample of everything available, and one lunchtime indulged in a lengthy tasting session. Some of it was of almost gourmet quality. I picked out what I liked, we discussed quantities, and Julia then took care of all the provisioning. I planned for a passage of thirty-five to forty days and decided to take food for forty-five. Tinned chicken stew and curry, irradiated steaks, roast beef, roast pork, and chicken in tomato sauce, were piled into the food locker, along with a selection of tinned vegetables. The day before the start, fresh fruit, onions and garlic were stowed in the large mesh bag hanging by the bosunry. The "sweet bin" was filled with Mars bars, Toblerone, Smarties, jelly beans, and other little treats. Another bin was filled with fruit cake and a selection of biscuits. Julia was determined to hear no further complaints about lack of variety and between-meal snacks!

She had brought from England a number of new CDs to supplement my existing library and we shopped for more in Cape Town — so this took care of helping me to feed my mind as well as my body. Julia also sorted out, bagged, and stowed my extensive clothing inventory for the Southern Ocean: T-shirts and underpants, silk long-john tops and bottoms, thermal inner-layer tops and bottoms, thick-pile middle-layer thermal tops and bottoms, three suits of foul-weather outer gear, thick woollen socks and sweaters, woollen and fur-lined hats, gloves, mittens and boot liners. To all of this she added two hot-water bottles for use both in and out of my Everest sleeping bag, rated for sub-zero temperatures. She was determined I should have little excuse to complain of the cold either.

Meanwhile, Skip and Andy worked solidly on the boat and pulled in other local resources when they were needed. The mast was out within a couple of days of our arrival and they worked on it for a week. We had the Doyle loft in Cape Town build us a new headsail that would withstand the rigours of the Southern Ocean and the stresses of furler-reefing gear for which the Sobstad sails were clearly unsuitable. The wind generators were rebuilt and remounted. The compression struts had their ends refabricated, the gooseneck and vang were beefed up, the problem with the mainsail halyard lead into the mast was solved, and we had bronze slugs milled to attach the batten cars to the mast track to replace the worn aluminium ones.

As the days rolled by my good memories of the passage from Charleston began to overtake the bad ones. It seemed to improve every time I described it to someone new. All the competitors swapped "war stories" with each other in the Royal Cape Yacht Club bar and at the various social functions. Most of us had had a pretty rotten time of it on Leg One and it was good therapy to share the misery.

New friendships embarked upon in Charleston, many of which were nourished over the radio during the passage down, were blossoming here. I had watched this happen in all the previous BOC races, and I felt privileged to be a part of it myself this time round. A unique bond seems to develop between competitors in The BOC Challenge, much as happens between soldiers who have fought alongside each other. Presumably its basis is a prolonged, deeply felt, shared experience. But there is something uniquely special about the Challenge, not only because of its length and because it is singlehanded. I think it is also due to the character and focus of most of those involved with it — competitors, families, shore crew, and organizing team — which fosters a very real sense of "family" and interdependence.

It was partly this, I am sure, which prompted some conversations with Josh who arrived on *Newcastle* with Alan in a great splurge of publicity a couple of days ahead of me. Josh was now pondering what to do next with his life. Mark and I agreed he would make an outstanding addition to the short-handed race communications team in the "Langley" trailer in Charleston, and add value to the publicity effort – especially in relation to safety and communications at sea in which COMSAT had such a deep interest. It was a happy arrangement for us all, and it bought Josh a few more months to think through what options he might have for the future.

The social programme in Cape Town was as enjoyable as it was demanding of our precious time. On balance I think these interruptions to the work programme were beneficial – not least because they enabled us to mix even more with each other than we might otherwise have done. The Royal Cape Yacht Club membership and staff welcomed the event and its competitors with their customary and practised warmth and enthusiasm. It was the venue for several cocktail parties and receptions, and the club arranged a day-trip to the wine country for competitors, family and shore crew. BOC's South African company organized its traditional welcome *braii* for us all and some seven hundred other guests when most of us were in, as well as the gala prize-giving evening the night before the restart.

The "media machine" under Dan McConnell and Herb McCormick ensured unprecedented coverage of the event on television and in print around the world, as well as in South Africa. As start day approached, more international media came to town and the circus began all over again. The last three days in Cape Town, like those in Charleston, were exhausting – emotionally and phys-ically. It was one of the perversities of the event, and perhaps of all such events, that one has the least amount of time to oneself when one needs it the most! Without a doubt the competitor who suffered most from this was Neal Petersen. He arrived just a couple of days before the official restart, and sensi-bly took advantage of the rule that allowed him to take a week in port without incurring a time penalty. He was tired when he arrived, and exhausted when he left. He had to juggle with the different and often conflicting demands of the media, family, his girlfriend, local schools, and new sponsors – and prepare his boat and himself for the next leg. Harry Mitchell had a slightly easier time of it; but he only had four days in port after a passage of seventy days from Charleston. He arrived in Cape Town an hour after the official restart and left with Neal the following week. Simone Bianchetti was clearly a troubled young man when he arrived. He said his hull was delaminating and taking in water, and he was concerned about having the boat ready in time. In the end, he never rejoined the fleet. By comparison, my programme was leisurely.

The work list on *Sky Catcher* was completed on time, and I had had enough

shore leave to feel fairly ready myself. The second leg of the Challenge was tradi-
tionally the toughest and I think one would need an extraordinary lack of
imagination not to be apprehensive about one's first experience of the Southern
Ocean. Two days before the restart I was the after-dinner speaker at a customer
event for BOC's South African company. I told them that sailors of old used to
say that "below 40° south there is no law, and below 50° there is no God." I
told them it was the only place where the sea moved around the earth without
having its flow interrupted by bumping into land, and that this meant that waves
could sometimes be as high as apartment blocks. I told them that this early in the
spring, fog, snow and ice were likely to be encountered, especially by those who
chose to sail deep into the fifties. They probably thought I was mad to volun-
teer for such conditions in a small boat on my own.

My anxieties were further nourished the next morning when Skip told me
I would have to sail the leg with the mainsail I had used on the voyage from
Charleston. They had discovered serious stress fractures along the batten pockets in the fabric of the sail I had planned to use, and there was no one in Cape
Town who felt able to effect repairs in time. The old sail, which was due to be
shipped to Sydney for the Sobstad loft there to inspect and repair, was instead
inspected and patched in a hall near the Royal Cape Yacht Club. Once again, I
was going to start a long passage with a last-minute panic and what was to me a
potentially troublesome handicap.

This helped me resolve in my mind the vexed question of how far south to
go. If I had a suspect mainsail I did not want to risk prolonged periods of being
beaten up by storm force winds, which were more likely to be in the fifties
than the forties. In my mind I broke Leg Two into three "manageable bites". The
Admiralty chart covering the Southern Ocean between South Africa and
Australia folded in half conveniently through the Kerguelen Islands at 70° east.
Just below Kerguelen was Heard Island, which was a waypoint of the course that
we all had to leave to starboard. The first "bite" would therefore be from Cape
Town to Kerguelen. The second would be to where the same chart ends at the
Great Australian Bight. The third would be the last difficult five hundred miles
or so through the cluttered Bass Strait and up the east coast of Australia to
Sydney. I decided to leave open the option of going north or south of Kerguelen
until I was closer to it and could better judge what weather I might run into.
Certainly going south early in the trip would have enabled me to follow the
Great Circle route which was a few hundred miles shorter than sailing further
north and staying above Kerguelen; but above all else I wanted to finish in one

piece, and I wanted to enjoy the sailing.

The weather was perfect for the restart – sunshine, a light cloth of cloud on Table Mountain, enough wind to sail but not so much that the spectator fleet would have a rough time of it. We were towed out by Bill O'Reilly's son Tom. Skip, Andy and Julia were on board with me until half an hour before the start as we tacked to and fro, ate sandwiches and drank beer. Julia put a small cache of Christmas and birthday presents in one of the lockers; we hugged, said our good-byes, and they were whisked away to Tom's boat by a small rubber-inflatable tender. As they disappeared with waves and smiles, I mumbled some ill-remembered Shakespeare under my breath: "Once more unto the breach, dear friends . . ."

Only thirteen of us crossed the start line that afternoon. Neal and Simone were still in port working on their boats. Harry was less than ten miles from the finish line. Floyd Romack was still close to a thousand miles from Cape Town (and arrived too late to continue in the race). And minutes before the gun, David Scully was towed back to the Royal Cape with a blown out mainsail.

SOUTH AND EAST

The start gun fired from the deck of the South African Navy ship *Umkomaas*, and we made our way through the spectator fleet to open water. It must have been fun to watch. Again, just about everything that could float was out there to see us off; the navy turned on a helicopter flypast at the gun, and there was the usual flock of media helicopters buzzing around the fleet. The winds in Table Bay were fickle in both strength and direction, due to the influence of the mountains around the city; but two long tacks put us well clear and into a clean 20 knots from the southwest.

I was reefed down for stronger winds and was definitely going to sail conservatively until I had the measure of this awesome place called the Southern Ocean, whose reputation and spectre now lay heavily on my mind! My head was juggling with a mixture of anxiety, excitement and a simple fear of the unknown. I had heard and read such different tales of what it was like as a place to sail through. But could it really be so much worse than the storms I had experienced in the North Atlantic? I suppose the Southern Ocean had been on my mind from the day I decided to compete in The BOC Challenge. It was one of the reasons for doing the race, one of the things that would make it a significant and therefore worthwhile test of my character; one of the things that made it such a unique endeavour. Could it be that I had bitten off more than I could chew?

In the planning stages for the race, and even during Leg One, the Southern Ocean was somewhere I could be excited about as a prospect, not burdened by any sense of immediacy. My intellectual curiosity about it could be exercised and entertained by discussion and modest research. Now the veil of other distractions had been removed. The emotional journey had now traversed the plains of excited anticipation to the rocky ground of anxiety, and I was beginning to smell the fear of it. I knew I was well on the way to psyching myself into a state of desperation and I was going to have to work on this if it was not to have the better of me.

The first hurdle on this leg was the Agulhas Bank, a two-hundred-foot-deep shelf that protrudes far to the south of the land mass and is notorious for its currents, counter-currents and difficult seas in windy conditions. As the wind moved round from the southwest towards the south, there was really no way to avoid it. It was a lumpy ride in steep short seas, with the wind strength ranging from 20 to 40 knots. In fact it moved up and down within that range continually, sometimes completing a full cycle within the space of just an hour. Those at the front of the fleet would certainly be on deck most of the time, putting in and letting out reefs. I decided to set enough sail for the heavy wind and pay the price in boat speed in the lighter stuff. I told myself this was prudent, but I suspect there was a piece of idleness as well as caution in there.

The big boys had taken a different approach of course and some were paying for it already. Jean Luc Van den Heede blew out his mainsail and was waiting for calmer weather to stitch it up again. Christophe Auguin blew a headsail and had it wrapped around his mast. Arnie Taylor was caught in a gust which shredded his only headsail and left him with just his "blade" staysail for the rest of the passage. David Scully's problems were not over either. A few days out he discovered the set-screws in the stay extrusion of his furler-reefing system popping out about twelve feet up the stay. To screw them back in he had to hoist one of his thirty-five-foot-long spinnaker poles alongside the headstay and then climb along it from the mast. "It wasn't much fun, but the alternatives weren't all that great either," he said over the radio afterwards. "Thank goodness we're in the boring forties and not the roaring forties at the moment!"

My only problem had been a trip out along the boom to tighten the leach line that puts tension in the trailing edge of the sail and stops it fluttering. It was blowing 30 knots at the time and I was concerned the sail would fracture down its back seam, otherwise I would have waited for less wind. It was an easy job, and I had myself securely tethered to the boat with my safety harness. Only when I was back at the mast with the job done did I remember that the leach line ran down the luff of the sail as well, and I could have tensioned it from the base of the mast. It had given me a little adventure for the day though!

The first week rolled by with no sign yet of a "big blow". It reminded me of my days at boarding school. When we had committed some misdemeanour that warranted a caning we were sometimes left for days before the punishment was administered. The anticipation of it was almost worse than the pain when it finally arrived. I wondered if the Southern Ocean would be that way . . . certainly I was suffering in anticipation.

Nothing seemed to change much as we edged south and east. Some days were so fine and warm I would spend hours basking in the sunshine. Four days into the passage I noted in my diary: "The weather has been wonderfully kind to us in these first few days. In fact yesterday was so good, and with a clear sky, that I spent much of it in the cockpit sunning myself. Who knows when a chance to do that will occur again?!" We were even becalmed on a couple of occasions during the first week. Niah and Robin joked on the radio about my uncanny ability to find no wind, as happened so often in the first leg. Indeed, a week or so later in the passage when I had twice more found myself engulfed in a little high pressure system of my own, they asked that I send a man with a red flag and a bell ahead of me to warn of my proximity, and that of an inevitable windless patch! But it was not all balmy breezes and sunshine – we soon started to encounter fog and the nights were becoming ever more cold.

By the end of the first week my caution had allowed Niah to escape further east, and I had both Robin and Minoru snapping at my heels. Harry and Neal joined the fleet and had a rough time of it crossing the Agulhas Bank. Further south and east of us, however, much worse was about to happen. The wind was kicking up a storm down there, with big seas. David Adams said it had become "really filthy stuff down here now". In the middle of it, Isabelle's *Ecureuil Poitou Charentes 2* took a bad knockdown and lost her mast at the deck.

Poor Isabelle. Like her mast and sails, her dream of a BOC win was in tatters around her. This would be a real test of her character and resourcefulness. Her nearest safe haven was a thousand miles further east, the French Kerguelen Islands, where there was little more than a weather station and a few people. We were all emotionally involved with Isabelle's disaster, and David diverted to where she was in case she needed help. At the time, David and Giovanni Soldini had their horns locked in combat for the lead in Class II. Herb McCormick followed events from race headquarters:

At first glance they are the Odd Couple, the differences between them so blaringly obvious as to almost be comical. David Adams (True Blue) and Giovanni Soldini (Kodak) will never be mistaken for a set of twins separated at birth and reunited by chance decades later. They might well be nicknamed "point" and "counterpoint".

Adams stands a hand above six feet and sports a John Newcombe moustache in, well, "true blue" Aussie style. He is equipped with shoulders as broad as the Outback and a slashingly quick wit that is just as dry. His sailing style is based on relentlessness and experience, as he proved as a competitor in the 1990-91 BOC when he wrestled a heavy 60-footer designed for a full crew around the world almost by sheer willpower — and which he underscored with his dramatic Class II comeback victory in the first leg of this edition of the race after falling behind by hundreds of miles.

The only things big about Soldini are his personality and his talent. A compact bundle of perpetual motion, the young Italian is a brash, confident wiseguy, in the best sense of the term. When moved by the occasion, he wields his high-pitched wail of a voice humorously, loudly and often. If Soldini holds an opinion on a matter deemed important, one needn't wait long to be acquainted with its essence. He does not, cannot, push a boat like Adams, so he must rely more on learned, enthusiastic finesse.

Given all that, the incredible trait that unites Adams and Soldini is their uncanny ability to sail across thousands of miles of open ocean and consistently arrive at their destination within hours of one another. Oh yes, and the fact that it drives both of them crazy.

Adams took the first "set" of the duel, which now had all the earmarks of a classic confrontation, by twenty hours. It did not take long for the pair to re-engage at the start of Leg Two. Both sailors headed immediately south from Cape Town, with eyes only for each other, as the majority of the fleet idled west in the general direction of Sydney. Adams, then Soldini, were the first competitors to dip below the fortieth parallel and into the infamous "Roaring Forties". Adams took the early lead, but before the end of the first week, Soldini scooted past.

And then, in an incident that had nothing to do with either of them, but which would alter both their BOC destinies, disaster struck. Six days after the start and 1,200 miles from Cape Town, the mast aboard Isabelle Autissier's Ecureuil Poitou Charentes 2 — *and the sweet dreams of her skipper — snapped and toppled into the uncaring sea.*

In a shoreside message, Autissier summed up her situation dramatically: "Thirty knots of wind, sea dark, sky crying. I'm working to clear off the deck and see what I can do. There is almost nothing left on deck, nothing left of my dream. But I won't think about that now. I am safe."

Though Autissier insisted she was safe and could carry on — which she would prove emphatically in the weeks ahead when she sailed under jury rig to remote Kerguelen Island, stepped a replacement mast, and rejoined the race — race officials deemed it prudent for the closest competitor to divert to the scene, make sure all was well, and file an unbiased situation report to race headquarters. That sailor, some sixty-five miles away, was none other than David Adams.

He arrived in the dead of a black, stormy night, and the pair could barely communicate — the batteries in Autissier's handheld VHF radio were low. "There wasn't much I could do," he said. "The sight of Isabelle struggling on deck with this grotty little spinnaker pole all by herself on this awful night . . . it got to me. For the next couple of days I was in a haze, I just couldn't get it together." Adams remained on station for about two hours in severe weather and then carried on in accordance with Autissier's wishes. The entire interlude had cost him about four hours. At the time, there was no way of knowing the short detour would have more lasting repercussions.

As Adams, Soldini and the rest of the racers pushed on across the Southern Ocean the weather continued to deteriorate. It would still be weeks before they all realized they'd survived the worst conditions on an individual leg in the storied history of the BOC Challenge. For now, all they knew was that the low pressure centres were marching through in rapid succession, bringing winds in excess of 50-60 knots and wicked cross seas as the endless fronts wound the breeze around from the northwest through to the southwest.

Two weeks into the leg, in the first of two extended gales that would wreak havoc with the fleet, Adams reported: "The gale is going on. I'm absolutely stuffed. Been twenty-four hours at the wheel in 40-60 knots. Had four knockdowns, with the mast in the water. Once we went down a wave like that, on our ears. It's just survival out here, not racing."

*The damage reports coming into race headquarters were awesome. Sails had been shredded, autopilots fried. Steve Pettengill (*Hunter's Child*), J.J. Provoyeur (in his renamed* Novell South Africa*) and Chaniah Vaughan (*Jimroda II*) all reported broken booms. Adams had one too — the result of the mainsheet slipping out of a self-tailing winch, allowing the boom to fly forward unchecked into the shrouds — but he kept the news to himself. He did not want Soldini to know, he would not present him with anything that might provide a tactical or psychological boost.*

Autissier, who counts both sailors as her friends, describes them thus: "Little Giovanni, big David; the Latin and the Anglo-Saxon; the effervescent versus the cool; the extrovert versus the circumspect." As she sailed towards Kerguelen, each sailor confided in her via COMSAT Standard-C faxes.

From Adams: "The sea is awful, a while ago a wave threw me overboard in a gust of snow. I was wearing my harness but had trouble getting back. I feel wet and tired, like some poor old kangaroo . . ."

From Soldini: "Adams! What a shit! He got one hundred miles ahead yesterday . . . but he's mad, he never stops steering outside. It's a crazy risk. I won't do it. I don't want to kill myself."

On and on they sailed: obsessed with each other like jealous lovers, living and dying with each mile gained or lost, alone but together.

The day after Isabelle's dismasting the seas began to kick up a bit for us too, but I continued to edge south. I planned to sail south of Crozet Island, to leave open my option of going north or south of Kerguelen. That decision was taken for me, however. On the radio chat-hour that morning, I discovered that Arnie had taken a knock in heavy seas a couple of hundred miles ahead and slightly north of me; he had lost his rudder and had "a bit of a mess" on deck as well. Niah was seventy miles to the south of Arnie, but it was an easier sail for me to divert to him in the prevailing winds. Arnie was not asking for help, but we all agreed it would be prudent to have someone closer at hand, at least until he had fixed, and was satisfied with, an emergency steering system.

Thursday's Child has a rudder that hangs off the back of the boat. This makes it a bit more vulnerable, but easier to deal with if it breaks. Arnie had an emergency rudder on board which he bolted to the undamaged fittings on the transom, and halfway through the following day said he felt confident about proceeding to Fremantle or some other port on the west of Australia for a proper repair. By then I had to round north of Crozet, which also meant staying north of Kerguelen, a decision I probably would have made on my own anyway as more foul weather unfolded further south.

Isabelle's character and resourcefulness were soon in evidence. She had jury-rigged some sail using a spinnaker pole as a mast and was proceeding at five to six knots to Kerguelen. There she would have a mast from a smaller cruising boat fitted, and she would sail to Sydney where her sponsors would arrange for a new mast and sails to await her arrival. She would be ready for the next leg, and would be taking no hostages then, for sure!

By the time I reached Kerguelen, however, the casualty list had grown alarmingly. Both Harry and Neal took knockdowns in bad weather at the back of the fleet; but for Neal his near-capsize cost him his mast and flooded his main cabin. He pumped the boat out, jury-rigged some sail on what was left of the mast, and limped slowly up towards Port Elizabeth a few hundred miles to his north. I talked with him over the radio the day after he was knocked down. He was exhausted and dispirited, but his incurable energy and optimism were already shining through. "You know, Nigel, I've had many setbacks in my life and this is another one. I've always overcome them and I'll overcome this one too. My dream is shattered now, but not for ever. My goal is to have a properly funded campaign for the next BOC, with a boat I don't have to build myself. There's lots I can do in South Africa now while this race is still on and I plan to take full advantage of it. By the time I get to port I'll have an action plan – I am going to fulfil my dream, hopefully next time in four years."

To Neal, a poor man was not one without money in his pocket, but one without a dream.

A few days later the front-runners in the fleet were being decimated by winds up to 60 knots, and some had snow as well. Steve Pettengill, who had earlier made five trips up the mast of *Hunter's Child* to jury-rig a problem with one of his Kevlar shrouds, took a bad knockdown. J-J Provoyeur broke his boom on *Novell* in a knockdown and was having autopilot problems. David Adams, leading Class II and up with the 60-footers, suffered four knockdowns in one day aboard *True Blue*. Damaged sails and broken gear were commonplace among the front-runners now. They were in a different game to me, playing by different rules, and this passage through the Southern Ocean underscored the gulf between us in attitude and expertise. Of course, we were all "out there" competing in the longest race on earth, and in one of the most desolate and forbidding places on the planet. But most of the skippers of the Class I boats, and the two leading Class II, were out there and "on the edge" as well. It was this relentless quest around the clock for that extra fraction of a knot of boat speed, shaving margins for error to the finest limit they knew how, that put them in a league of their own. This was the source of their torn sails and broken gear, not carelessness or any lack of skill. I was in awe of them now as I had been of those in the first Challenge – in fact more so, because now I had a better understanding of what they were dealing with, what they were up against, what being "out there" and "on the edge" was really about.

Much closer to me, Minoru had lost the use of both his electric autopilots, and a fitting on the main shaft of his windvane self-steering gear was damaged. We discussed the possibility of him diverting to Kerguelen for repairs, but he chose instead to sail to Fremantle: "I know Fremantle, can get fixed there for sure. Kerguelen too difficult, too cold, and no spare parts there. Fremantle two weeks maybe – I go there." Minoru was a tough fighter, he proved that in the first leg; but he sounded glum and he must surely have felt he was having more than his share of ill fortune in this race.

By now, the fleet had two reliable sources of information on what was happening to us all: reports passed down the line through the radio chat-net, and the almost daily "Trailer Gazette". This owed much to Larry Brumbach who, like the other members of the "Langley gang" in the race communications trailer in Charleston, had a strong empathy for those of us at sea and our needs. It was not long before most of the competitors were sending in snippets for publication in Larry's excellent journal – along with ideas for impossible improvements like cartoons, pictures and a colour supplement! One day I sent Larry a small advertisement for a "Lost and Found" column I thought he might like to start: "Lost. Wind. Usually returns within hours but feared lost altogether now. Big reward if returned at full strength to *Sky Catcher*." We all had fun with the Gazette, and it was something else to look forward to each day.

My passage to Kerguelen had been painless if singularly unspectacular, although I felt prepared psychologically for the worst. *Sky Catcher* was behaving well even though I was not driving her at more than about sixty per cent of her full potential. This bothered me a little, but my emotional passage through this potentially treacherous ocean had delivered my mind to a curious state. It felt as if my feelings were cushioned from any excesses, good or bad. That part of my mind that could sense extremes of excitement or fear had been closed down. It was an odd state to be in and the strange thing about it was that I was very aware of it – as aware as I would have been if my feet and hands had gone numb.

Perhaps all of this was just as well, because things on *Sky Catcher* were about to change significantly for the worse.

KERGUELEN TO SYDNEY

FURTHER EAST

On the morning of 13 December the slumbering giant of the Southern Ocean finally awoke close by, and breathed foul fog and drizzle over us in ever stronger breaths. As he stirred himself at last, the seas moved towards us in great and growing hills until finally their snowy white peaks were being torn off and scattered across the rest of the ocean. At last a taste of a "Southern Ocean blow" – the caning for which I had been waiting!

I was woken just after midnight (GMT), after a couple of hours' sleep, by the jolt from a crossing wave. The grey light of dawn was seeping into the cabin. I stuck my head out from my sleeping bag and my breath hung over me in a light mist. It was cold. I twisted my head round to peer at the instruments by my navigation desk and could see we had 30 knots of wind. I stared up through the deck hatch and could see the mainsail straining with its last reef still out. Every now and then a wave would catch our stern and slew us round up into the wind. The staysail would flog uncontrollably and the main would billow in its back-draft. I screwed my eyes up tightly. Surely the wind would ease soon.

Moments later *Sky Catcher* eased herself upright. The sea seemed smooth and silent. We were suspended, weightless. Then I could hear the dull crackle of a breaking wave. It caught us full on our side and we went over – not a full knockdown I suspect, but enough to throw me out of my bunk and across the cabin in a graceless somersault, trailing my sleeping bag half with me. I landed more or less painlessly, however. My feet hit the deckhead handrail, my head landed on the starboard seat cushion, while my back took the weight of the fall against the pipe-berth, which was fortuitously stowed in its upright position. The three large underside pouches which broke my fall were stuffed with sweaters and quilted jackets.

As *Sky Catcher* came upright again I was thrown back towards the centre of the boat. I scrambled to my feet, sat down, shook my head. "OK, OK," I said aloud to the giant of the Southern Ocean. "Time to take in that last reef, I know."

With more than 30 knots pressing it against the rig, reefing the sail was a slow process. I pulled the boom back a little, then gradually, a foot at a time, let out the halyard and ground in the separate luff and leach lines. This way the sail did not flog or bend back, but it was a long job.

I brewed a cup of coffee and sat in the companionway seat from which I had good all-round vision. This was surely a grey and forbidding place! The hills of ocean rolled across our stern quarter, lifting the transom and shoving us both forwards and slightly sideways. As the morning passed, the wind and seas built inexorably under the thick grey sky. It blew 35-40 knots and gusted at more. Soon more waves were breaking around and against us. These breaking waves, if they caught us just right, would give us a little burst of speed, beyond 15 knots sometimes. Then we would settle down in the trough between the waves and wait for the next one.

If the wind had been steady in both speed and direction we would have had a good ride. But its direction moved around as much as twenty-five degrees, and its speed wandered randomly between 30 and over 40 knots. This delivered confused seas and irregular wave patterns. The combination of a contrary breaking wave and a sudden gust of wind played merry hell with the windvane's ability to steer the boat properly. We were knocked almost horizontal two or three times. I was concerned that I might damage the rig if the boom dug into the sea with its "preventer" strapped too tightly, so I loosened it – enough I thought to let it ride up in a knockdown.

I had left it too loose. We were caught by a breaking crosswave and a sharp wind shift at the same time. The stern of the boat was thrown sideways and the wind got behind the mainsail. It swung across the back of the boat with a tremendous crash, snatching the preventer line from its loose grip on the winch, and fetching up against the port side running backstay. How it all stayed together I shall never know, and before I could get to the tiller the boom was on its way back to starboard with a whistle and a loud crack. I hastily secured the preventer and quickly checked the obvious places for damage – the sail, vang, gooseneck, standing rigging, compression struts, running backstay. We had been very fortunate. This was how booms and rigging were broken, and how masts were lost. I went below and touched the Bible that the Rev David Roberts had given me in Falmouth. The "Good Angel" to whom he had referred in his inscription had surely looked after us this time!

The emotional numbness that had gradually enveloped me in the early stages of the passage from Cape Town was still with me and I was still very aware of it. My curiosity about it was now tinged with irritation. While it was clearly a subconscious protective mechanism in my mind, and no doubt a significant contributor to my ability to deal effectively with a Southern Ocean passage, I was feeling deprived of the very intensity of experience for which I had signed up with my entry in the race. I found myself unable to reach my true feelings and emotions, and to this extent felt that I was being cheated. It was like visiting an expensive new restaurant with the promise of a lavish gourmet dinner, and finding that it all tasted as bland as mushroom omelette.

The difficult weather stayed with us through the night and not much sleep was had on board *Sky Catcher* because of it. The cold was penetrating, even down below, and the cabin filled with steam when I cooked dinner. This was quite an exercise in itself, but I took no short cuts. I peeled and fried an onion and garlic, then added irradiated roast pork, potatoes, mushrooms and asparagus, mixed herbs, pepper and a dash of red wine. Remarkably little of the ingredients ended up outside the saucepan. Although the slumbering giant was doing his best to throw us at the wrong moment, he succeeded only once. There were too many potatoes in a tin for one meal anyway, and the few that leaped behind the stove that evening could stay there till we were in calmer waters. I sat braced in the companionway to eat an excellent meal, and washed it down with the remaining half of an even better bottle of red, given me the day of the start by Jean Luc — half having been consumed the previous evening after passing Kerguelen. I had kept it specially for that occasion.

As I stared at the grey heaving ocean under that dark frowning sky, I realized why the sea was in such a state. The wind was strong, of course, but I had been in stronger in the North Atlantic many times before. Why was the sea so different, so much more turbulent, down here? Two things were going on that were beyond my experience before. In the first place the wind direction varied with the wind strength, which itself was on a fairly short cycle of change. Thirty-five knots northwest would become 45, gusting to 50, out of the north, then go back again — all within less than an hour. At the same time the relentless and natural march of the ocean westwards, causing a continual westerly swell to run, was being challenged by rolling wind-created waves from the north. The net result was confusion, with the run of the swell and the wind and the waves in conflict with each other. It made for an uncomfortable and unpredictable passage.

After a few hours, the wind subsided to the low thirties again, and I was ready to take advantage of its relative stability in my sleeping bag. The giant of the

Southern Ocean slept for a while that morning as I did. But his sleep, like mine, was an uneasy slumber destined to be short-lived. At dawn I decided to do a quick "deck check" before he started flailing his arms and the sea at us again.

I wish I had had the video camera rolling. While standing at the toe-rail near the mast, tidying some lines, we took another tumble. Before I knew it, I was thigh deep in sea water and being pressed against the shrouds. I was tethered to the boat by my safety harness and line, so I felt in no danger; but I had not bothered to seal the bottoms of my foul-weather trousers and the icy water was pouring into my boots.

Back in the cockpit, I furled in some more headsail, engaged the electric autopilot and disengaged the windvane. This involved a quick trip into the stern scoop to lift and secure its water paddle. It was really asking too much of the Monitor to handle these conditions, and I felt they were bound to get worse. I set a compass course that would take account of the shifting wind and ease our passage through the confused seas. I then went below to change everything from the waist down and have a quick body-wash with a handful of baby wet-wipes! I felt better for it, and the change of clothes was overdue anyway.

With *Sky Catcher* as settled as she ever would be in these conditions, I took off my boots and lay on my bunk under my sleeping bag. Sleep was impossible, and it was not long before our motion became ever more violent in the rising wind and seas. I would have to do something about this. I already had the deep reef in the mainsail; but I should furl up more headsail and perhaps think about dropping the main altogether.

I put on my shiny new dry boots and foul-weather gear, and was just stepping up into the companionway, when we were caught, lifted and rolled by a huge breaking wave in a full-blown knockdown.

The sound of the angry and exploding water flow around us was roaring in my ears. We were soon horizontal and I lost my footing. I was pinned against the companionway with my face pressed against the leeward cuddy window and the blood rushing to my head. I could see only the turbulent turquoise and white water. It poured into the cockpit, then between my legs down into the boat. The boom was digging into the sea with a rooster-tail of foam behind it. As we reached the bottom of the wave we began to come upright again, just as the leeward wind generator was about to be wiped out, and just before we would have lost everything at the top of the mast. We came upright as quickly as we had gone over, and we were on an even keel before I had time to panic. But what now?

I took in more headsail on the furler and decided that dropping more of the reefed main with 45-50 knots of wind pressing it against the rigging would be a risky business, and might create more problems than it solved – especially knowing how sensitive to wear and chafe the Sobstad Genesis sail material was. I did not like the idea, but I decided to leave it where it was. I was pleased to find there was very little mess down below. Everything that had been loose in the cabin (some tape cassettes, a bottle of water, a couple of torches, pair of spectacles, hot-water bottles) was on the leeward cabin seat. The cutlery tray had emptied itself across the galley onto and around the stove. Other than that, and with less water to pump out than I recalled had poured into the boat, we were in good shape.

The storm lasted a few hours. I stayed in the companionway seat ready for action, but with not much of a clue as to what might be required of me. This was very much "on the edge" for me, and I was far too close to losing control of the situation. We had a few more near knockdowns from waves breaking over our side. But of more concern to me now was surfing down the waves coming at us from behind. Bursts of 13-15 knots were routine and exhilarating; but every now and then a really big wave would come along, pick us up, and throw us down its face like dice on a craps table. We would hurtle down, dig our nose in at the bottom, then get lifted again. Our top speed in one of these joyrides was a coat of paint under 20 knots! This was close to being dangerous. More wind would mean bigger seas, steeper and longer waves, faster surf-rides, and a real risk of digging our nose in at the bottom deep enough to be tossed head-over-heels. That, or being thrown sideways to the waves and capsizing. Yet, to heave-to or run under bare poles in these conditions was probably just as dangerous – it was important to keep the boat moving with the flow of the sea.

I counted myself lucky that the worst of this lasted only a few hours, and I had even more respect for those at the front of the fleet. They had had to contend with worse weather, stronger winds, bigger seas, more knockdowns, and surf-rides in the high twenties – and much of this through driving snow in very limited visibility.

For us the wind eased quickly. I sent a message to race headquarters: "My compliments to whoever is in charge of things; but I've had my taste of the Southern Ocean, thank you very much. Just give me the 'been there and done that' sticker, and a gentler ride to Sydney."

Our only damage from this experience was to the teeth of the bronze cogs which connect the windvane shaft to the water paddle shaft of the Monitor.

The water paddle had been swiped by the wave in our knockdown and forced right over to one side. In doing this it wrenched its set of bronze cogs away from the upper set. It would not take long to fix once we had some calm waters in which to work; but to save it from further damage, I went over the back and removed the water paddle altogether for the duration of the storm.

Over the radio later in the day, however, Minoru reported having several knockdowns and some broken deck gear. Robin Davie, to the south of me, said he had lighter winds, but sleet. To the north of us, Arnie said the sea was unsailable with his emergency rudder and he was running under bare poles. Niah, ahead of us a couple of hundred miles, said thanks for the warning! His turn was a few hours later and he suffered a similar pasting to *Sky Catcher*.

But the curtain had yet to drop on this drama. I had an urgent message from race communications in Charleston. Arnie's Emergency Position Indicator Radio Beacon had been activated and he had not sent them a message to explain why. I was asked to divert to his position and try to raise him on the radio. Others in the fleet were also asked to try to contact him. Knowing that Arnie was running with no sails in dreadful seas, I feared the worst. But a couple of hours later race headquarters called off the dogs – Arnie messaged them to say his EPIRB must have been set off when it was submerged by a breaking wave. All was well on board, if a little uncomfortable! The relief felt on board *Sky Catcher* was such that I felt obliged to open a half-bottle of champagne.

Again, we were experiencing the unpredictability and rapid change in the Southern Ocean weather. I noted in my diary on 19 December: "The wind down here is like London buses – none for ages, then more than you can possibly use come all at once." Soon after midnight the next day we were literally becalmed again. Or perhaps I should say we had no wind, because things were still far from calm. The seas from the storm were still large and uncomfortable, and we were being thrown around with no forward motion or pressure on our sails to steady us. I dropped all sail and sat in the cockpit in the drizzle for a few hours, waiting for something to happen. The storm had brought winds from the north and northwest. When the wind returned it was out of the southeast, about 10 knots. We were moving again, close hauled, and heading for Australia once more.

FURTHER EAST AND NORTH

It was not clear to me then, but the giant of the Southern Ocean had been merely toying with *Sky Catcher* and me – just slapping us around a little to size us up. This was not his idea of serious harassment at all. I, and others, were to discover that over Christmas, when he decided to give us his full and undivided attention, and he was not going to be satisfied until he had exacted some painful sacrifice from the fleet. He bagged four of us in one foul and terrifying temper tantrum several hundred miles west of Tasmania. But in the two weeks before Christmas we again had some truly great sailing, swept along on the westerly swell in moderate winds.

One of the things that makes the Southern Ocean different to anywhere else I have sailed is the quality of the light, especially that from a cloudless sky. Everything under the sun is so clear and intense and sharp. The sky is a brilliant even blue. The sea is a dark turquoise with every ripple and wave sparkling in sharply defined three-dimensional relief. In my diary for 22 December I noted: "Rowe's Southern Ocean Sunshine Cruises at their best! Balmy eight to 12 knots of breeze from the west, clear sky, day spent grabbing rays in the cockpit and doing light chores. But another day of unspectacular progress, and I'm amazed how little this is bothering me. Must be getting sensible in my old age – 'perspective' I think they call it. It helps that the sailing is so enjoyable too."

We had some good day's runs during this period as well, but I was still sailing cautiously and did not entirely trust the Monitor after my makeshift repairs – the all-important bronze cogs that help to transfer a message from the wind-vane to the tiller by way of the servo-paddle were not meshing properly. Sometimes the system was slow to react and sometimes the cogs stuck. It meant I had to be vigilant at all times and on hand to help it at a moment's notice. This probably had a small walk-on role in another knockdown just a day after my diary reference to Sunshine Cruises. On 23 December I wrote: "Just had another knockdown followed by a long out-of-control surf and a crash-gybe. Over on our ear, water everywhere. Wrestled us round again and tried to put the Autohelm 7000 to work (great timing for it to be out of action again!). How the Monitor is still working at all in these conditions I don't know. The knockdown cost us our vang – its boom attachment broke open; what force that must have taken!"

Perversely, it was my caution in sailing this leg – the course I chose and the amount of sail I elected to carry – that eventually put me in a position of what seemed at the time to be some considerable peril.

Towards Christmas Niah was well ahead of me, and Robin was moving ahead too. Robin had taken a more southerly route along 50° south where, as it happened, the wind held fairly consistently and he sailed his boat aggressively well. I was a few degrees further north and was plagued by long periods of little or no wind.

As we began to move up towards Tasmania and the Bass Strait only four boats were behind me and *Sky Catcher*. Harry was some two thousand miles to the west. Isabelle was just a few hundred miles west and a bit south of us. North and slightly west of her was Minoru. North and slightly east of us was Arnie.

For *Sky Catcher* and me the drama began late on Christmas Eve GMT – Christmas morning local time. I heard a loud crash on deck and rushed up to find a huge brown-black gull dead and dangling from the lines on the foredeck guardrail. No doubt sailors of old would have taken this as a bad omen – and I should have heeded it myself perhaps, for that is when our troubles began. I shuddered, could not bear to touch the poor dead creature, and simply cut it loose with a little prayer for its soul.

We had 20-40 knots of wind that day, building with the seas. Now, the wind from the north was driving waves across the strong westerly swell to create a very confused and uncomfortable sea. Sleep was virtually impossible as we rolled and surged through and over the waves, taking the occasional breaker over the deck.

The other factor inhibiting sleep, and indeed interfering with working the boat generally, was the increasing pain I was feeling in my upper left arm and shoulder, the result of straining it while fixing the wind generators in the first leg. Lifting my arm above my head had become a problem, and it was delivering sharp stabs of pain whenever I used it too much.

The following day we had a full gale on our hands with 30-45 knots of wind still out of the north. I furled the staysail altogether and we sailed with just the deeply reefed main, with the wind slightly behind us.

A message on the computer via COMSAT gave me brief details of a disaster elsewhere in the fleet a couple of days earlier. Jean Luc, sailing up the east coast of Australia and within a spit of Sydney, lay his head on a winch for a few moments' rest. He was exhausted from the difficult passage through Bass Strait. The next thing he knew he and his boat were being washed up Kembla beach. Herb McCormick takes up the story:

The helicopter lifted off from Mascot Airport, on the outskirts of Sydney, on a hazy Australian summer afternoon. Christmas was just two days away. The downtown streets teemed with last-minute shoppers. Sixty miles south, on a sandy beach near the small town of Port Kembla, Jean Luc Van den Heede — arguably the world's most experienced single-handed ocean racer — was convinced he was about to lose his boat.

The chopper found the coastline, lost altitude and settled into a low course parallel to the sheer, imposing cliffs defining the southeastern boundary of the continent. The steep rock walls stretched on for miles and miles, and offered not a hint of shelter. Here, in the thick, settled haze, visibility was a scant two hundred metres. The pilot made a comment: "He's lucky he didn't put her up here."

The aircraft rounded the headland marking the northern point of the long, half-moon beach, and conversation stopped. There, way inside the foamy white stripes of breaking surf, lay Van den Heede's distinctive red yawl, Vendée Entreprises, hard aground on its port side. From aloft, the keel and rudder appeared high, mostly dry and clearly visible; the two masts were nearly perpendicular to the sea. The mainsail was torn and awash. A tiny Jean Luc clung to the topsides. It was a ridiculously short wade from his deck to dry land.

The bird landed and race director Mark Schrader hit the ground running. His immediate thoughts did not encompass the vision of Vendée again sailing swiftly in open water. He knew the tide was falling, night was coming, and the honest chance of saving the yacht was slim. "First I wanted to be sure Jean Luc was safe," Schrader said. "After that, it looked like it might be a question of salvaging all the gear we could from the boat before she was a total loss."

Riding the pitching vessel, Van den Heede was thinking the same thing. "The Port Kembla water police had already tried to tow the boat off, but the tow rope broke so I was back on the shore," he said. "I thought it was time to empty the boat, to save the maximum number of things. I knew at night I would not be able to do that."

Van den Heede also knew he could blame no one for his predicament but himself. Robbed of sleep as he negotiated the tricky, hazardous waters through the Bass Strait, the veteran solo sailor — just shy of the halfway point of his fourth race around the world alone — committed the sport's cardinal sin. He fell asleep while making landfall. "I had just tacked for the beach," he said. "I put my head down on the winch, just for a few minutes I told myself. I slept for one half-hour. I woke when I hit the sand."

But the time for unbolting hardware and electronics had not yet come. "There were about twenty people on the beach, and I gave them a rope so they could pull the back of the boat around so the bow was facing the seas," Van den Heede said. "I prepared a new shackle on the front of my boat, a big one. The water police brought me a new rope, and they started to try again."

Ashore, Schrader watched the swells and, as a fresh wave rolled under Vendée and lifted her ever so slightly, he signalled the persistent crew of the Port Kembla Water Police vessel Sea Hawk to put the throttle down. "Slowly, with each wave, the boat was going a little bit, a little bit," said Van den Heede.

And then, suddenly, miraculously, Vendée lurched over a sandbar, righted herself, and was free. Simultaneously, Van den Heede's fists sprung toward the heavens. "I did not *think it was possible," he admitted. "It was unbelievable."*

Though the boat had suffered torn main and mizzen sails — as well as a lost mizzen boom, port stanchions and bow pulpit — the hull, keel and rudder emerged unscathed. Van den Heede rested overnight in Port Kembla while a team of shore crew members from competing yachts inspected the boat and affixed a borrowed mainsail from a French sailboat competing in the Sydney-Hobart race.

The next day, just sixteen hours after his BOC bid had nearly ended for the sake of some slumber, Van den Heede sailed into Sydney Heads to complete Leg Two on Christmas Eve morning. "I had enormous luck," he said. "I saw that today when I sailed past the cliffs and the rocks between Port Kembla and Sydney. If I had hit those instead of the beach, I would have been dead. Yes, enormous luck."

But even with his vast good fortune Van den Heede could do no better than second. Four days earlier, fellow Frenchman Christophe Auguin (Sceta Calberson) had steamed into Sydney and served notice that his title defense — and his bid to equal the accomplishment of legendary sailing soloist and countryman Philippe Jeantot, who had won back-to-back BOCs in 1982-83 and 1986-87 — was alive and well.

For Auguin, whose crack and unequalled shore crew had spent long hours putting Sceta right in Cape Town before the outset of the voyage, Isabelle Autissier's dismasting had opened the door to sweet vindication. His winning time of just under twenty-five days, like Autissier's on Leg One, set a new record for the leg (by over a day). But it had not been easy, though he had made it appear so with a string of 300-mile-plus days in the final stretch of the voyage.

"My boat is a big boat, it's not small," Auguin said. "But it seemed like a very small boat on this leg. The seas were enormous, with waves fifteen to thirty metres high, the biggest I've ever seen."

Auguin's and Van den Heede's arrivals set the stage for one of the most remarkable days in the eventful history of The BOC Challenge — Christmas Day 1994, a literal yuletide festival of sail.

A little past two in the morning, Steve Pettengill sailed into Sydney to take third in Class I. The resourceful American had literally rebuilt wholesale portions of his 60-foot Hunter's Child. A broken shroud nearly cost him his mast, but he managed to shore up his rig after countless trips up the spar. His autopilots required major work, and his ripped mainsail needed mending, but that was kid's stuff. The most harrowing moment came when the yacht was knocked down and the cabin so deeply submerged that the skipper's ears popped from the pressure. The upshot of that occasion was a boatful of water via a stoved-in deck hatch: the remedy, much pumping, a bit of planking.

But from a competitive standpoint — the bit that really mattered to Pettengill — the worst of it all was a broken boom, which buggered his sail plan and forced him to alter course radically. "I went a week and a half without a mainsail," he said. "I had to get back in warmer conditions to fibreglass the boom. Every time I started laying glass it started sleeting and snowing. It made it difficult. It was a tough leg. I don't know if it could get much rougher next leg. I hope not."

Twenty-five minutes later, Giovanni Soldini (Kodak) crossed the line to pip David Adams (True Blue) to the post by two short hours. "I feel great, just great," said Soldini, bubbling like a bottle of shaken champagne, after his smooth, trouble-free voyage. "I don't do crazy stuff. When there is too much wind, in heavy weather, I slow down. If you don't, one day or another you will have trouble with yourself or your boat. I attack in lighter winds in the high pressure. That is where I got my lead on this leg."

Though Adams's homecoming at first light on 25 December should have been a joyous experience, the imposing Aussie — whose tired, squinting eyes cast him as some sort of Ghost of Christmas Present — could only shuffle along the deck like the definition of the word "weary". At the end of the day, his own broken boom had proven to be too much of an impediment, and he had no answer for Soldini when he passed him in the final stages of the leg.

Adams did not mince words: "It was the worst experience of my life, just bloody terrifying, especially the seas, which were gigantic. There were times I thought, we're not going to get out of this. But Giovanni sailed a great race. He deserved to be here first. He looked after his boat and he made it."

Soldini's victory, however, proved to be a moral one. After reviewing Adams's logs, the race committee granted him a four-hour time allowance, which enabled him to skip past Soldini on elapsed time and again earn Class II line honours for the leg. It only set the stage for the next confrontation.

David Scully (Coyote) and J.J. Provoyeur (Novell South Africa) were the fourth and fifth sailors to finish on that memorable Christmas Day. Scully, sailing the late Mike Plant's salvaged, controversial Open 60, had registered a terrific voyage. And Provoyeur, driving a heavy, dated design, showed that he was one of the more tenacious and talented sailors in his own right, squeezing every ounce of speed from the boat even after he also broke his boom.

For those still at sea, however, it would be a Christmas season to remember for far different reasons.

I was beginning to feel that tingling sensation down my spine and a knot in my stomach that day – "chaos theory" was at work. The string of ill-fated coincidences and the bad news were only just starting. At last the nerve-endings of my feelings and emotions were coming back to life. Perhaps it was simply the passage of time that had worn away the numbness, or maybe it was that the unfolding situation was deteriorating to new levels of experience that was penetrating my defences. Strangely, I found this a welcome development. It would have been dreadful to have come all this way and not experience true raw fear!

The next two days were a living nightmare on *Sky Catcher*, and more so elsewhere in the fleet.

On *Sky Catcher* it started with a crash-gybe in 50 knots of wind. A link rod in the self-steering gear had become dislocated and we were thrown sideways by a breaking wave. The violence of the throw broke the tiller just below where it attaches to the self-steering lines, and the rudder was jammed under the hull.

I quickly pulled down the mainsail and then managed to free the rudder after a strenuous half-hour. I then discovered that the Autohelm 7000 autopilot had "locked" – so now I had no effective self-steering at all. I hove-to and set to work in the cockpit and stern scoop to repair the Monitor self-steering and jury-rig a new tiller to the stump of what was left of the original one. I did this using the shaft of the keel-bolt wrench, a tube from the Monitor spare-parts kit, and other bits and pieces including my emergency tiller arm. It took hours. I was wet and cold from the frequent soakings to which I was subjected from waves breaking over the side of the boat. What a crazy sight it must have been – like some stupid television programme, while bouncing on a trampoline and having someone throw buckets of cold water over you!

We now had 50-60 knots of wind. Sailing under bare poles, we ambled along at five knots and surfed on the waves at 15.

That night the wind rose to 60-70 knots, topping out at 74. We were in hurricane-strength winds. We took a huge wave on our side and went crashing over and down its frothing slope. When it passed, we were still pinned over on our side. I discovered the windvane on the Monitor had been broken at its base and the servo-paddle had sheared right off.

As I leapt through the companionway into the cockpit I was blown back against the cuddy by the sheer weight of the wind. As I gasped and opened my mouth, my cheeks filled with the wind like a balloon. I could hardly breathe. It started to rain, and it felt like gun-shot. The rain turned to hail and it *was* gun-shot! But two things had to be accomplished before I could go below again. First, I had to lash the tiller to one side to steady the boat and reduce the risk of further damage. I also had to remove the severed servo-paddle, now thrashing around at the end of its tether line at the stern of the boat. With the tiller lashed we were semi hove-to and the boat's movement was a little easier. Fetching the servo-paddle was a bit of a circus act, but it was achieved with only minor cuts and bruises. I clipped my harness to the backstay as I clambered over the transom and slid across the antenna dome in the stern scoop. Wedged between the dome and the windvane frame, I leant over the stern and pulled in the paddle which was thrashing like a fighting fish. The jagged edge of its broken tube gashed my left hand.

Back in the cabin, I secured the companionway hatch boards and closed the boat up. I turned the CD player on and pushed the volume to high, to drown out the screeching howl of the wind and the sound of crashing on deck every time we took a wave. The Hilliard Ensemble's "Officium", the Estonian Philharmonic Chamber Choir's "Te Deum", and a selection of "opera classics" had enough stirring passages in them to steady the soul a little. I stared out through the small cabin window above the navigation desk – it looked unreal!

I decided to send another status report to race headquarters. I logged into the computer. There was a message from them to me: "Nigel: Two EPIRBs on Isabelle's boat have been activated. No other communications with or from her. We cannot poll her position. Please stand by and cease sailing further east."

My imagination went into overdrive. My heartbeat raced away and my anxiety level went into overdrive too. Tension pains gripped the muscles at the top of my spine. I prayed for her safety, and I prayed for the rest of us caught in the storm.

To her north and slightly west, Minoru had lost the use of all his self-steering systems. North of me Arnie had no steering at all, his emergency rudder having been ripped off by a passing wave. We were all walking-wounded at best – and *Sky Catcher* had the least damage of the four of us.

There was one point when I became conscious of being perilously close to panic. I found myself sweating, breathing in shallow breaths, and clutching the sides of the companionway while staring mindlessly at the advancing ocean. My stomach muscles were tensed involuntarily around a continuous ache below my rib cage. The seas, which had been huge, were now towering citadels of black ocean marbled with turquoise and foaming white – sixty, maybe eighty, feet high. The sound was deafening – the dreadful screech of wind in the rigging, the rolling thunder of the tumbling seas. The air was thick with spray that smelt dank and salty. Every sense in my body was under attack.

A lot of praying was done in the ensuing twenty-four hours or so, not only on *Sky Catcher* but elsewhere in the fleet and around the world I suspect. Herb

McCormick was at race headquarters in Sydney and followed every move as the drama of Isabelle's plight unfolded:

On 28 December, in a remote cauldron of storm-tossed seas some 850 miles southwest of the wild Australian island state of Tasmania, the worst month of Isabelle Autissier's life spiralled even further downward.

It happened instantly; after all, the great irony of fate is its ability to change a lifetime of waiting and planning in a single moment. Mercifully, Autissier did not witness the giant wave that turned her life and her wonderful 60-foot yacht Ecureuil Poitou Charentes 2, *quite literally, upside down. But she was not spared from the sound of its thunder.*

"I could hear the noise of it coming," she said. "Luckily for me, I was down below in a narrow passageway leading from the aft compartment to the nav station. Outside, the wind was blowing over 50 knots, and I was making eight knots with all my sails down. Then the boat did a huge roll."

Later, Autissier would try to piece together the dynamics of her flight. "The boat went right over through 360 degrees," she said. "I could feel it rolling. I fell against the bulkhead, then on the ceiling, then on the other bulkhead. When I opened my eyes the boat was full of water."

The devastation to Ecureuil *was as sure as it had been swift. "All the steering systems were gone," Autissier remembered. "The masts were gone. Overhead in the main compartment it was absolutely open air. There was a four- or five-square-metre hole in the deck where the coach roof used to be. Everything was wet. I don't know if the rudders were gone because the aft compartment was full of water and I had to shut the bulkhead to keep the rest of the boat safe and floating."*

Ever the optimist, Autissier said, "I was lucky. If I had been on deck, or sleeping at my bunk, or at the chart table, I would have been washed away. Everything that was at the navigation station and the berth was sucked out of the boat."

Autissier harboured a brief illusion of cleaning the mess up, raising an emergency spar, and carrying on. The entire leg had already been a study in perseverance. Dismasted in early December in the early going, she had built a jury rig with her spinnaker pole and sailed to the French Antarctic research station on Kerguelen Island, where her shore crew had shipped a replacement rig which in theory would allow her to sail to Sydney where a proper racing stick could be stepped.

But then reality set in. "I was very tired, and there was no steering," she said. "With the state of my boat and my personal state, I knew it would not be safe to try and get to Sydney." With the decision made, Autissier activated the pair of EPIRB distress beacons which, by race rules, all competitors are required to carry.

The BOC Challenge has a long history of fellow racers coming to the aid of competitors in distress. In the first race in 1982-83, Francis Stokes had liberated Tony Lush from a crippled vessel, and Richard Broadhead seconded the act later in the event when he rescued Jacques de Roux from his sinking boat. In the 1990-91 Challenge, it was South African Bertie Reed who came to the aid of countryman John Martin. And of course Alan Nebauer's assistance to Josh Hall had been one of the premier stories of the current BOC race.

In this instance, however, the two closest sailors — Nigel Rowe and Minoru Saito — were well over 250 miles away and battling through survival conditions in the same massive low pressure system that had doomed Ecureuil. Though Saito was ultimately (and briefly) diverted by race officials, the Maritime Rescue Coordination Centre in Canberra — the government arm that was contacted after the distress signal was received, and which had the task of driving the rescue effort — decided they were too far away and too few in number. The call for the cavalry was raised.

At Air Force bases near Sydney and Adelaide, flight crews scrambled long-range Orion- and Hercules-class aircraft on missions to locate Autissier and evaluate the situation aboard Ecureuil. Autissier's ace shore crew Serge Viviand was aboard for the initial sortie. "The boat was bobbing like a cork," he said. Though he was unable to speak directly with Autissier he also reported that, with a section of the remaining spar, she had managed to rig a boom tent above the missing coach roof to halt the ingress of water.

Soon after, near Fremantle, the 140-metre Australian Navy frigate HMAS Darwin prepared to get under way. Three days after the rollover, as dawn broke on the first day of the New Year, Autissier was airlifted from the deck of Ecureuil by a Sea Hawk helicopter dispatched from the ship.

A day later, she faced the press at Edinburgh Air Force Base near Adelaide. "The rescue happened very quickly," she said. "The wind was only blowing 20 or 25 knots. The seas were not too rough. One guy came down with a line, and put a harness around me. And we were winched up very quick." Regarding her own plans, Autissier said, "I do not know what I will do right now, but I do know I will race again."

Autissier was philosophical about her epic BOC experience: "After the first leg everything was so wonderful for me. I had a big lead. But I have done the BOC before. I know what can happen. But this time the Indian Ocean was very tough for me. It did not like me and it did not want me there."

Autissier's insurance company commissioned a salvage operation for Ecureuil, but soon after the deep-sea trawler Petuna Explorer left Hobart en route to the stricken sailboat, the EPIRB batteries weakened and then died. The mission was eventually called off after several days when the boat could not be located.

Isabelle Autissier's historic BOC run was over. A breakthrough yacht had been lost forever. But a great sailor had been saved to sail another day.

With Isabelle's rescue well under way, race headquarters stood *Sky Catcher* down and allowed us to continue sailing. Given the damage to our steering I had decided to head for Hobart, some six hundred and fifty miles east. I did not want to risk finding myself in the Bass Strait with no self-steering, in an uninsured boat and with a life on board I had come to value quite highly! Both Arnie and Minoru were heading there too. Minoru was having to hand-steer virtually all the time, and Arnie was doing a remarkable job of steering his boat by trimming the sails and using warps and chain over the stern. The three of us kept in touch over the radio every four hours, and I continued to be Minoru's link with race headquarters since he was having difficulty working the Standard-C data communications system.

In the middle of the storm, on 28 December, I wrote in my diary: "I am tired. I have had very little sleep for several days. With the steering problems, I had already decided to divert to Hobart, but that's still days away. Everything is wet below, we've been knocked over so many times. I'd be lying if I said there have not been times when I was scared in the huge seas at the height of the storm. They were awesome and capable of delivering the worst imaginable."

Finally, the wind began to subside and the passage to Hobart was spent in what the weather forecast described as a "vigorous westerly airstream with firmly embedded fronts. Seas very rough. Swell high." It was no joyride but it was bliss compared to the pounding we had endured in the storm.

Isabelle's rescue had been international news, and the arrival of *Sky Catcher* in Hobart made national television news in Australia. Media interest in the race and its casualties was high: "What was it like in the storm? . . . Did you fear for your life? . . . How big were the waves? . . . Will you continue in the race?" I was both surprised and flattered by the attention.

The rescue operation for Isabelle had stirred up a hornet's nest of political controversy. Or, perhaps more accurately, an opposition politician in the Australian parliament took the opportunity to use it as a stick to stir up a hornet's nest. With the use of a great deal of polemic and hyperbole, her argument was that Isabelle's rescue had cost the Australian forces millions of dollars and the bill should be paid by Isabelle, her sponsor, insurance company, or even the organizers of the race. This may or may not have been good politics for the home audience, but it certainly turned the public relations coup of a textbook

Top *Jean Luc Van den Heede and* **Vendée Entreprises** *being towed past the Sydney Opera House after finally finishing Leg Two on Christmas Day.* (JACQUES VAPILLON)

Bottom *Australia Day celebrations just before the start of Leg Three gave Sydney and the BOC competitors the most spectacular fireworks display the city had ever seen.* (JACQUES VAPILLON)

Previous page *Smoke from the cannon aboard* New Endeavour *at an almost windless start of Leg Three at the mouth of Sydney Harbour.* (JACQUES VAPILLON)

Top Sky Catcher *and me ploughing through a calm sea in a rising breeze on one of those days I wished would go on for ever.* (CEDRIC ROBERTSON/PPL)

Right *Part of the daily routine on a long passage, a tour of the deck to check that everything that could come apart hasn't.*

(RONALD LOPEZ/PPL)

Former commodities broker and America's Cup sailor David Scully on board the fast and elegant Coyote,
which he had chartered for the race. (JACQUES VAPILLON)

Above Henry (Harry) Mitchell
blowing his horn on Henry
Hornblower. Mitak *was what
he called the boat originally.
Then he called her* We Are
Lovers, *changing it to* Henry
Hornblower *for The BOC
Challenge.* (BILLY BLACK).
At 70 years old, Harry climbed
his mast like a 17-year-old and
inspired us all with his zest for
life. (JACQUES VAPILLON)
Left Arnie Taylor on Thursday's
Child, *a man with more grit and
humour than most.*
(JACQUES VAPILLON)

Top *Merfyn Owen, yacht designer and builder, and shore crew for* Thursday's Child, *helping to build a new rudder for* Newcastle Australia *before Alan Nebauer's arrival in Punta del Este.* (BILLY BLACK)
Bottom *The rudderless* Newcastle Australia *crossing the finish line in Punta del Este at the end of Alan's nightmare passage from Sydney.* (BILLY BLACK)

rescue by the Australian services into an embarrassment internationally. The argument, of course, ignored several important factors – not least the international treaty obligations for search and rescue – and the unfortunate fact that in the same week several Australians had to be saved at sea by the French authorities. The real cost of Isabelle's rescue (mostly fuel and overtime) was a small fraction of the "millions" claimed – the point being that defence forces have to have ships and aircraft, and sailors and aircrew have to be paid, whether or not they are active at sea. In addition to this, without the occasional real rescue to deal with, air/sea forces around the world have to create simulated exercises to practise and refine their skills. Taking into account the training and international public relations benefits of Isabelle's rescue, it would not be difficult to construct a case that the investment more than paid for itself.

Hobart was in festive mood; it was New Year and the crews of more than three hundred boats in the Sydney-Hobart race were in town celebrating. The long sail down Storm Bay, then the tow down the wide Derwent river to the town, was a wonderful experience in a light breeze and sunshine. Skip was there among several old friends to help effect repairs quickly. We berthed at the Royal Yacht Club of Hobart, alongside *Spirit of Sydney* in which Ian Kiernan had competed in the 1986-87 BOC Challenge, and in which good friends of mine, Don and Margie McIntyre, were about to leave for Antarctica (Don sailed in the previous BOC Challenge). It was a surprise to me that they were still in Hobart, and they left the day before me for their epic adventure. They planned to spend a year alone down there in a small purpose-built hut, in a spot recognized as the windiest place on earth. Winds in winter reach a staggering 200mph. Having experienced 74 knots, I found that unimaginable.

I wished I had time to explore neat and friendly Hobart and its remarkably beautiful surroundings; but my priority had to be to reach Sydney as quickly as possible and finish the leg. All the welding and other metalwork on *Sky Catcher* was completed swiftly by InCat, world leaders in the construction of catamaran ferries, thanks to a friend of Ian Kiernan's. Sail damage was repaired quickly also. Our departure was delayed a day by lack of wind, but we were finally under way for the six-hundred-mile jog up to Sydney.

The wind was strong and out of the east as we headed north along the Tasmanian coast, then across the cobblestones of a lumpy Tasman Sea where it connects with the western end of Bass Strait. As we approached the mainland coast of Australia, the wind turned nor'-nor'-east and presented me with two unpleasant alternatives. Either I could short-tack up to Sydney in the busy and narrow corridor between the mainland and the strong southerly current about five to eight miles off shore, or I could sail east across and out of the worst of the current before heading for the finish line. I was tired, having slept only a few hours since leaving Hobart, and chose the safer route. We took an eighty-mile tack out into the Tasman Sea, then turned north. Ten to 25 knots of wind kept us moving at a fair clip, and the warm sunshine afforded me the luxury of allowing my legs to see daylight for the first time in almost two months!

Mark, Skip and Andy were among the welcome party on the boat that greeted me at Sydney Heads. People on other boats hooted and waved as we crossed the finish line. I felt desperately relieved to have Leg Two behind me, and hoped that someone would have remembered my urgent need for ice cream and chilled champagne.

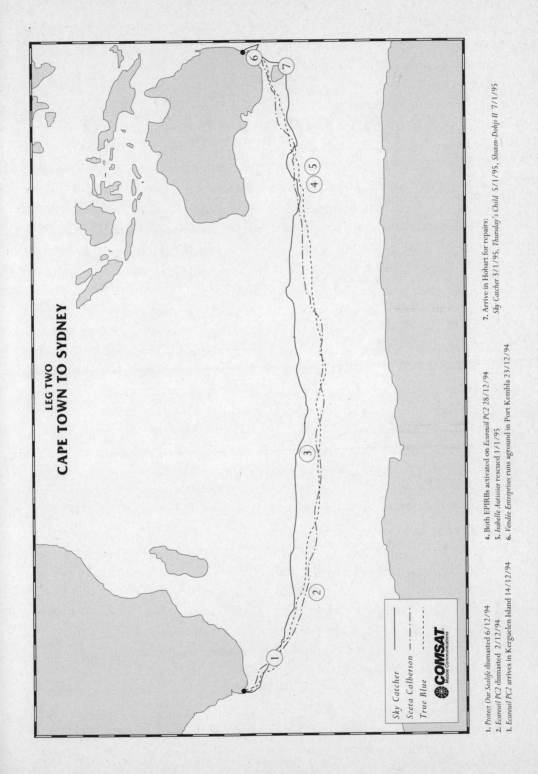

LEG TWO
CAPE TOWN TO SYDNEY

Sky Catcher
Sceta Calberson
True Blue

COMSAT
Mobile Communications

1. _Protect Our Sealife_ dismasted 6/12/94
2. _Ecureuil PC2_ dismasted 2/12/94
3. _Ecureuil PC2_ arrives in Kerguelen Island 14/12/94
4. Both EPIRBs activated on _Ecureuil PC2_ 28/12/94
5. _Isabelle Autissier_ rescued 1/1/95
6. _Vendée Entreprises_ runs aground in Port Kembla 23/12/94
7. Arrive in Hobart for repairs:
   Sky Catcher 3/1/95, _Thursday's Child_ 5/1/95, _Shuten-Dohji II_ 7/1/95

SYDNEY AND BEYOND

The sun was shining from an almost cloudless sky as we were towed down the most spectacular harbour in the world that I have ever seen to the BOC Marina. Passing boaters hooted and waved. Passengers on the big ferries between Sydney and Manly at the other end of the harbour, waved and called to us as well. Sydney's remarkable skyline, dominated by an eclectic mix of skyscraper architecture and the Centre Point viewing-tower with its revolving restaurant 300 feet up in the sky, unfolded before us as we proceeded down the harbour. The white ceramic roof tiles of the Sydney Opera House, jutting into the water on its own little promontory, glistened in the late morning sun. We passed under Sydney Harbour Bridge and turned left towards the Darling Harbour complex of tourist shops, fast-food restaurants, gardens, fountains, amusements and vast exhibition halls, and pulled into the newly completed BOC Marina just behind the aluminium-and-glass Maritime Museum. A small gathering of friends, race officials and competitors were there to applaud our arrival, watch me drink champagne and eat ice cream. It was good to be ashore and with people again.

Having had the unscheduled stop in Hobart, I was not as drained emotionally as I had been when I arrived at the end of the first leg in Cape Town. In fact I wasn't really sure how I was feeling. I was happy to be in Sydney, probably my favourite city in the world, and among old friends. I was pleased to have Leg Two, and half the race, behind me. All of this, especially the bad storm that sent us scuttling for Hobart, gave me a lot of confidence in both the boat and myself. But I had the same anxieties as virtually everyone else in the fleet about the next leg. Even Christophe Auguin was openly concerned and fearful about another trip (for him) deep into the Southern Ocean and through the ice to round Cape Horn. Isabelle's dismasting and rescue was fresh in our minds, and we all knew that being in a disabled yacht on the next leg could be a real problem. From New Zealand to the Horn we would be crossing the most desolate ocean in the world, for some of it would be beyond the reach of rescue services and there would be virtually no shipping. This was lurking at the back of all our minds, I'm sure, but it was not discussed much. Besides, we all had a lot of work to do on our boats, and we were owed some shore leave!

Sydney was in holiday mood. It was the middle of the annual Sydney Festival – a three-week feast of international culture, from vast rock concerts and opera in the park, to plays, musicals, ballet, modern dance, street theatre, and endless parties. It was therapeutic! Julia arrived a few days after me, and it was wonderful to be with her again.

Skip and Andy began working their way through the list of projects we had agreed. High on it was dealing with the mainsail we had shipped from Cape Town so we could use it on the next leg. It had been sold to me as being "bulletproof" for the Southern Ocean. The batten pockets were reinforced and chafe patches were stuck all over the sail in areas where it might rub against anything. It was a good-looking sail and I hoped it was finally going to live up to its original promise. The other major project was to haul the boat and replace the bottom rudder bearings, which were badly worn. The choice was to have new roller-bearings fabricated or use nylon sleeves as many of the other BOC boats had. We decided on the latter, mainly for speed and cost.

The last to arrive in Sydney was Harry Mitchell, about a week before the restart. Poor Harry had had only four days in Cape Town before setting off from there, and then a pretty unpleasant passage through the Southern Ocean. Now he had only a week in which to sort out himself and his boat before Leg Three. He was exhausted when he arrived and then went down with flu. There was no shortage of help, however, and within hours of berthing he had more volunteers on his boat than he knew what to do with.

As restart day approached, I could sense the anxiety levels of my fellow competitors rising. Shortening tempers and forced humour were telltale signs in some. Others appeared to be just too relaxed – and I suspect I was one of these. *Sky Catcher* was ready. I was looking forward to the next leg with a healthy mixture of excitement and dread. Like everyone else, I just wanted to get on with it and get to the Horn. I was past the point of worrying about any of it. One of the things I had discovered about myself throughout this whole project was that my mind had the ability to worry about things while there was something I could do about them, and to bury my anxieties when I felt I was past that point. It was a useful trick.

Australia Day was two days before the restart. The BOC Challenge competitors were picked to lead the parade through the thronging crowds in Darling

Harbour and into the specially constructed temporary arena, where the Premier, State Governor, other dignitaries and several thousand spectators were gathered for an orgy of national self-congratulation. A small troupe of school children was assigned to walk ahead of each of us with our national flags. The little girl allocated to me was in floods of tears because she had to carry the Union Jack – a sure sign, I thought, that the movement to make Australia a republic was winning hands down. The day ended with a reception for several thousands in the Darling Harbour exhibition centre, and the most wonderful fireworks display I have ever seen. What a send-off we were having, even if it was not all arranged just for our benefit!

Julia did her usual fine job of packing and stowing my clothes on board and loading the boat with provisions. She was keeping her anxieties under control, but I could tell it was not easy.

We had brilliant sunshine for the start. Julia, Skip and Andy were on *Sky Catcher* for the tow out to Sydney Heads, where a spectator fleet was slowly gathering. The start cannon was aboard the barque *New Endeavour*, a remarkably fine replica of the ship in which Captain Cook first sailed to Australia. The fleet milled around in the dying breeze as noon approached. We crawled at a snail's pace across the line and out through the Heads, where we began to pick up some wind. Boats were hooting, spectators waving and shouting, and as we sailed past *New Endeavour* I got a rousing cheer from the BOC people on board her.

Media boats and helicopters buzzed us a few times, and almost the last boat to pay us a visit was the one carrying the fleet's shore crew and families. Julia and I blew kisses to each other, and then the boat's skipper gunned her engines and she was whisked away from me in a cloud of spray.

As the spectator fleet and Sydney's skyline disappeared behind us, and the BOC fleet spread out across and over the horizon ahead and behind me, a deep melancholy settled over *Sky Catcher*. I expected it. It had happened at the beginning of each leg of the race. I put it down to the sudden isolation after so much socializing in port, and the prospect of another six or seven weeks alone at sea so soon after the previous leg. Each time it was taking me three or four days to settle into a rhythm again, and I suppose I was bound to be at my most vulnerable emotionally during those first few days. It was the worst time for anything to go wrong.

We were on a rhumbline course for the bottom of New Zealand, reaching in 10-12 knots of breeze on a gently undulating sea. The electric autopilot was on the helm and we had all available sail up. I spent the late afternoon in the cockpit, nursing a half-bottle of champagne and a can of peanuts. This was going to be the "big one" – across the most desolate ocean on the planet, through iceberg territory and around the infamous Cape Horn. In past BOC races the weather on Leg Three had always been better than on Leg Two, and in any event I thought it unlikely that we would experience the 70-knot storm conditions we had had over Christmas. But the big risk on Leg Three was unquestionably the stretch of ocean between New Zealand and the Horn. At the halfway mark, we would be two thousand miles from anywhere and beyond the reach of Search and Rescue aircraft. With almost no shipping in the area, the only help in an emergency would probably have to come from another competitor. We all knew that, and perhaps that was one of the strongest reinforcements for the friendships that developed.

I was not very hungry that night, but I forced myself to cook a good dinner – chicken, potatoes, peas and carrots, along with the customary onion and garlic. I ate it in the cockpit in the dark, under the stars and a thin moon.

I dozed on and off in the cockpit during the night and watched the sun come up. The wind picked up a bit during the day and I turned the helm over to the Monitor windvane gear. We kept wandering off course, and at first I could not fathom why. Finally I realized what was happening – every now and then the tiller would stick and not respond to the commands from the self-steering gear. I unhooked the Monitor from the tiller and hand-steered. It was really stiff and not at all smooth. At certain angles the tiller would stick and it would take some effort to shift it. It did not take me long to figure out that the problem was with the new bearings.

This was not good news. I did not fancy doing this leg with no windvane self-steering. I turned the helm back to the electric pilot and sat glumly in the cockpit, staring at the tiller and wondering how to deal with the problem. Maybe it would wear itself in over time; but was that a chance I wanted to take? I concluded that I could leave a decision on this until I was approaching New Zealand. If the new bearings hadn't worn themselves in by then, I'd have to pull in somewhere and get them fixed.

The wind rose from very little to the high teens by nightfall and I decided to put a reef in the mainsail. As I got things organized in the cockpit to do this, I stared up at the sail before letting the halyard out. I could not believe my eyes. The sail had a tortured shape to it and a gaping black hole a third of the way down. It had torn from luff to leach, just below the third reefing point! It was beyond belief that this could happen to my "bullet-proof" Southern Ocean sail

135

in less than 20 knots of wind. I rounded up more into the wind so the sail would not flog against the spreaders, and dropped it all the way to the third reef.

I slumped in the cockpit again, feeling more depressed than I could ever remember. This was disastrous and I had no choice but to pull in somewhere for repairs — if indeed repairs were a practical option on either the rudder bearings or the sail. I messaged race headquarters on the Standard-C unit, and phoned Mark on the Standard-M satellite phone.

Minoru Saito was heading for the fishing port of Ulladulla because his Trimble equipment was not working and race headquarters could not track his position. I decided to go to Ulladulla as well. Although it meant sailing well north of west, almost diametrically opposite the direction in which I needed to head for New Zealand, there was a slip there where we could haul the boat and it was a reasonable drive to Sydney to deal with the mainsail.

We had 30-40 knots of wind and a very brisk sail to Ulladulla, arriving late at night. Everything was set up there for me. A Rescue Service launch met us half a mile from the entrance to the harbour, with Skip, Andy and Mark on board, to tow us in. Minoru was already there and I tied up alongside him. By now I was fit to be tied. Anger, especially about the mainsail, had overtaken my depression.

With the sail still on the boom we could see that not only was there a jagged tear right across it, it was torn in other places too. The next morning, when we got the sail off the boat and spread it out, we could see stress fractures and little tears all over it. The fabric was simply disintegrating and repairing it was out of the question.

I was ready to throw in the towel. Mark and I went for a walk. The boat needed a new mainsail whatever I decided to do, he said, so why not postpone a decision on continuing in the race until a new one could be sourced and the rudder bearings fixed? Maybe the decision would be taken out of my hands anyway if all of this was going to take a long time. It was good advice and I accepted it.

Through Ian Kiernan we arranged for Hood to make a new mainsail in Dacron. Skip took the old mainsail up to Sydney for them to use as a template and we left Merfyn Owen, who was helping out as shore crew for *Thursday's Child*, in charge of dealing with the sail loft. Back in Ulladulla, we had the boat hauled and both Skip and Andy worked on the rudder-bearing problem. We had the shaft milled and polished to ensure an absolutely smooth and even surface, and then refitted the bearing sleeves. While all of this was going on, Mark and the people from COMSAT fixed up Minoru's Standard-C problem and he was back in the chase, albeit a long way behind the others.

I spent a few days in Sydney, waiting for the mainsail to be finished. I fired off a fax to Sobstad, telling them what had happened and letting them know they could expect me to make a claim against them. They didn't reply.

The new mainsail arrived and we bent it onto the boom for a test sail. It was a great-looking sail, almost half the cost of the one from Sobstad and really well made. The tiller was still stiffer than it had been with the roller bearings, but the windvane gear worked it well and it wasn't inclined to stick any more.

I thought through the situation carefully to decide whether or not to continue. I hated the idea of not finishing the race but a little voice inside my head was telling me to pull the plug. This was the one part of the race where the risks were multiplied if one was too separated from the rest of the fleet, and I was now a week behind. I had to admit to myself if to no one else that although the race had been an enormously interesting and rewarding experience thus far, I was not enjoying the sailing anything like as much as I had expected to. The fact that I was having to sail the race uninsured was still plaguing me. So too were the physical problems I was having with my arms.

I was sure that most of the remaining skippers in the race would not have let any of this stand in their way, and would have continued. But I concluded that the right thing for me to do was retire. To find oneself way behind the fleet in the Southern Ocean would be bad enough. To put oneself there deliberately was not wise, particularly if the rewards of enjoyment were not there to compensate for the price of risk.

I had discussed this possibility with several people in the days before. Most of my sailing friends urged me to continue and felt sure I would regret not doing so in the months and years ahead. One told me of a mountaineer he knew who pulled out of an Everest climb when he was three-quarters of the way up, and spent the next ten years in therapy! My closest friends, however, told me to think it through, decide what was right for me, and bugger what anyone else might think! One of my concerns was obviously Jim and Nick at the Carbide Graphite Group who had given my project such enthusiastic support. They both said the same thing. "We're your friends. The only thing you should be thinking about is your safety and what you think is right for you . . . we'll back whatever you decide."

As we sailed back to Ulladulla I told Skip and Andy what I had decided, and why. If it bothered them, they didn't show it. Maybe they were expecting it; they didn't say and I didn't ask. We tied up the boat and went to the local cinema to see *Terminal Velocity* – an action thriller that required no brain-power at all; just what I needed.

Skip and Andy stayed on the boat that night and planned to leave early to sail her back to Sydney. Eight dollars bought me a dark and depressing little room in a local hotel, with a creaky narrow wooden bed, a sink in the corner, green walls and a naked light bulb hanging from the ceiling. I had taken a half-bottle of champagne from the boat and lay on the bed staring at the ceiling, sipping the wine from a grubby tooth mug I found by the sink. This was not a fitting place to end what had certainly been the grandest adventure of my life. The thought made me feel miserable at first; but then I started to laugh. I had failed to accomplish the task I had set myself, but I felt good about the decision and I knew a lot of other people would be relieved. In any event, it had long been my view that if one could not handle failure one should not take any risks in life, just stay at home and grow roses. Besides, failure could be a valuable and enlightening experience too. By the time morning arrived, I was already beginning to make plans for the rest of my life . . . there was a lot to look forward to.

I suspect this was all a lot easier for me to deal with than it might have been for others in the fleet whose whole lives were centred on the sport. People's reactions to me and my decision were quite different. Some talked to me as if I had just lost a close member of my family; others expressed deep relief, particularly my family and Julia. Several said they thought it must have been a lot tougher to decide to stop than to carry on.

I just hoped that my own comfort with the decision would last; and indeed it was not long before it was actually reinforced. I decided to have both the boat and myself "surveyed". The boat was done in Sydney. It revealed that she was in excellent condition in almost every respect. But it also exposed a structural fault in the lower spreaders that would almost certainly have resulted in the mast coming down had we hit bad weather. Back in England for a brief visit, an examination of my arms revealed a lot of tendon and other damage in both. This required excruciatingly painful injections of steroids into the joints of both elbows and my left shoulder, and a warning from the doctor that I should take no exercise with them for three months.

~~~~~~~~~

It was February and it was brutally cold in England. The thought of spending the rest of the leg in Punta del Este, back in my old seat of helping to manage the race, had lots of appeal, even though it meant another protracted parting from Julia. Events like The BOC Challenge can, and often do, put an enormous strain on the relationships of those involved – principally but not only those of the competitors and their partners. Thankfully, ours was holding up well.

Since returning to Ulladulla, I had been following the fortunes of the rest of the fleet with half my mind. Now I could give it my full attention. I read through the files of press releases and messages between the fleet and race head-quarters. I looked at what was happening with the weather and the courses each had elected to take. It was clear that this leg too was already shaping up to be another "Demolition Derby".

The gale that I had experienced on my way to Ulladulla was more severe further south and bagged all of the fleet for a couple of days. It took a hefty and almost unexpected swipe at those leading the parade towards New Zealand. At the head of Class II, David Adams reported to race headquarters over the COMSAT Standard-C service: "I was resting when 60 knots came through. Quite a storm. It nearly wiped me out . . . the headsail tore and the furler got caught and tried to rip the mast out." Two days later he added: "Weather appalling, atrocious. Bloody awful seas."

The conditions produced a flood of similar tales from other skippers. Jean Luc Van den Heede reported: "The sea is starting to be rude . . . very hard on boat and man." J-J Provoyeur commented: "The sea is wild"; and David Scully, with his customary humour, said it was "Blowing dogs off chains . . . Windex gone, masthead unit gone, keeping busy bailing."

As the damage reports came in, mostly torn sails and some broken deck gear, Arnie Taylor, further back in the fleet, decided on prudence: "We've backed off in the theory that I've got five-to-six weeks to break things – why do it all in the first week?!"

By the end of the first week I was not the only casualty. Both Alan Nebauer and David Scully were heading for Bluff, on the south coast of New Zealand's South Island. Alan couldn't get his alternator to work – the same problem that sent him into Simonstown soon after starting Leg Two from Cape Town – and David had a mainsail that he said was beginning to look like a venetian blind! This was the same sail that had blown out at the start of Leg Two and had been shipped to Sobstad in the US to be repaired. It sounded like he was having the same problem I had had, and I knew exactly how annoyed and frustrated he must have been feeling. He had chartered the boat to do the race, complete with sails. He did not think the sails were suitable for the kind of sailing involved in a solo circumnavigation in the first place, and now he was kicking himself for not insisting on them being replaced. Having a new sail built now was out of the question from the point of view of both time and money, but he was able to keep himself in the race by borrowing an old mainsail from David Adams's 50-footer. It was shipped and waiting for him in Bluff when he arrived. Just as on Leg Two, he was having to sail this leg with a mainsail about three-quarters of the size his mast could carry. He must have felt like he wanted to strangle someone.

News of my withdrawal was slow in reaching the fleet but it seemed to be a matter of some interest. Arnie messaged the race communications centre in Charleston: "Received a fax from Stateside indicating *Sky Catcher*'s shore crew are looking for a new berth. A number of us in the fleet have been trying to reach Nigel and express our support for whatever his decision is and we have been a bit concerned about the lack of news . . . "

I must confess to being touched and a little flattered by the reaction. In a later message to race headquarters Arnie said: "It must have been an inordinately difficult call for him to make, perhaps tougher than continuing." J-J said: " . . . really sorry to hear about Nigel. He must have struggled to make the decision." There were a number of other messages along the same lines; but the one that amused me most was from the laconic David Scully: "Sorry to hear about *Sky Catcher*'s withdrawal. I will miss Nigel very much because whenever I was very wet, cold and uncomfortable, my spirits were buoyed by reminding myself that not too far away someone was opening a bottle of Puligny-Montrachet to the accompaniment of a Rachmaninov concerto. 'I wonder what Nigel is having this evening,' I would say to myself as I spooned down my freeze-dried."

I have no idea how he knew the name of my favourite white wine, but I made a point of opening a bottle that evening and drinking a toast to the entire fleet. I was going to miss being with them "out there", I was sure of that.

By now the calmer weather had settled over the whole fleet, from Christophe at the front to Minoru bringing up the rear with Harry Mitchell. It was back to being a Southern Ocean Sunshine Cruise again. As I walked through the driving rain in a bitterly cold London, I was beginning to wonder about the wisdom of my decision. Niah Vaughan was probably reclining on his after deck, blowing smoke rings from a small Havana cigar. Robin Davie would be nursing a cup of tea in his tiny cockpit. Harry would be stretched out naked on his side deck, working on his tan. Up at the front of the fleet the big boys would be fiddling and fine-tuning to squeeze the last drop of available speed from their machines – and indeed the front-runners were reporting some truly fabulous average speeds. David Adams and Giovanni in their 50-footers were making close to 300-mile days, and some of the 60s were doing well beyond that. Christophe was knocking off consecutive daily runs of around 340 miles. Giovanni messaged to race headquarters: "I learned in the last leg how to go in the Southern Ocean. The most important thing is some good seas and one nice bottle of red wine per day, so now I am very well organized. The bottles I have are little, only two glasses like on an airplane, so don't think I'm crazy all the time!"

While they and I knew the good weather would not last for long, it must have been a welcome respite from the pasting they had had crossing the Tasman Sea. To add to everyone's sense of at-oneness with the world, the fleet also soon had some special family news to celebrate and a nice little problem to contemplate. David Scully was probably blowing the dust off the best bottle in his cellar as he reported to race headquarters: "Latest addition to the *Coyote* team arrived 10.00 Zulu, Paris, France. Wind is on the beam and we are making 18 knots. *La vie est belle!*" The nice little problem the fleet was invited to contemplate was what the new daughter should be called. Several names were suggested, including "Bluff" in honour of David's last port of call; another was "Tasman" to celebrate the place where the fleet had been beaten up the previous week. But it transpired that David's wife Véronique had already set her heart on Blanca, and reported that her first gurgle sounded like "sponsor".

Even though I had pulled out of the race and was gradually sliding back across the great divide into a race management role, I still felt a part of the family and my spirit was out there with them. It was great to see that serious attention was also being paid to the spirit of competition with some quite elaborate bets being wagered. The most complex was devised between Niah and Arnie with a points system based on: first across the date line, nearest to the race waypoint at 59° south, 130° west; first to see ice, the furthest south; first to see the Horn, nearest to the Falklands; first to speak to Falklands radio; and the first to see Uruguay. *Phew*! It was going to take some sorting out over a few beers in Punta del Este.

The spirit of competition was more fierce than fun at the front of the fleet. Giovanni was leading David Adams in Class II by a whisker in the most hotly contested battle of the race. Remarkably, they were running in third and fourth place overall in the fleet on this leg, with four 60-footers behind them. Jean Luc was only miles behind Christophe at the front of the pack. Steve Pettengill was not far behind and he had J-J and David Scully breathing down his neck. It was not long before the generally fine weather gave way to increasingly colder temperatures, then fog, and finally ice.

Jean Luc was the first to spot it at about 58° south, 153° west. The morning light was bouncing off it about five miles away. He guessed it was about four miles long and one hundred feet high, and he sailed about two miles to the south of it to take some photographs. His sighting was reported to the rest of the fleet. The Southern Ocean Sunshine Cruise was definitely over. Now it was getting serious again.

Jean Luc's message sent a shiver through the fleet. The ice was further north than it had been in previous races, and there was still a long way to go to the Horn. Everyone would be sleeping a lot less easily and spending more time in the cockpit keeping a good lookout, at least during the day. It would be a nerve-racking couple of weeks. With fog, and frequent rain and snow squalls, visibility was often very poor. The radar might pick up an iceberg, but the chances are it would not unless it was big and close. For every iceberg out there, there would be hundreds of "growlers", and the chances of seeing them in time were about zero. Staying in the cockpit for long periods was impossible – even with good thermal clothing every skipper would have to go below to thaw out fairly frequently. At night in particular it would be even more of a game of Russian roulette.

Anxiety among the fleet took many forms, from expressions of genuine fear to humour. Robin suggested the fleet should fall into line behind Jean Luc to the Horn and everyone would have to promise not to queue-barge!

It was not long before there were other sightings. J-J saw a berg at 57° south, 121° west, and said it was a really eerie experience. Jean Luc saw another "with plenty plenty growlers". David Adams saw one ". . . very tall. Looked great. Had some children. Now I've seen my 'berg I can go home!" Giovanni saw ice as well, and every skipper who did not see any knew they must have passed some along the way.

The Southern Ocean had not finished with the fleet in terms of bad weather either. It still had a few tricks up its sleeve. After what he described as "a bonus points knockdown" that up-ended his "wine cellar" and scattered broken glass and wine around the cabin, David Scully remarked with resignation, "the Southern Ocean is doing what it's supposed to do – enormous waves, snow squalls, plenty of breeze." He later reported that life aboard "feels like a ride in a front-loading washing machine!" Alan was thrown across his cabin in a terrifying knockdown that left him bruised and bleeding, and blackcurrant jam everywhere. Steve was in his cockpit watching "square waves with spray flying continuously over the decks" when *Hunter's Child* was knocked down. He was thrown across the cockpit and landed with his back on a winch, leaving him in agony and requiring him to sail the rest of the leg in a surgical brace, which he had with him as a precautionary measure because of a previous back problem.

Things were no better further back in the fleet. About fifteen hundred miles to the west of the front-runners, Harry, Robin and Arnie all suffered knock-downs in a series of rapidly moving frontal systems, screaming across the "Furious Fifties". Harry said the seas were "diabolical" and getting to be as bad as those he had experienced during Leg Two. Barometric pressure had plummeted to the mid-970s and the isobars on the weather map were close enough to be bumping into each other. All hell was about to break loose.

As Christophe and the fleet leaders were just a few hundred miles from the Horn in an ever-lightening breeze, the wind and the seas began to mount for the tail-enders. The first casualty was Robin. Two thousand miles from the Horn, *Cornwall* was running with her Genoa poled out. A snow squall came through and the boat rounded up in the wind shift. The wind went forward of the poled-out sail and the mast broke about seven feet from the deck, falling backwards. It was a single clean break.

On Sunday, 19 February, Robin messaged race headquarters: "*Cornwall* was dismasted at approximately 10.00 GMT in a big squall . . .No assistance required."

Robin tethered the fallen rig to the deck to stop it doing any more damage, and sat in the cockpit nursing a cup of tea while he worked out a plan to jury rig the boat. When the squall passed and the wind eased a little, he cut away the disabled mast and rigging with a hacksaw and bolt cutters. He removed the sails and dropped the mast over the side. It was a struggle. Now he would see if his plan for a jury rig was going to work. Everyone in the fleet had worked out in advance how they would deal with a dismasting – it was part of the scruti-neering process prior to the start of the race that we all had to describe how we would deal with such emergencies.

Robin had two spinnaker poles on board, both the same length. His plan was to construct an A-frame with the poles. He tied the base of each to the toe-rail about level with the mast, tied the tops of them together and hoisted the A-frame, using wire halyards as a forestay and backstay. He then hanked on his small jib and got under way again.

His messages to race headquarters were buoyant, almost defiantly so in their tone. While he obviously would not have wanted to be dismasted, it would be in character for Robin to see it as more of an opportunity than a problem. He had sailed the last BOC Challenge and was disappointed to be having to sail this race in the same boat. He was sailing aggressively and was certainly extracting a performance from her that almost no one else could; but to him it probably seemed like just a repeat performance. The dismasting made the voyage different, got him into the newspapers, and gave him an opportunity to exercise and demonstrate his seamanship skills.

The decision of where to go was an easy one. With the prevailing wind and current, and the added attraction of having to round Cape Horn under jury rig, the Falkland Islands was the obvious place to head for. With a great deal of help from Josh Hall in the Charleston race communications centre, a new mast and sails were sourced in England and flown down to the Falklands to await his arrival. At the same time, fans in Charleston and elsewhere were raising the forty thousand dollars this was costing. Robin said he thought he should rename his boat "Charleston" in gratitude.

A few days after Robin's dismasting, Arnie reported a serious problem with his deck-stepped mast. It was twisting on its base and a hairline crack was beginning to move up its side. As the days went by the problem got worse and he wove a cat's cradle of Kevlar line around the base to hold it together. To reduce the stress he was proceeding under headsail alone, slowly – and to the Falklands too. His handiwork with the mast was given a severe test not long after: "Things continue wild and woolly. Yesterday in 30-40 knots of wind, the port steering cable snapped at the sheave, turned us broadside to a twenty-foot breaker and rolled us 180 degrees. Boy, was I surprised to see the mast still there. The interior looks as if it were decorated by Attila the Hun."

Just a few days later, a 40-knot squall some six hundred miles west of the Horn tore into *Newcastle* and snapped her mast about seven feet above the deck. Reporting this to race headquarters, Alan kept his humour and said it was becoming "the trendy thing to do!" He fashioned a similar jury rig to Robin's, then he too set off for the Falklands. It was becoming quite a procession, and Josh now had another customer for getting a replacement mast to Port Stanley. Since it had been Alan who had rescued him from his sinking boat in Leg One, he was happy to have an opportunity to begin repaying the debt. While Josh was organizing the logistics of the shipment, fund-raising efforts were under way in Alan's home town of Newcastle, Australia.

While all of this drama was unfolding, the front-runners were beginning to round the Horn.

First was Christophe, the day after Robin's dismasting. He had dipped south in his approach to avoid a big high pressure system and passed some forty miles to the south of the Horn. He didn't see a thing, and was making course in light winds for the Straits of Lemaire – a narrow channel between the mainland and the tiny island of Isla de Los Estados. He had a lead of about 360 miles over Jean Luc who was next to pass almost two days later, at night and in a brisk 25 knots of wind. This was his fourth rounding of the Horn alone.

Steve rounded next, less than a day later, and messaged to race headquarters: "I'm psyched. It was perfect weather for rounding Cape Horn, 35-45 knots of wind and I was humming along at 18-25 knots through the water – maybe just a little bit out of control. I was four miles off and could just see the halo of the lighthouse." He had been round Cape Horn twice before, but this was his first time alone and he was really pumped up by the experience. His first trip round the Horn was in 1989 and on that occasion he left the ashes of his old dog Frodo there. This time he had a long talk with Frodo, who had often sailed with him, about old times, what was going on in his life, how he was feeling, and the weather! According to Steve, Frodo would love the weather around Cape Horn.

Not long after Steve, Giovanni, J-J and David Scully went round. In their different ways, all three had produced remarkable performances.

Giovanni was in the toughest of all battles with David Adams, which was forcing them both to squeeze the last drop of performance from their boats. Most remarkable of all was that Giovanni should be fourth in the fleet at this stage of the leg in a 50-footer.

J-J's performance was impressive too, given the fact that he had the oldest and by far the heaviest maxi boat in the fleet. He said that when he saw the Horn he felt a sudden and unexpected sense of achievement, a sense of exhilaration and pride. "I'm not a religious person but I told God that if he had anything to do with its creation he'd done a wonderful job."

For David Scully to be where he was at this stage of the leg truly represented a great performance, given his detour to Bluff and the fact that he was sailing with a seriously undersized mainsail. To this must be added the fact that he had been hand-steering for the past fifty hours because his three autopilots had crashed, a problem that was to dog him for the rest of the leg. He found the Horn desolate, horrible, forbidding – it seemed to him that even the sun was trying to avoid looking at it. "I decided this was the place where the sea meets the land and find they hate each other," he said. "It was a very impressive sight but I just wanted to get away from it as fast as possible."

Christophe Auguin held onto his lead and crossed the finish line in Punta del Este just under thirty days after leaving Sydney. It had been a record-breaking run. He had smashed Alain Gautier's Leg Three record from the last race, and produced a record day's run of more than 350 miles. As he crossed the line in the company of several spectator boats and helicopters, a fix-winged plane circled above towing a banner "BIENVENIDOS SCETA CALBERSON". He was a happy man, and deserved to be.

His sponsors organized a press conference the following day. He was asked all the obvious questions about his trip and how he felt. Then someone asked him a very "Gallic" question that produced an answer I could not have scripted better myself. "What," he was asked, "do you think is the philosophy, the concept of 'Le BOC'?"

Christophe thought for a moment and stroked the designer stubble on his chin, then said: "For me it is a unique blend of competition, camaraderie, technology, solitude, fear – but above all else adventure. It is the greatest race of all." He had summed up the whole thing in a few words.

Two days after Christophe, five more boats crossed the line in the space of just a few hours. Steve was the first to arrive. Jean Luc was less than an hour behind him. Two hours later Giovanni finished, and David Adams was an hour and a half after him. In some ways it was a fitting end to Leg Three for these two. After leading most of the way in Leg One, Giovanni lost out to David in the last week or so, but finally beat his Australian rival across the line. Giovanni had been first into Sydney at the end of Leg Two, but was bumped into second place when David was awarded a four-hour bonus to compensate him for the time he spent diverting to Isabelle Autissier when she was first dismasted. On this leg, Giovanni had again led most of the way, but David had stolen a lead over him through making better decisions about the weather just before Cape Horn. David had stayed ahead until just a few hours short of Punta. Now he had an overall lead of twenty-one-and-a-half hours over Giovanni – exactly the same as Alain Gautier's lead over Christophe in the last BOC Challenge, and Christophe went on to win by two days! This race within a race between David and Giovanni was far from over.

An hour and a half after David's arrival in Punta, and barely six hours after Steve in second place, came J-J. To have this happen after more than seven thousand miles of sailing was testament to the intensity of the competition. David

Scully came in the next day, having hand-steered most of the time with little sleep in the previous five days.

But the mood of celebration was short-lived. What was about to unfold was the worst drama of any BOC Challenge, the worst nightmare for anyone of us involved in the race as a competitor or administrator.

HARRY

It had not been good news at the back end of the fleet for a few days. Minoru Saito was the back-marker and was struggling with problems that seemed endemic to his boat – his autopilots were down and he was low on power again. The net result was that he was having to hand-steer a lot and he had turned off his Standard-C unit, something that was strictly against the rules of the race. Harry Mitchell too was having power generation difficulties, partly because his wind generator had been disabled in a knockdown. He was a couple of hundred miles ahead of Minoru. Because of their power problems and atrocious propagation conditions, their radio communications with race headquarters were only intermittent. Every now and then Robin Davie, some three hundred miles further on with a jury-rigged wire aerial, would pick them up on the radio and have a brief conversation.

In fact Robin had been in fairly regular contact with both for most of the leg, and those of us in the race management team were enormously encouraged with his reports of Harry's progress. He had left Sydney with the tail end of a bout of flu a day after the official start. As the days rolled by, his spirits seemed to improve. He reported via Robin that he was eating and sleeping well, and beginning to enjoy the passage again. He was making the boat move faster on this leg too and seemed to be very much on top of things.

No one had heard from Minoru, including Robin, since the very end of February, and with his Standard-C unit switched off we were unable to track his progress. Then, at 22.00 GMT on 2 March, one of the two 406 EPIRBs on Harry's boat was activated and, in effect, he went missing too. No one could raise him on the radio and his Trimble unit had stopped functioning. This meant we could not message him via Standard-C or track his position. Robin, a few hundred miles closer to the Horn, said the weather conditions in the area were dreadful and looked like getting worse. This was certainly confirmed by the weather data we had looked at. According to meteorologists in France and California, Minoru and Harry were in an area of severe winds with gusts up to 70 knots.

The 406 EPIRBs, when activated, send a continuous stream of data to earth stations via a network of six satellites – three US, three Russian – circling the earth a thousand miles up in space. The EPIRBs are guaranteed to work for a minimum of forty-eight hours. Our race rules required all competitors to carry at least two on board (one of which was supplied by the race organization with part sponsorship from the manufacturers, Alden) to provide extended coverage in the event of just such an emergency as this. A 406 EPIRB provides position data that is accurate to within a radius of less than three nautical miles. To add another feature to each competitor's inventory of safety equipment, the race organization also supplied every boat with an Alden Search And Rescue Target (SART) unit – a clever piece of electronics that acts as a homing device for any ship's radar within a radius of ten miles.

Harry kept his Alden EPIRB in his cabin, under his bunk. His second EPIRB was a Lokata, which was taped up and bolted to a stanchion at the stern of the boat. At first, there was speculation that the Lokata might have been washed overboard; but when we checked the identification number of the EPIRB that had been activated, it turned out to be the Alden. This almost certainly meant that Harry had taken it from under his bunk into the cockpit and set it off.

Knowing Harry, activating his EPIRB would mean he was in serious trouble, with no chance of sailing his boat towards land. He was an experienced and resourceful sailor and it would take more than a dismasting and disabled steering to knock him out of the race. His modest and self-effacing personality would also prevent him from seeking help unless it was his only option.

It would have been late afternoon where he was when the EPIRB was activated. The Maritime Rescue Coordination Centre (MRCC) at naval headquarters in Valparaiso, Chile, was responsible for search and rescue operations in this area of ocean, and was alerted first by the US MRCC headquarters in Maryland. Pete Dunning at BOC Race Communications Centre in Charleston was next on the list. It was Pete who phoned Mark Schrader at race headquarters in Punta del Este, where we were all about to go out for a drink.

Mark phoned the MRCC in Valparaiso to determine what plans were being put in place for a search. The first thing they had to establish was what, if any, shipping there was in the area. The US MRCC unit in Hawaii and the British unit in Falmouth were brought into the picture to help with this aspect. Valparaiso at first said they would send one or two planes to search the area, but later cancelled the operation because visibility was too poor. The Lockheed P3 aircraft used by the Chileans were not fitted with colour or temperature infrared sensing equipment. Besides, they had a range of two thousand miles there and back, so they would have only a few hours of search time in the area.

By the following morning it had been established that another British yacht, the *Spirit of Birmingham*, was three hundred miles east of Harry's position. She was being sailed alone by Lisa Clayton, who was attempting to become the first British woman to sail around the world solo and non-stop. She had storm damage to her boat already and it was deemed to be both unwise and unsafe to send her to search for Harry. Later in the day the MRCC in Valparaiso and Falmouth were trying to make contact with a Grenadan-registered 150-metre bulk carrier, the *Francesca Shulte*, which was almost five hundred miles northwest of Harry and on her way to Punta Arenas in Chile. Contact was established that afternoon, and her master was instructed to divert to the position of the EPIRB signals. At full speed in the prevailing conditions he estimated his ship was twenty-five hours away.

Robin kept race headquarters informed of his weather conditions. "A very rough last twenty-four hours with 30-40 knot winds . . . the problem has been the breaking beam seas from the north, made worse by heavy cross seas from the west and southwest, and a heavy westerly swell. On three or four occasions we have been picked up and chucked sideways onto our beam ends."

These were exactly the same conditions we had had in the storm over Christmas. Armed with that experience, it did not take much imagination for me to know how painfully miserable it would be on a dismasted or disabled yacht. If this indeed was the condition of the *Henry Hornblower*, Harry would be having a very rough time of it.

The deteriorating weather slowed down progress on the *Francesca Shulte* and she did not arrive at Harry's position for thirty-two hours. On her way there, just after dusk, the officer on watch spotted a small yacht a few miles off. The skipper of the yacht had spotted the ship also and turned on his VHF radio. It was Minoru on *Shuten-Dohji II*. He said he had virtually no electrical power, his generator having failed and there being too little daylight to produce much from his solar panels. Other than that, he said all was well on board and he was heading for Cape Horn.

The *Francesca Shulte* arrived at the position from which Harry's EPIRB was still sending out a signal in the middle of the night, and started to search an area of ten by thirty nautical miles in the traditional "expanding square" pattern. Halfway through the day, at 13.03 GMT, some sixty-four hours after it had been activated, Harry's EPIRB coughed out its last position. The *Francesca Shulte* completed two full searches of the area by the following morning, using her fog horn and flares during the hours of darkness to attract attention. Mark was in frequent contact with the MRCCs in Valparaiso, Hawaii and Falmouth, and was now in direct contact via COMSAT Standard-C with the master of the *Francesca Shulte*. In one message Mark thanked him for undertaking such a thorough search in such appalling conditions. He replied: "Assistance at sea is the normal practice of seamen. My crew and I are trying to do our best to locate and rescue this brave man."

BOC race headquarters in Punta del Este, and the communications centre in Charleston, were on twenty-four-hour watch to follow and assist the search process. In Punta we stuck a photograph of Harry on the office wall. It was of him at his most characteristic, laughing, a twinkle in his eye, waving a Union Jack. Each evening we stood in front of it and drank a toast to our friend. I am sure I was not alone in saying a little prayer for his safety under my breath at the same time.

After two searches of the original area were completed, the MRCC in Valparaiso then moved the focus some way to the southwest, based on their own calculations of likely drift and the set of the current. As all the EPIRB positions over the whole period were within three miles of each other (a big mystery in itself, given the wind and currents in the area), it was a controversial decision. While the *Francesca Shulte* was combing the new area, the satellite spat out two more positions from Harry's EPIRB in the same area as the original search. This "new" data later turned out to be a regurgitation of old information, but the *Francesca Shulte* was ordered back to the original search area. The master of the ship messaged to Mark: "I hope we are searching for a lost EPIRB, that all of Mitchell's communication equipment has failed, and he is now on his way to Punta del Este."

The *Francesca Shulte* completed another search in winds of over 50 knots, horrendous seas and visibility of under a mile, and was then released by the MRCC in Valparaiso. Before heading for Punta Arenas, her master agreed to follow the track Harry would have been taking if he was still sailing for the Horn. It was still a possibility, if perhaps an unlikely one, that the EPIRB had been activated by mistake and fallen off the boat, and that Harry was still sailing.

Almost two days later, six days after the first alert, another ship was diverted to search. She was the 270-metre Liberian-registered bulk carrier *Doceriver*, on her way from Australia to Brazil with a full load of coal. The search position was defined after consultations between the MRCCs in Valparaiso, Hawaii and

Falmouth, and with race director Mark Schrader. The *Doceriver* reached the area two days after being diverted. Having combed it for thirty-six hours, she too was released for her own safety in a 60-knot storm and mountainous seas.

Although another ship was later diverted through the search area, and the Chilean Navy undertook to keep a good watch at Cape Horn, that was effectively the end of the search for our friend Harry. What happened will remain something of a mystery. My own theory, perhaps because I want it to be true, is that it happened quickly and he would not have suffered much. The sea state must have been at least as bad as that we had had over Christmas, and the kind of rogue wave that rolled and disabled Isabelle then could easily have done the same or worse to *Henry Hornblower*. The boat would probably not have survived long in those conditions if she was badly disabled. With the sea temperature just a few degrees above freezing, hypothermia would have rendered even the fittest person unconscious in minutes.

I had known Harry for almost ten years. I'd been sailing with him. He taught me how to fix a position with a sextant. It is hard to think of not seeing Harry again with his mischievous smile and sparkling eyes, not being able to tease him about his baggy shorts and bandy legs, listen to his tales of adventures from earlier days, become infected by his own zest for life and uncritical enthusiasm for humankind. He was a lovable man with a generous spirit. He received and deserved the loudest ovation whenever the skippers in this race were presented at prize-givings and other receptions. He never sought but always enjoyed the notoriety he attracted. It's a cliché, but he truly was one of a kind.

～～～～～～～

As the *Doceriver* was released from the search, Niah Vaughan was crossing the finish line in Punta del Este to take third place in Class II. He had sailed consistently and skilfully, keeping up a good average speed given the age and weight of *Jimroda II*. But he had not escaped the wrath of the Southern Ocean and came into port with a good deal of damage to the back end of his boat. Just after rounding the Horn, just when he was beginning to heave a sigh of relief at the prospect of calmer and warmer waters in the South Atlantic, he decided to take the short cut through the Straits of Lemaire. He had not been in there long when a front came through with 40-50 knots of wind. In the relatively shallow waters the seas soon became large, steep and confused. Night fell and it was pitch black. He decided to hand-steer, and clipped his harness to a U-bolt in the cockpit. Minutes later an enormous wave collapsed on the boat and sent her into a 120-degree knockdown. He was under water for ten seconds, and it must have seemed like ten minutes. When the boat righted herself again, the sails were torn and the stainless steel antenna arch at the stern had crumpled around the backstay. Everything had been wiped off the top of his mast.

As Niah was licking his wounds and sailing for Punta, Arnie Taylor was fixing his mast base in the Falklands; Alan Nebauer arrived there too in *Newcastle* to rig his new mast. It was cold, wet and windy most of the time, but they got the work done with the help of the British military there and quickly became celebrities with the locals. Alan left soon after Arnie for the final thousand miles to Punta, just before Robin arrived at the islands for his new mast.

But Alan's problems were far from over. A little more than two days out, and at 03.30 hours (local time), he was in serious trouble. He was dozing in his bunk. Suddenly, his off-course alarm went off and *Newcastle* rounded up into the wind. He thought he must have run into a big kelp bed because he had seen a lot of it around the previous day. But, up in the cockpit, he soon realized he had no steerage at all.

When he went into his watertight aft compartment to check the steering cables, it began to dawn on him what must have happened. The compartment was half filled with water and there were cracks around the lower end of the rudder post tube. He must have hit something quite hard. His rudder had snapped off, leaving a stump of rudder post protruding from the hull. Alan patched up the cracks in the aft compartment to stem the flow, but he still had to pump it out every two or three hours. Then he set about fashioning an emergency rudder with a whisker pole over the back of the boat, hinged at the transom and with first a piece of line, and finally a wooden paddle, tied to the end of it to provide some steerage. He messaged race headquarters: "Under present conditions it works . . . I need a gentle breeze and a flat sea."

It took him eight days to cover the remaining six hundred miles to Punta. When he arrived on 25 March, his wife Cindy's twenty-ninth birthday, he said that sailing those last few hundred miles had been the most demanding thing he had ever done in his life – emotionally and physically, as well as technically. The loss of his rudder must have been a savage blow after everything else he had had to contend with in the race to date. Dealing with a dismasting was easy by comparison: "You can always jury rig something to get a boat moving, but not being able to steer the thing leaves you helpless. I tried everything and finally found that the best solution for my boat was the whisker pole with a paddle strapped to the end of it, and then trying to balance the boat with the sails as well. But then any change in wind direction or strength would change the boat; we'd round up into the wind and it would take me a couple of hours to get her going again. It was an absolute nightmare!"

He added that he had been both humbled and overwhelmed by the assistance he was receiving from other skippers and shore crew to keep him in the race. It was, he said, "one of the unique characteristics of this race that the other competitors become your mates and help out when you need it. After everything that the people back home in Newcastle had done for me in fixing me up with a new mast, I thought losing the rudder would be hard to deal with in terms of time and money. Now I'm here in Punta I can't believe what everyone's doing for me."

Almost as soon as Alan had reported the loss of his rudder, David Adams and his shore crew Phil Lee were working with Cindy Nebauer to get hold of the original drawings for the part. They organized other skippers' shore crew to build another rudder and work out how it could be fitted without needing to haul the boat. A haul-out would require taking the boat to Montevideo, a day trip each way; time and money Alan certainly could not afford.

Alan's new rudder was just about ready when he arrived in Punta. A huge crane was used to haul the stern of *Newcastle* out of the water for it to be fitted. It was an excellent piece of teamwork, and Alan was almost in tears.

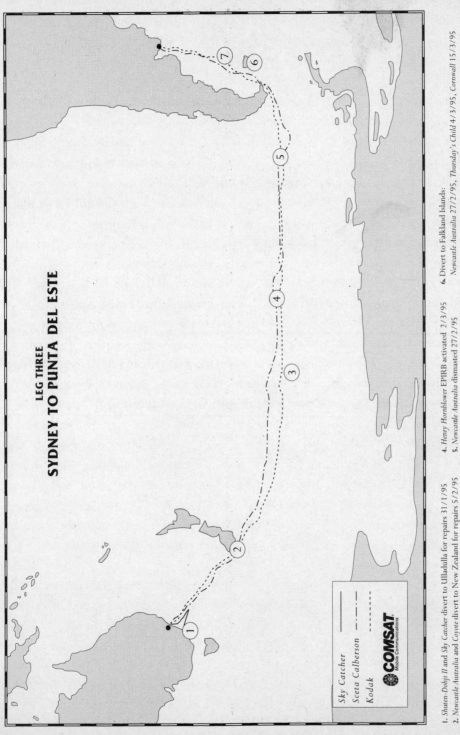

LEG THREE
SYDNEY TO PUNTA DEL ESTE

Sky Catcher
Sceta Calberson
Kodak

COMSAT
Mobile Communications

1. Shusen-Dohji II and Sky Catcher divert to Ulladulla for repairs 31/1/95
2. Newcastle Australia and Coyote divert to New Zealand for repairs 5/2/95
3. Cornwall dismasted 19/2/95

4. Henry Hornblower EPIRB activated 2/3/95
5. Newcastle Australia dismasted 27/2/95

6. Divert to Falkland Islands:
   Newcastle Australia 27/2/95, Thursday's Child 4/3/95, Cornwall 15/3/95
7. Newcastle Australia loses rudder 17/3/95

PUNTA TO CHARLESTON

U ruguay likes to be thought of as the Switzerland of South America. Certainly its secretive banking regulations make it a haven for foreign capital and, partly as a consequence, it is something of a playground for South America's rich and occasionally famous. Punta del Este is its principal resort and it is stacked to the gunwales with foreign visitors from Christmas till March. During that period its population of a few thousand grows ten-fold. Most of the high-rise apartment blocks along the seafront, and huge mansions in well-manicured gardens, are owned by Argentinians and other South Americans. For nine months of the year these properties lie empty and the town almost literally closes down. The discos and casinos close. So too do most of the shops, hotels and restaurants. They even turn off the traffic lights from Easter till Christmas!

The BOC fleet began to arrive in Punta del Este in late February, just as the town's holiday season was beginning to go off the boil. Still, countless millions of pounds' worth of luxury yachts crowded the marina and harbour. The streets were also still clogged with visitors, their excited chatter and designer clothes, their cars, mopeds, bicycles and roller-blades. The endless white-gold beaches were thick and alive, like anthills, with tanned bodies in string bikinis. It had a strong resemblance to the best of the Mediterranean coast in high season. But by the middle of March the town was in rapid seasonal decline. By the end of the month, as the tail-enders of the BOC fleet arrived, it was in hibernation.

Robin Davie was the last to arrive, on *Cornwall*, before the restart and at about the time we finally had welcome and long-awaited news of Minoru Saito, who had not slipped around Cape Horn undetected as we had thought. When he arrived in Punta he told us he had been contacted by the Chilean Navy over the VHF radio. He said they asked him, "Are you panicked?", and he told them in typical fashion: "Radio no work. Radar no work. Steering no work. I'm OK. Not panicked. But boat is panicked!" For some reason this contact was not reported by the Chileans and we knew nothing of Minoru's whereabouts or his safety until he was spotted by a fishing boat off the Falklands. Over his VHF radio there he reported that all was reasonably well on board, despite drained batteries and having to hand-steer most of the time.

The Punta del Este Yacht Club staff and members were being excellent hosts to The BOC Challenge once again, and the mood among the skippers in port was relaxed and convivial. My arrival meant that Kent Martin could withdraw from his role as event director and return to his other duties with BOC. We were fortunate to have Carole Marsh on the event management team through to the end of the race, having joined us in Sydney.

Those who had survived the race thus far knew they were about to embark on what should be the easiest as well as the shortest leg. They had all "climbed Mount Everest" by rounding the Horn and were now close to the gentler reaches of the descent.

While I still had no serious regrets about retiring from the race, it was becoming more difficult for me to control my sense of personal failure in not completing the course. I kept debating it in my mind and always concluded that my withdrawal had been both sensible and inevitable for me. Having invested so much time, money and effort in the project, pulling out when the job was only half done was not a satisfactory outcome. The dreadful conditions encountered by those at the tail end of the fleet between Australia and the Horn, however, was a perverse comfort to me and helped confirm the wisdom of my decision; but Harry's demise was a savage price for it. It left me with a strange sense of guilt I could not explain. It was not easy still being so close to the race. I began to wonder if I should not have organized my life so I could distance myself from it a bit, at least until my emotional involvement with it had worked itself through. Then again, maybe staying this close, though not without its pain, was going to help "lay the ghost".

For those left in the fleet there was still a race to be sailed, and none of the skippers was prepared to take anything for granted. Leg Three had left most with big repair projects to be completed and the front-runners in both classes were still trying to psych each other. There was a fair bit of good-humoured needling going on between David Adams and Giovanni Soldini for example. David's lead of twenty-one hours over Giovanni was certainly not an unassailable margin. In Class I all the front-runners were hard at work planning how they could be first into Charleston. Second-place Steve Pettengill, for example, removed almost six hundred pounds of weight from his boat in Punta in an effort to gain a competitive edge. He was going to take only the bare necessities for a fast passage and little in the way of spare parts or extra sails, just enough food and no little luxuries.

Start day approached. As it did, the weather began to change. The often blistering heat gave way to chill breezes, torrential rain and the occasional spectacular burst of thunder and lightning. With hindsight, April 1st was probably not the best day to pick to do anything very much; but this was the day we had selected for the restart, and this was the day Punta decided to serve up its first big storm of the season. The sky was leaden, heavy with wind and rain. Along the seafront, the waves were pounding up the beach and hurling thick clouds of sand and spray across the road. The two navy ships and the Uruguayan sail-training tall-ship *Capitan Miranda*, which was to be the start vessel, were sheltering in the lea of the small island in the bay about a mile from the marina.

The race committee gathered in the office just before seven in the morning; we then leaned into the storm as we trudged down the dock to where the BOC boats were straining and pulling at their mooring lines. It was a ritual visit, followed by a formal discussion and an inevitable decision. The restart would have to be postponed until noon the following day. In fact if the weather forecast was at all accurate, we might not be able to have the fleet at sea for another two days.

This was the first time we had ever had to postpone a start in The BOC Challenge in twelve years of running the race. It was a disappointment to sponsors and others who had flown in and would now have to leave before the restart. It was a disappointment to some of the competitors who wanted to use all that wind to sweep them up the coast towards the finish line, especially those who had boats that thrived in strong wind and lumpy seas. But no one questioned the decision. Just pulling the boats out of the marina would have been a major problem, and no one wanted to take that sort of risk at this stage of the game.

We all spent the rest of the day anxiously kicking our heels and hoping the forecast was wrong. Looking at the weather pictures, Punta was close to the centre of a storm with very tightly packed isobars. The question was, how quickly would it blow itself off shore?

Doors and windows rattled through the evening and early part of the night. The sea was in turmoil, and the BOC boats were struggling at their lines, heeling and complaining in every strong gust. But by morning the storm had passed, the sun was forcing its way through the thinning cloud and the wind was down below 20 knots. The gun would fire at noon after all!

Pulling the boats out of the marina was not an easy task but it was tackled with patience and skill for the most part. The luckless *Coyote*, however, did not escape unscathed. David Scully had been plagued by problems throughout the race. Finally he had a new mainsail that was likely to last the leg. This was going to be his first opportunity to demonstrate the kind of performance of which he knew the boat to be capable. But as he was being pulled from the dock, *Coyote*'s keel snagged on a mooring buoy line and a yacht club tender rushed too quickly to her aid. The bow of the tender pierced the side of the hull two feet above the waterline. The spectators lining the dock squealed in disbelief, and *Coyote* was towed to a buoy outside the marina.

Within an hour David and his shore crew had the hole patched. He demonstrated more good humour, patience and politeness than I would have thought possible in the circumstances – and he managed to make it to the start line with the rest of the fleet.

NORTH AND EAST

The eleven BOC boats bobbed around behind the start line in 15-20 knots of wind and a sea-state that was still very lumpy from the previous day's storm. Most were reefed down for ease of manoeuvring and for the stronger winds they would surely encounter beyond the island that had to be rounded after crossing the line. Not David Adams, though, who was carrying full sail on *True Blue* and throwing her around as if she was a 15-foot dinghy rather than a 50-foot ocean racer. He played the start like a dinghy race too, and was first across the line.

The less-than-friendly conditions soon had J-J Provoyeur using his championship dinghy-racing skills and his heavier *Novell South Africa* to advantage too. He led the fleet round the island and out to sea. But it was not long before the list of fleet standings had a familiar ring to it. Christophe Auguin was soon in the lead again. Steve, David Scully and Jean Luc were huddled together and locked in a battle for second and third place that was to last almost to the finish line. David Adams and Giovanni kept their tussle for first place going at full tilt too, and it was not long either before Alan Nebauer and Niah Vaughan realized they were fighting at close quarters for third place in Class II. This was a scrap that was to frustrate both of them and last most of the leg as well.

The fleet stayed bunched together for several days at the beginning of the leg as the wind lightened. These were now conditions in which the skills of each sailor would make more of a difference than the relative merits of each boat, save for the obvious advantage that the lighter craft would have over the very heavy ones. In these conditions extra boat speed could be extracted from skilful sail trimming, keeping the spinnaker full, and endless hours of hand-steering. These were the conditions that prevailed for most of the leg, in fact, with the occasional burst of tropical storms and squalls, and prolonged periods in the trade winds only when the fleet was in the northern hemisphere.

The unpredictable weather patterns experienced in the first leg were back to torture the fleet once again, and several of the skippers complained when it was all over that Leg Four was the worst and most frustrating of the entire race. As the reports came in from the boats of daily runs in the low double digits, hours of being becalmed and then being hit by a sudden 30-knot squall, my mind returned to the torment of the first leg and I felt a sympathy for the fleet that few others could share. They were back to the Chinese water torture of gear clanking and sails slatting from side to side as their boats rolled in the swell. I remembered the times it got the better of me, and had me standing in the cockpit screaming to the heavens for more wind. I recalled the agony of finding myself in yet another "windless hole", all the while believing that everyone else was racing away in a good stiff breeze. Suddenly, it was hurting less not to be out there on this leg!

But the light and fickle winds were not the only problems with which some of the fleet had to contend. Just as Minoru was finishing Leg Three before dawn on 6 April, with Punta del Este in total darkness suffering one of its occasional power failures, Giovanni lost his forestay. He had managed to edge *Kodak* just ahead of *True Blue* when it happened. It was a cruel blow for the young Italian who had sailed so competitively throughout the race and who would now have to divert to a port in Brazil for repairs. He arranged for a new stay to be flown to Vitoria several hundred miles away, used headsail halyards to help keep the rig up, and did his best to maintain boat speed with his small staysails. His best turned out to be good enough to retain his lead over David for a long while. Two days later David said he thought someone had forgotten to tell Giovanni he had no forestay. In a message to race headquarters he quipped: "I can't believe Giovanni. He's without a forestay and he's absolutely flying! According to the weather forecast, I'm the one who's supposed to have the wind."

It seemed that Giovanni might still be able to keep himself in the race for first place; but then he faced another setback. Two days later he sent a message to race headquarters: "When I was seventy miles south of Vitoria I received a telex telling me that the plane bringing my forestay from Spain had left it in Lisbon! The real problem is that I spent twenty-four hours diverting to Vitoria so I have lost very much time. I don't have much luck but I will have the forestay sent to Recife and will do the job there." Once in Recife it took him only three

Above The BOC fleet moored at the almost deserted Punta del Este Yacht Club marina. In high season the harbour is wall-to-wall boats. (JACQUES VAPILLON)

Right Not the most flattering photo, and looking a bit like Siamese twins, race director Mark Schrader and me on one of those days when everything was going right! (BILLY BLACK)

Above *David Adams, winner of Class II, driving his* True Blue. *He always made it look like he was sailing a dinghy.* (JACQUES VAPILLON)

Right *Robin Davie on board* Cornwall, *the oldest boat in the fleet. This was their second BOC Challenge together.* (JACQUES VAPILLON)

Below *Niah Vaughan sailed consistently well to bring* Jimroda II *into Charleston third in Class II, and the first unsponsored boat in the Class.* (BILLY BLACK)

Top Sceta Calberson *powering through the ocean. Having produced a "fleet best day's run" of 350.8 miles, Christophe Auguin and a crew managed a staggering 447.5 miles in 24 hours during his return to France after the race, smashing the previous record by a Whitbread boat.* (JACQUES VAPILLON)
Bottom *High-tech electronics for communications and safety featured on all the boats, not least on Class I winner Christophe's. His broad navigation station featured an array of gadgetry, including two computers.*
(JACQUES VAPILLON)

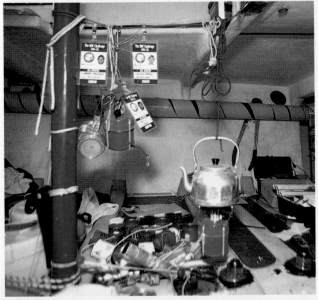

Above *The effervescent Giovanni Soldini during a burst of speed on board* Kodak. *He was not pleased with his second placing in Class II, but won the coveted Spirit of The BOC Challenge Award.*

(JACQUES VAPILLON)

Left *Top prize to Giovanni and* Kodak *also for having the least comfortable accommodation and cooking facilities below decks.*

(BILLY BLACK)

Above *Fans queued for hours in Charleston's Marion Square Park for the autographs of the BOC finishers. The queue for Christophe Auguin's stretched right across the park.* (JACQUES VAPILLON)

Below *Media relations director Dan McConnell (right) and media relations manager Herb McCormick made this BOC Challenge one of the top ten events in the world in terms of global media coverage.* (BILLY BLACK)

Top David Adams (left) and
Giovanni Soldini, locked in
combat for line honours in Class II
all the way around the world,
arm-wrestling in Punta del Este.
It was a draw!
(GARY-JOHN NORMAN)

Above Christophe Auguin
popping a bottle of Mumm after
winning the race. (JON NASH/PPL)

Left Steve Pettengill, Christophe
Auguin and Jean Luc Van den
Heede in the City Marina,
Charleston. No prizes for guessing
who was first, second and third!

(JACQUES VAPILLON)

Top *Mark Schrader and I compèred the gala prize-giving evening in the University sports hall and brought the curtain down on The BOC Challenge 1994-95.* (JACQUES VAPILLON)

Bottom *BOC's CEO and deputy chairman Pat Dyer (centre) presents The BOC Challenge perpetual trophy and line honours prize of $100,000 to Christophe Auguin.* (JACQUES VAPILLON) hours to get the task done and be back at sea again. He wasn't going to give up or ease up until he was over the finish line.

A week into the race saw David Scully in more trouble too. He had to make a trip up the mast to mend the tang that held the swivel of his headsail furling gear in place – the five-millimetre titanium strap had simply snapped in half! He celebrated a job well done and his "return to earth" with a tot of Calvados in his coffee.

The competition at the front of the fleet had become what one would expect in a day-race, not an ocean marathon. This message from Steve to race headquarters gave us all a good feel for its intensity: "The winds have turned against us – 20 knots on the nose. And it's coming from precisely where I want to go. One time I saw Christophe ahead of me, and a few hours later I saw Jean Luc behind me. But once the wind turned against us the fleet scattered like an eight-ball break in a pool game. Auguin turned left and crossed over to the Brazilian side of a contrary current that you don't want to be in. Ahead and to our east is a high pressure system that I also don't want to be in. David Scully took off on a port tack way to the east, while I headed up the middle, tacking on each wind shift."

The boats further back in the fleet were also often in sight of each other. Alan cheerfully informed race headquarters: "I'm enjoying the lovely weather in company with Niah Vaughan. My borrowed and second-hand sails are a bit of a handicap in this light windward stuff so old *Jimroda* is becoming a bit of an eyesore!"

While every skipper in the fleet was working overtime to squeeze the last drop of performance from their boats, Minoru and his helpers were battling round the clock to repair his electronics and radio equipment, radar, self-steering gear and rigging. His Tokyo shore crew were joined by members of the Punta del Este Yacht Club and other local supporters to get the work done. Five days later, and nine days behind the rest of the fleet, this indomitable sailor was back at sea again.

As the BOC boats approached the equator the tropical weather, with its squalls and calms, played with the fleet as a cat plays with a mouse. The big challenge now was to find the quickest route through the doldrums and into what should be steadier trade winds. By now the whole fleet was well behind where it had expected to be, and race headquarters began to extend its estimates of likely arrival times.

NORTH AND WEST

Christophe was first through the doldrums and raced away towards Charleston at a blistering pace. He had day's runs of more than three hundred miles, with a leg best for the fleet of 350 miles on Easter Sunday. An astonishing performance in itself but one he was to beat during his return sail to France, with a crew, after the race – he clocked a staggering day's run of 445 miles, smashing the previous record held by a Whitbread boat.

The battle for second place continued about two hundred and fifty miles behind him, with David Scully some forty miles ahead of Steve who was still just ahead of Jean Luc. But now Steve was in trouble. He had had to make more trips up his mast during the race than most sailors make in a lifetime, and this weekend he had to make a few more. The starboard cap shroud of *Hunter's Child* had broken between the second and third spreaders while he was screaming along with his spinnaker on a broad reach. He was lucky that his Bergstrom-Ridder rig, like that on *Thursday's Child*, *Sky Catcher* and *Cornwall*, had a lot of redundancy designed into it with reverse-diagonal struts as well as the more conventional shrouds; but it was a tribute to his considerable seamanship that he did not loose the rig over the side. He used multiple turns of quarter-inch Kevlar line to effect repairs and was soon under way again, determined to be in no worse than second place on this leg as well as in the overall standings.

The weather split the fleet into two packs. All the 60-footers except *Thursday's Child* were in the front group with the two 50-footers of David Adams and Giovanni. The second group was about a thousand miles behind, led by Alan and Niah who were still often in sight of each other. More than three weeks into the leg Alan sent this to race headquarters: "I awoke this morning to what is becoming a familiar sight . . . a funny white boat (*Jimroda*) on my horizon! Niah is getting pretty excited about the prospect of a full-on match race all the way to Charleston – eat your heart out Dennis Conner!" (Unknown to Alan, Dennis Conner was not going to see much close racing in his forthcoming defense of the America's Cup and was about to experience the most resounding thrashing of his life. He and his crew were humiliated in a 5-0 defeat by the New Zealanders in San Diego.)

The front group was fairly well spread out, though. Christophe, with around two thousand miles to go, was about 230 miles ahead of his nearest rival. David Adams had opened up a staggering five-hundred-mile lead over Giovanni. But this "race within a race" was far from over. David had been struggling with a recalcitrant generator and it eventually packed up altogether and would not start. He had no other means of generating electric power for his instruments and autopilots. A terse and despondent message to race headquarters said it all: "Cannot start generator. Will divert to Antigua." He had to hand-steer virtually the whole way. His shore crew Phil Lee was there waiting for him. The generator was dead and no amount of skill, tinkering and kicking it in the right places would get it going. Phil rigged up a second-hand petrol generator in the cockpit to feed the boat's spare alternator. He also put on board a brand new battery charger, donated by a local cruising sailor. Nine hours after pulling into port, David was under way again with a healthy margin over Giovanni still intact.

As the miles rolled under their keels, and as the finish line came ever closer, the mood on board most of the boats seemed to change. The racing was still fierce. There was still a lot to race for. But the messages from several of the boats to race headquarters were becoming longer and more philosophical. With the race nearly over, the enormity of their accomplishments was beginning to seep into the consciousness of the brave few left in the fleet.

J-J had battled round the world in a boat that was at least one generation behind most of his competition, but he had sailed with great skill and determination and extracted a remarkable performance from her. He had been meticulous in his preparations and carried this through to life on board. On *Novell South Africa* everything had its designated place, and everything was in its place. He ran a clean ship. He had not been much given to conversation, least of all any expressions of emotion, during the race. But with the end in sight he was loosening up a little. He sent this to race headquarters:

Crossing the equator was a very significant milestone for me. Back in the tropics I can now look back and wonder at the long route I have travelled, and contemplate my good fortune at having managed to come through unscathed. It is a tough race and this one has taken its toll even more than usual.

My passage from Punta del Este has been hard, harder than any other part of the race, with the ever-changing winds and thunder and heavy down-pours of rain, all of which do not make for easy sailing. To make matters worse I slipped back from the leaders because my trusty yacht doesn't have the speed. This gap was enough to lose phase with the favourable winds so I watched helplessly as the leaders pulled away . . . Still, crossing the equator is always fun, so for the occasion I cooked a favourite meal – sauerkraut, potatoes and country sausage, which I allow to simmer for a long time so the ensemble is very tasty! Together with a "dinky" of red wine (my first for the trip) it was a fitting celebratory meal and I enjoyed it.

So life on board is full of exciting happenings which are enhanced by the fact you are racing and therefore trying to get more speed all the time. I would not have it any other way . . . I am trying my best as we all know it's not over " 'til the fat lady sings!"

The race for second place on the leg ran until the last few hours, and David Scully was leading this little parade by a short head for a lot of the time. He had been the most wittily eloquent of the whole fleet and his turn of phrase was now becoming quite poetic:

There is no wind here. The stray puffs that tantalize the hanging spinnaker are the tail ends of the soft sighs of a sleeping ocean. Moving slowly, with the precision of a Japanese artist, we gather these breaths until there are enough to deceive the boat into motion. She gathers way, the wake just scratching the glazed surface of the ocean.

Two knots, three knots, the ocean is immense at three knots of speed. Still, for the last twenty-seven thousand miles we have nibbled at her size. Less than one thousand remain. We are now crossing tracks we made at our departure seven months ago. *Hunter's Child* and *Vendée Entreprises* are so close that in these fickle breezes, either or both could pass me, and be passed again, many times. Only *Sceta* is sure of success. Christophe's rocket ship makes our boats appear trundling transports as she flies toward victory.

Although I had more fun in the boisterous seas of the far south, on this leg I have had the satisfaction of finally learning about my boat. The first leg, following our hurried blaze of preparation, was, for me, a lesson in how to race down oceans instead of across them. In the second and third legs, *Coyote* was handicapped by the undersized mainsail we used when ours failed. Finally, on this leg, equipped with a beautiful new main, I am discovering how to sail her to her true potential. And that is exciting.

The long race wanes, the finish waits. I am satisfied that I have accomplished my objectives in this race. I have sailed the Atlantic up and down, crossed the equator, passed the three great capes of the world by sea, and brought my boat back safe to land. But, still, every thought I have of this race produces an echo in my mind that asks how to do it better. Next time.

*

Christophe was more technical than philosophical as he approached the finish line. His analysis of the race was, well, more analytical! *"Sceta Calberson* is a very good boat in reaching conditions. When reaching I have around six per cent more boat speed than *Hunter's Child* and *Vendée Entreprises*. I do think that *Coyote* has the same boat speed as *Sceta* in those conditions with a properly sized mainsail. In all other conditions the differences between the boats are less than three per cent."

Modesty prevented him from giving himself much direct credit for the four-hundred-mile lead he had at the end of this leg of the race: "My lead can be divided into different parts. One hundred miles is due to the boat itself. Another hundred miles is due to sailing in different weather conditions. Still another hundred miles is due to the tactics. Fifty miles is credited to the autopilots and fifty miles to my sails."

Christophe crossed the finish line as the sun came up to greet another day of warm Southern hospitality, almost twenty-five days after leaving Punta del Este. His total elapsed time for the race was 121 days, 17 hours, 11 minutes and 46 seconds – some nineteen hours longer than it had taken him to win the event four years earlier. His victory was witnessed by a fleet of thirty spectator boats, two helicopters and a fixed-wing aircraft towing a sign "BIENVENUE CHRISTOPHE". Hundreds more lined the dock and applauded his arrival, before pouring into the Charleston Yacht Club for his press conference, where he was greeted with a standing ovation.

He had not slept much in the past couple of days, but he looked fresh and relaxed. His open smile was never far from his lips and, whereas at the beginning of the race he had often called on his girlfriend Véronique to translate for him, he now had the confidence to rely on his own English to answer questions. He was courteous and thoughtful in dealing with both the predictable questions (How do you feel? . . . Is it good to win the race twice in a row? . . . Were you ever scared?) and the more difficult ones (Has this race changed you? . . . What will be your next adventure?). He handled himself like a champion and with none of the arrogance that often attaches itself to winners in major sports events.

The contest for second place for the leg was settled only in the last few hours of the race. The night before the finish, Steve Pettengill tacked away from the other two contenders to pick up the stronger winds of a weather front moving in. It was a good call and this piece of tactical skill brought him across the line several hours ahead of David Scully and Jean Luc, who crossed the line just an hour apart from each other.

Steve had sailed a brilliant race; and despite the substantial investment Hunter Marine had made in improving her hull shape, keel and rig, *Hunter's Child* was still a nine-year-old boat. Steve was a "skilled mechanic" as well as a competitive "driver". This had helped him keep his boat together while sailing "on the edge" most of the way around. He had made a great study of weather and tactics too, and he had made few mistakes. Scores of children from local schools who had been following his progress around the world showed up for his press conference and asked the best questions. Yes, the race had probably changed him. Yes, he wanted to do it again – there was still room for improvement! The only question that seemed to throw him was, "What are you going to do after this press conference?" He looked at his wife, smiled, and couldn't quite find the words.

David and Jean Luc held a joint press conference after their finish. Jean Luc announced that after four solo circumnavigations he was going to retire from racing alone – it wasn't that he didn't like the sport, he just liked people and wanted to cruise. David said he wanted to do the race again and, yes, he was sure it had changed him, hopefully for the better. Indeed, he said it would be a great disappointment to have undertaken and completed such a task and not be changed in some way by it.

David Adams arrived the next day. At his press conference he was generous in his praise for Giovanni, and he was modest enough to acknowledge that he had won with the advantage of having done the race before. He said it had been a tough race and he wasn't sure if he wanted to do it again.

J-J crossed the finish line in the middle of the night, but looked like he was on his way to a yacht club function – clean shaven, hair brushed, and wearing his Royal Cape blazer and "new South Africa" tie. When he stepped ashore, he announced his intention to sail the race again. He said it had been a remarkable experience and it had surely changed him – "I feel I am a better person for having done it, but don't ask me just how. Ask my wife in a few months!"

Giovanni was next across the line. He said he would be back at the start line next time, though. Second place wasn't good enough for him but the race had been the greatest adventure of his life. He looked back on his campaign with some pride, something he could share with those who had helped him put the boat and his whole project together in the first place.

More than a week later Alan Nebauer finished. He was followed in the early hours of the next morning by Arnie Taylor, and not long after him Niah crossed the line. They had been sailing in close company for several weeks and it was clear that Niah had been gently needling Alan over the radio for a lot of the way, no doubt in a spirit of friendly competition! Alan said he finally stopped coming up on the radio. "I figured that if I let them talk to each other all day I could be up on deck driving my boat a bit faster . . . and it seems to have paid off." All three said they'd like to do the race again – in different boats and with adequate commercial sponsorship to cover the costs of a proper campaign. Alan said it had been a "privilege" to sail in the race and he had been overwhelmed by the support he had had from his home town.

Robin Davie crossed the line at night and in the worst weather he had had for the entire fourth leg, a flash storm with heavy wind, thunder, lightning and a couple of water-spouts. He pledged to return for the next race, hopefully with enough sponsorship to build a boat that would give him a fighting chance of winning.

Last in was Minoru Saito. His dreadful passage around the world had been a tribute to his remarkable perseverance. He wasn't sure about the next race. For now, he was going to rest a few weeks in Charleston, then sail for England – to take home the soul of his friend Harry.

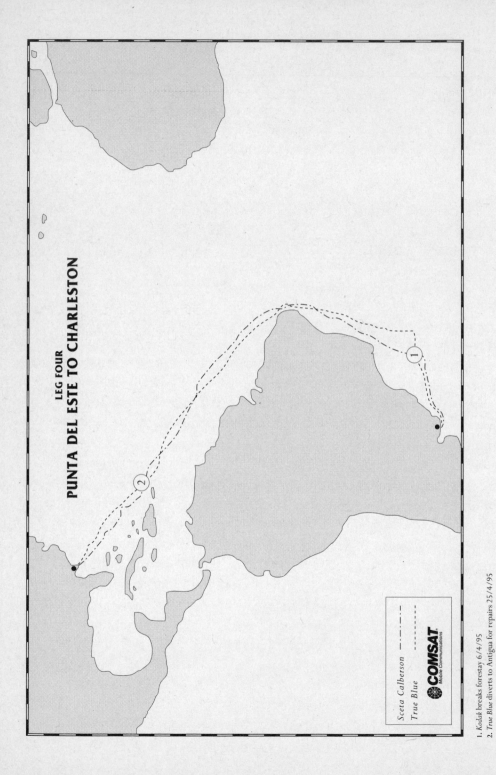

LEG FOUR
PUNTA DEL ESTE TO CHARLESTON

Sceta Calberson
True Blue

1. *Kodak breaks forestay 6/4/95*
2. *True Blue diverts to Antigua for repairs 25/4/95*

LAST THOUGHTS

Charleston saw to it that everyone involved in the event had an abundance, a surfeit even, of parties and other social activities to ensure The BOC Challenge 1994-95 ended with a bang and not a whimper. The curtain was finally dropped on Saturday, 20 May, in an orgy of celebration and congratulation. It began in the morning with a public presentation of all the finishers in the race to the community of Charleston in Marion Square Park. Thousands, half of them schoolchildren, showed up and many queued for hours to get the autographs of their favourite skippers. At one point the queue for Christophe Auguin stretched right across the park.

In the evening we took over the Charleston University sports hall for a gala prize-giving for which we had built a huge and elaborate set. Mark and I compèred the evening together. As we introduced each skipper to the audience, they appeared from behind the set to thunderous applause. I could not help thinking how odd each of them looked in this setting – bright-eyed, freshly shaven, well-groomed, trousers pressed, some even wearing ties and jackets. What a contrast this was to the way I had become accustomed to seeing them in the various ports of call and as they had come into Charleston at the end of the race, exhausted and for the most part bedraggled. It was a fine evening that ended with an open air party catered by a group of local restaurants. The dancing and excited chatter outlasted the champagne well beyond midnight.

I called in at the race office the next morning. There was an air of sombre melancholy about the place as a small group of our volunteers started to dismantle the displays, take down the banners, and pack up our files. Some of the competitors were preparing to leave too.

I went down to the waterfront park, sat on one of the swing seats and stared out across the glistening bay. I wondered what this event had achieved, both for me and for singlehanded sailing. Certainly the event had not been without its critics – those who felt its inherent risks were too high, those who made politics with silly claims about the cost of search and rescue, those whose mean view of personal endeavour and high adventure lacked even a modest understanding of what nourishes the human spirit. Every time we had run the race the experience had suggested new ideas for improving it, not least in terms of its safety. No doubt this process would continue; but it would have to ignore the carping of those who had little to contribute beyond a deep-seated prejudice born mostly out of ignorance. The sad fact was that most of the so-called disasters in this edition of The BOC Challenge were the result of the exceptionally bad weather, specifically two horrendous storms packing hurricane-force winds. But even that would have to be taken into account in framing rules for future events.

Public interest in the event, especially in those countries touched by the race, had been considerable. Thanks largely to Dan McConnell, Herb McCormick and the rest of the media team, the race had reached a huge audience around the world. They helped to make The BOC Challenge one of the top ten multi-venue events in the world in terms of global media coverage. Through television, radio and print media the event had reached a cumulative audience of close to ten billion in one hundred countries. About a third of the coverage had been in the US, with Europe, Japan, Australia, South Africa and South America accounting for most of the rest. In all, some 1,200 hours of broadcast programming on the race had been seen or heard around the world. It was a great achievement.

(Media coverage in Charleston had helped to make The BOC Challenge a big community event in the city. Further proof of that came not long after the end of the race with the official opening of Charleston's internationally acclaimed Spoleto arts festival. All manner of celebrities were there and some were introduced to the crowd thronging the streets in front of City Hall. Having missed the prize-giving weekend celebrations because of his late arrival, Minoru Saito was presented to the crowd and received a deafening round of applause which far outweighed even that given moments earlier to that icon of American culture, Bob Hope!)

For me, one of our greatest achievements was the manner in which we had managed to preserve the unique spirit of the event, balancing the two directions in which others wished it to move. Some wanted it to be a more "by-the-book" yacht race, following all the conventional yacht-racing rules and procedures. Others wanted it to be an adventure pure and simple. It had been tough to maintain the middle ground between these two extremes but, thanks largely to Mark Schrader and the vast majority of the competitors, this was achieved.

The BOC Challenge had contributed to a wider society in many important ways, too, and I believed we could all feel justifiably proud of that.

The race had made enormous contributions to the development of more reliable and safer equipment and materials, and to boat designs that combine safety with better speed. All of this had already been of direct benefit to the average family-cruising sailor throughout the world – particularly in the development of more robust and user-friendly gear for boat and sail handling and for navigation. After all, most family cruising is done, in effect, singlehanded or short-handed. Very often only one or two on board in those circumstances are actually competent sailors.

The Student Ocean Challenge, pioneered and fostered by The BOC Challenge, has made an unarguable contribution to the teaching and understanding of a wide range of subjects in many countries. Thousands of schools have participated in the programme over the years, with teachers around the world praising its unique ability to bring excitement and energy to subjects as diverse as maths and the sciences, geography and history, and what the Americans call "life skills", throughout the academic year. The programme's founder and director Mame Reynolds deserves the credit for this; but it would not have happened without The BOC Challenge and The BOC Group.

Few would deny the positive effect of our efforts over the years to use the race to enhance the protection of our coastal and marine environment. This has included clean-up and awareness programmes in ports of call and elsewhere, logging pollution in the oceans and an insistence on "best practices" among the fleet in not throwing plastics and other non-biodegradables overboard, and the spawning of many other environmental programmes.

Of course, there can be no denying the inherent risks of singlehanded ocean sailing. Indeed, part of its attraction to those who do it is the challenge of managing the risks involved. It requires, though, the ability to distinguish between a risk and a gamble, as well as courage, stamina, and a wide range of sailing and seamanship skills. Is it an activity in which the participants can lose their lives? Of course it is, however rarely . . . but name a physically demanding sport that isn't. Certainly there are many sports that have a far worse safety record than single-handed sailing – indeed, in Britain anyway, more people drown [sic] horse-riding than sailing! But the essence of good seamanship is safety, and safety remains a key preoccupation of those of us who have and will continue to organize this event and others like it. New ideas and new technology will continue to improve its safety into the future, without interfering with the fundamental attraction of such a challenging undertaking as sailing around the world alone.

All of these areas – education, the environment, safety – have good scope for further development, growth and improvement. It is an exciting prospect.

As I sat staring across the bay and reflected on my own endeavour, the balance sheet was certainly not one-sided but it was overwhelmingly positive. I could not deny a strong sense of disappointment and failure at not achieving what I had set out to do. However, my decision to withdraw in Leg Three had been as unavoidable for me as it had been prudent. This apart, I looked back on the whole project with a powerful awareness of having been changed, enriched and educated by it.

Maybe I had been driven to competing in the race by a subconscious sense of mid-life crisis and a desire to do something out of the ordinary with my life. Perhaps a long and materially rewarding existence in the corporate womb – despite the fact that it had provided me with the very means to follow my dream – had left me with a sense of imbalance in my life, and a need to redress that through some other challenge. It could also be that I had been feeling bored, burned out. I was sure all of these things were true; but that part of my life now seemed so long ago. I had stopped the world and got off, and I cannot exaggerate to others the benefits of doing so, given the chance.

Preparing for and participating in The BOC Challenge enabled, indeed forced, me to discard the routines, disciplines, conventions, constraints and pressures of a normal everyday life ashore. The long periods of solitude allowed me to examine the entrails of my life and its effect on others. On balance this had left me with a sense of wellbeing and a few regrets about things I wished I had not done, things I wished I had not said. Certainly I now had a different perspective on what mattered, what my priorities should be. They don't have much to do with wearing a suit five days a week or with being hostage to other people's opinions.

Competing in The BOC Challenge 1994-95 had left me much poorer materially, but richer spiritually. It had given me a stronger sense of freedom and perhaps a better understanding of who I am. I believed it had also left me more sensitive to the importance and needs of others, and I was sure I could smell bullshit at a greater distance than hitherto!

Not a bad result.

THE BOC CHALLENGE

1994–95 COMPETITORS

Profiles by Herb McCormick

CLASS I

CHRISTOPHE AUGUIN

SCETA CALBERSON

BORN: 10 DECEMBER 1959

COUNTRY: FRANCE

SCETA CALBERSON: LOA 18.2M (60'); BEAM
5.5M (18'1"); DRAFT 4.5M (14'9");
DSPL 9,652 KG (21,280 LB); RIG SLOOP;
DESIGNERS JEAN MARIE FINOT/PASCAL
CONQ; BUILDER JMV INDUSTRIES;
YEAR BUILT 1994.

After capturing the 1990-91 BOC in record fashion, professional yachtsman Christophe Auguin from France returned for a second go with a singular ambition — to win back-to-back BOCs and equal the accomplishment of countryman Philippe Jeantot, who won the first two editions of the event. To realize his goal, Auguin once again sought the expertise of naval architect Jean Marie Finot, who had designed his previous *Groupe Sceta*. Finot's "fourth generation" Open 60 was built of a carbon/Nomex sandwich and exhibited the radical "aircraft carrier" shape — low freeboard, and a remarkable beam/length ratio of almost 3:1 — optimized for fast reaching in heavy downwind conditions. Auguin's longtime sponsor Sceta Calberson, the French transportation and tourism conglomerate, bankrolled the project.

ISABELLE AUTISSIER

ECUREUIL POITOU CHARENTES 2

BORN: 18 OCTOBER 1956

COUNTRY: FRANCE

ECUREUIL POITOU CHARENTES 2: LOA
18.2M (60'); BEAM 5.4M (17'8"); DRAFT
4.5M (14'10"); DSPL 8,430 KG (18,734 LB);
RIG SLOOP; DESIGNER JEAN BERRET;
BUILDER CHANTIER MARC PINTA;
YEAR BUILT 1993.

The only woman to have completed a BOC Challenge (finishing 7th in Class I in 1990-91), and the only female competitor entered in the 1994-95 event, trail-blazing French singlehander Isabelle Autissier commissioned yacht designer Jean Berret to produce a boat capable of winning the big-boat division and overall titles. Berret responded with a hull constructed of a carbon/foam/glass laminate, and featuring a hydraulically-controlled canting keel. With it, Autissier and a crew of three tuned up for the BOC by smashing the sailing record from New York to San Francisco via Cape Horn. An engineer and marine science professor, Autissier had dual backing from Ecureuil Bank and the Poitou Charentes region of France.

MARK GATEHOUSE

QUEEN ANNE'S BATTERY

BORN: 21 AUGUST 1949

COUNTRY: ENGLAND

QUEEN ANNE'S BATTERY: LOA 18.2M (60'); BEAM 5.3M (17'6"); DRAFT 3.6M (12'); DSPL 11,902 KG (26,448 LB); RIG KETCH; DESIGNER GUY RIBADEAU-DUMAS; BUILDER JEANTOT MARINE; YEAR BUILT 1986.

The son of Richard Gatehouse, the founder of the noted marine instrument company Brooks & Gatehouse, English skipper Mark Gatehouse is the operator of his Class I 60-footer's namesake and sponsor – Queen Anne's Battery Marina in Plymouth. A lifelong competitive sailor aboard boats ranging from dinghies to offshore catamarans, for the BOC Challenge Gatehouse entered the Guy Ribadeau-Dumas design that was sailed to first place in the 1986-87 race under its former name, *Credit Agricole III*. To gain a competitive edge, Gatehouse added a mizzen mast and lightened the aluminium boat by almost two tonnes. Aboard the boat, Gatehouse took a close second behind winner Yves Parlier in The BOC Transatlantic Challenge in the summer of 1994.

JOSH HALL

GARTMORE INVESTMENT MANAGERS

BORN: 18 MAY 1962

COUNTRY: ENGLAND

GARTMORE INVESTMENT MANAGERS: LOA 18.2M (60'); BEAM 4.7M (15'4"); DRAFT 3.6M (11'10"); DSPL 12,398 KG (27,550 LB); RIG SLOOP; DESIGNERS BOUVET/PETIT; BUILDER CAPTAIN FLINT BOATYARD; YEAR BUILT 1986.

Another veteran BOC competitor – he took 3rd in Class II in 1990-91 aboard *New Spirit of Ipswich* – Josh Hall came back for a BOC encore aboard a classic campaigner: his *Gartmore Investment Managers*, built of foam sandwich construction, scored a 2nd in 1986-87 as Titouan Lamazou's *Ecureuil d'Aquitaine*, then another 2nd in the 1988-89 Vendée Globe as Loick Peyron's *Lada Poch III*. She was sailed by José de Ugarte in the 1990-91 BOC as *BBV Expo*. Hall, who got his start on the professional sailing circuit as a member of Robin Knox-Johnston's *British Airways* crew, was backed by Gartmore Investment Managers as title sponsor, with a consortium of local businesses as secondary donors.

STEVE PETTENGILL

HUNTER'S CHILD

BORN: 20 MAY 1951

COUNTRY: USA

HUNTER'S CHILD: LOA 18.2M (60'); BEAM 4.9M (16'); DRAFT 4.2M (14'); DSPL 8,325 KG (18,500 LB); RIG SLOOP; DESIGNERS HUNTER DESIGN TEAM/B&R DESIGN; BUILDER PARAGON COMPOSITES; YEAR BUILT 1989.

Originally a Great Lakes sailor who moved to Newport, Rhode Island, in the late Eighties to begin a career in boat-building, deliveries and professional ocean racing, Steve Pettengill set a record from New York to San Francisco aboard the trimaran *Great American* in 1989 (a record later broken by fellow BOC sailor Isabelle Autissier). Later, Pettengill was rescued off Cape Horn when his tri was capsized on a return record attempt. Sponsored by the US sailboat manufacturer Hunter Marine, *Hunter's Child* was originally built for company president and accomplished solo sailor Warren Luhrs to race in the 1990-91 BOC. But Luhrs's plans changed, and Pettengill's entry was the first round-the-world race for the radical carbon/Kevlar speedster.

JEAN JACQUES PROVOYEUR

NOVELL SOUTH AFRICA

BORN: 24 DECEMBER 1950

COUNTRY: SOUTH AFRICA

NOVELL SOUTH AFRICA: LOA 18.2M (60'); BEAM 4.6M (15'); DRAFT 3.4M (11'3"); DSPL 12,247 KG (27,000 LB); RIG SLOOP; DESIGNER RODGER MARTIN; BUILDER J.J. PROVOYEUR; YEAR BUILT 1989.

Though South African J.J. Provoyeur was a first-time BOC competitor, he already had a special link with the race – he built the boat he would sail in the Challenge for countryman Bertie Reed, who drove it to an 8th-place finish (as *Grinaker*) in 1990-91. Provoyeur, a savvy small-boat racer and former South African Yachtsman of the Year, stripped over a ton of unnecessary weight and equipment from the Rodger Martin-designed, carbon/Kevlar/foam-constructed vessel prior to the start. Provoyeur started the race as an unsponsored entry, but that changed during the Cape Town layover when he secured a sponsorship package from Novell South Africa.

DAVID SCULLY

COYOTE

BORN: 10 SEPTEMBER 1955

COUNTRY: USA

COYOTE: LOA 18.2M (60'); BEAM 6.4M
(21'); DRAFT 4.2M (14');
DSPL 9,450 KG (21,000 LB); RIG SLOOP;
DESIGNER RODGER MARTIN;
BUILDER CONCORDIA CUSTOM
YACHTS; YEAR BUILT 1992.

A native of Illinois and a former commodities broker in Chicago before moving to France to devote himself to competitive racing, David Scully's eclectic sailing background covers a span from the America's Cup to offshore multihulls. Scully's chartered Rodger Martin design was built for fellow Yank Mike Plant, who was lost at sea when the ballast bulb on the boat parted with the keel and the yacht capsized on the maiden voyage. After a salvage operation the carbon-rich composite foam/Kevlar hull — at 6.4 metres (21ft) the beamiest of all BOC boats — was reinforced with additional carbon stringers, and fitted with a lighter keel and taller carbon-fibre mast.

ARNET TAYLOR, JR

THURSDAY'S CHILD

BORN: 4 MAY 1950

COUNTRY: USA

THURSDAY'S CHILD: LOA 18.2M (60');
BEAM 4.5M (14'8"); DRAFT 3.6M (12');
DSPL 8,325 KG (18,500 LB); RIG SLOOP;
DESIGNERS LINDENBERG/BERGSTROM;
BUILDERS LINDENBERG/BERGSTROM;
YEAR BUILT 1983.

American Arnie Taylor grew up in a sailing family, and continued with the sport as both vocation and avocation with stints in boat-building and yacht deliveries — during which he acquired a 100-tonne commercial Master's license — as well as extensive singlehanded sailing. When it was built in 1983 for the following year's OSTAR, *Thursday's Child* was the most radical monohull of the era. Built of lightweight composite construction and featuring an unusual articulating rudder, skipper Warren Luhrs proved the worthiness of the concept by winning the monohull class and challenging the top multihulls. Luhrs fared worse in the 1986-87 BOC aboard the boat, when he retired in Sydney. More recently Alan Wynne Thomas entered the boat in the 1989-90 Vendée Globe, though he too retired from the race in Australia — where Taylor acquired the vessel for the 1994-95 BOC.

JEAN LUC VAN DEN HEEDE

VENDÉE ENTREPRISES

BORN: 8 JUNE 1945

COUNTRY: FRANCE

VENDÉE ENTREPRISES: LOA 18.2M (60'); BEAM 3.8M (12'6"); DRAFT 4.3M (13'); DSPL 7,934 KG (17,632 LB); RIG YAWL; DESIGNERS HARLE/MORTAIN; BUILDER CHANTIER C.D.K.; YEAR BUILT 1991.

A former mathematics teacher and sailing instructor, French competitor Jean Luc Van den Heede is one of the world's most experienced singlehanders – his 1994-95 BOC would be his fourth race around the world alone (including two non-stop Vendée Challenges and the 1986-87 BOC, in which he finished 2nd in Class II). His 60-foot *Vendée Entreprises*, built of straightforward fibreglass construction with a foam core, was the narrowest of all Class I contenders at a slim 3.8 metres (12ft 6in). Van den Heede was sponsored by a group of small businesses in the Vendée region of France.

CLASS II

DAVID ADAMS

TRUE BLUE

BORN: 16 DECEMBER 1953

COUNTRY: AUSTRALIA

TRUE BLUE: LOA 15.2M (50'); BEAM 4.4M (14'6"); DRAFT 4M (13'2"); DSPL 6,114 KG (13,480 LB); RIG SLOOP; DESIGNER SCOTT JUTSON; BUILDER JB SAYER YACHTS; YEAR BUILT 1993.

With over 150,000 offshore sailing miles to his credit – including a 4th-place finish in the 1990-91 BOC Challenge aboard the Class I 60-footer *Innkeeper* – Australian David Adams returned for the 1994-95 race seeking top honours in Class II. To that end, he commissioned American born/Sydney-based yacht designer Scott Jutson to deliver a light- to moderate-displacement 50-footer that would perform well in all conditions – from light-air beats to screaming downwind reaches. Built of strip-planked cedar under epoxy Kevlar skins, and rigged with a state-of-the-art carbon fibre mast, *True Blue* possessed a thoroughbred's blend of strength, simplicity and power. Adams's effort was sponsored by a consortium including State Street Bank, Yalumba Wines, Crown Casinos (Melbourne, Australia), Panasonic and MMI.

SIMONE BIANCHETTI

TOWN OF CERVIA — ADRIATIC SEA

BORN: 20 FEBRUARY 1969

COUNTRY: ITALY

TOWN OF CERVIA — ADRIATIC SEA: LOA
15.2M (50'); BEAM 3.5M (11'6");
DRAFT 3.0M (9'10"); DSPL 6,604 KG
(14,560 LB); RIG SLOOP;
DESIGNER ROBERTO STARKEL;
BUILDER PIER 12 NAUTICAL YARD;
YEAR BUILT 1987.

Twenty-five-year-old Simone Bianchetti, the youngest entrant in the 1994-95 Challenge, began his offshore sailing career as a bowman aboard maxi-yachts *Congere* and *Kriter* before a two-year stint in the Italian military coastal patrol. Aboard his lightweight, Kevlar-reinforced 50-footer *Nonsisamai* (translation: "You Never Know"), Bianchetti found considerable success in crewed racing in his local waters of the Adriatic Sea before renaming the boat and outfitting it for solo BOC sailing. For the round-the-world race, Bianchetti found sponsorship from the town of Cervia, Italy, and the Pier 12 Nautical Yard.

ROBIN DAVIE

CORNWALL

BORN: 2 NOVEMBER 1951

COUNTRY: ENGLAND

CORNWALL: LOA 12.2M (40'); BEAM 3.6M
(11'8"); DRAFT 2.1M (7');
DSPL 8,130 KG (17,920 LB); RIG CUTTER;
DESIGNER LARS BERGSTROM;
BUILDER HURLEY MARINE;
YEAR BUILT 1973.

A veteran of the 1990-91 race, when he sailed to a 2nd place in the Corinthian Class (abandoned for the 1994-95 contest), Robin Davie first took to sea on the training ship *Sir Winston Churchill* as a sixteenth-birthday present. Later, he embarked on a career as a professional mariner while serving as an officer in the Merchant Navy. Davie's *Cornwall* (the former *Global Exposure*), a twenty-one-year-old IOR-rated cruiser/racer, was the oldest and smallest boat in the fleet. Davie, whose campaign was largely self-funded through the sale of T-shirts, posters, and postcards which he carried round Cape Horn, also received some financial backing from supporters and businesses in Cornwall and Charleston.

HARRY MITCHELL

HENRY HORNBLOWER

BORN: 4 APRIL 1924

COUNTRY: ENGLAND

HENRY HORNBLOWER: LOA 12.2M (40'1");
BEAM 3.0M (10'); DRAFT 2.3M (7'6");
DSPL 7,934 KG (17,632 LB); RIG CUTTER;
DESIGNER IAN NICHOLSON;
BUILDER ANGLO NORDEN;
YEAR BUILT 1985.

At seventy, the oldest competitor in the 1994-95 Challenge, Harry Mitchell was back for his third attempt at the round-the-world race — his first, in 1986-87, ended when he ran aground in New Zealand and his second, in 1990-91, was over before it started following a collision in the English Channel on his qualifying voyage. Mitchell, a lifelong sailor who took up singlehanding in earnest in his fifties after careers in aviation and in his family's car hire business, entered the race to fulfil a dream of rounding Cape Horn alone under sail and piercing his ear with a golden earring in celebration. His 40-foot cutter was built for short-handed racing in 1985.

ALAN NEBAUER

NEWCASTLE AUSTRALIA

BORN: 6 APRIL 1963

COUNTRY: AUSTRALIA

NEWCASTLE AUSTRALIA: LOA 15.2M (50');
BEAM 4.2M (14'); DRAFT 3.7M (12');
DSPL 6,000 KG (13,200 LB); RIG SLOOP;
DESIGNER DAVID LYONS;
BUILDER KANGA BIRTLES;
YEAR BUILT 1994.

A professional skipper who started sailing at the age of twelve and who stacked over 40,000 offshore miles onto his sailing résumé before the BOC race — including a voyage from Australia to Canada with wife Cindy, followed by several years of living aboard — Alan Nebauer sought out ex-BOC competitor Kanga Birtles to construct his maximum-length Class II entry *Newcastle Australia*. Designed by David Lyons, the moderate-displacement yacht was one of three new 50-footers — including David Adams's *True Blue* and Giovanni Soldini's *Kodak* — produced expressly for the 1994-95 BOC Challenge. Nebauer's campaign was financed by the city government and a host of businesses in his hometown of Newcastle.

NEAL PETERSEN

PROTECT OUR SEALIFE

BORN: 3 JUNE 1967

COUNTRY: SOUTH AFRICA

PROTECT OUR SEALIFE: LOA 12.1M (40'); BEAM 4.0M (13'); DRAFT 2.0M (6'); DSPL 6,000 KG (13,200 LB); RIG SLOOP; DESIGNERS GOULOOZE/PETERSEN; BUILDER MAGNUM ENTERPRISES; YEAR BUILT 1990.

A professional diver from South Africa who started sailing at the Royal Cape Yacht Club when he was a teenager, Neal Petersen fulfilled a longtime ambition when he submitted his entry form for the 1994-95 BOC Challenge. Based in Ireland prior to the BOC, Petersen added nearly a metre to the transom of *Protect Our Sealife* to conform to the minimum length requirement for Class II of the race. For Petersen it was not a daunting enterprise, as he both helped design the boat and was its principal builder, using the cold molded wood/epoxy technique for construction. Petersen participated in the 1994 BOC Transatlantic Challenge to qualify for the main event.

FLOYD ROMACK

CARDIAC 88

BORN: 6 MARCH 1928

COUNTRY: USA

CARDIAC 88: LOA 15.1M (49'8"); BEAM 4.6M (15'); DRAFT 2.3M (7'6"); DSPL 11,925 KG (26,500 LB); RIG CUTTER; DESIGNERS SOVEREL/CREALOCK; BUILDER SEAMASTER MARINE; YEAR BUILT 1990.

American Floyd Romack, a restaurateur from the seaside town of Cape May, New Jersey, named his boat after his 1988 heart attack. With an extensive background in long-distance cruising Romack had hoped to take part in earlier editions of the BOC, but he ran out of preparation time for the inaugural effort, and health problems forced him to miss subsequent runnings. For the fourth race, however, he obtained a solid, fibreglass 50-footer from the board of designer Mark Soverel which he outfitted with a versatile cutter rig. Aboard the boat, he took part in the 1994 BOC Transatlantic Challenge.

NIGEL ROWE

SKY CATCHER

BORN: 30 DECEMBER 1940

COUNTRY: ENGLAND

SKY CATCHER: LOA 14.7M (48'3"); BEAM
4.1M (13'6"); DRAFT 3.0M (10');
DSPL 9,000 KG (20,000 LB); RIG CUTTER;
DESIGNER HUNTER DESIGN GROUP;
BUILDER HUNTER MARINE;
YEAR BUILT 1988.

As the chief executive of corporate relations for The BOC Group, Nigel Rowe
was instrumental in securing sponsorship
for the first BOC Challenge, and oversee-
ing the company's stewardship of the event
in the races that followed. Rowe's business
involvement coincided with a burgeoning
interest in the sport from a participant's
standpoint, which originated with a solo
sail around the Isle of Wight in 1983.
Rowe prepared for entering the 1994-95
BOC race by competing in numerous
events including the C-Star, the Two-Star,
the Bermuda One-Two and the BOC
Transatlantic Challenge (1st in Class). His
Class II *Sky Catcher* was originally built as a
custom fibreglass racer by Hunter Marine.

MINORU SAITO

SHUTEN-DOHJI II

BORN: 7 JANUARY 1934

COUNTRY: JAPAN

SHUTEN-DOHJI II: LOA 15.2M (50'); BEAM
3.7M (12'); DRAFT 1.2M (4'1");
DSPL 8,618 KG (19,000 LB); RIG CUTTER;
DESIGNERS ADAMS/RADFORD;
BUILDER McINTYRE MARINE SERVICES;
YEAR BUILT 1990.

Though Japan's Minoru Saito is a relative
newcomer to the sport of offshore sailing –
he only took it up in 1987 – the 1994-95
BOC Challenge was his second go at the
event after a 3rd-place finish in his Class in
1990-91. A native of Tokyo, Saito also
participated in the 1987 Melbourne-Osaka
race and the 1989 Auckland-Fukuoka race,
and was on the organizing committee for
the 1988 Around Australia race. For his
BOC campaigns, Saito commissioned
fellow 1990-91 competitor Don McIntyre
to build a similarly sized and outfitted
sistership to his own 50-foot fibreglass
cutter *Buttercup*.

GIOVANNI SOLDINI

KODAK

BORN: 16 MAY 1966

COUNTRY: ITALY

KODAK: LOA 15.2M (50'); BEAM 4.2M
(14'); DRAFT 4.0M (13'2");
DSPL 4,959 KG (11,020 LB); RIG SLOOP;
DESIGNER JEAN BERRET;
BUILDER TOXIC BOATS; YEAR BUILT 1994.

A lifelong sailor and professional skipper with countless racing, cruising and chartering miles under his keel, Italian competitor Giovanni Soldini purchased 1990-91 Class II BOC winner Yves Dupasquier's *Servant IV*, and was racing it in the Quebec-St Malo Race, when the keel fell off the boat and he and his crew were rescued in the North Atlantic. Undaunted by the experience, and taken by the ultralight *Servant*'s easily-driven speed, Soldini commissioned designer Jean Berret to draw an even faster boat using the lessons learned from the *Servant* programme. Convincing the administrators of a drug rehabilitation centre that the work would be good therapy, Soldini built the boat from GRP with a crew of recovering addicts ("toxics" in Italian slang).

CHANIAH VAUGHAN

JIMRODA II

BORN: 23 FEBRUARY 1945

COUNTRY: ENGLAND

JIMRODA II: LOA 15.2M (50'); BEAM 4.2M
(13'9"); DRAFT 2.7M (9');
DSPL 10,886 KG (24,000 LB); RIG
CUTTER; DESIGNER RODGER MARTIN;
BUILDER MIKE PLANT; YEAR BUILT 1986.

A former professional rugby league football player prior to a career as a construction surveyor, English skipper Niah Vaughan entered the BOC with over a dozen years of sailing experience in the Irish Sea, the Mediterranean, and the challenging South African waters off the Cape of Good Hope. His 50-foot cutter *Jimroda II* – named after his parents – is one of the best-travelled of all BOC racing yachts. Built of a composite/GRP sandwich by American Mike Plant and sailed by Plant to a Class II victory in the 1986-87 BOC as *Airco Distributor*, the boat reappeared under the able guidance of Josh Hall and the new name of *New Spirit of Ipswich* for the 1990-91 race, where it took third in Class.

THE BOC CHALLENG

Elapsed Tin

COMPETITORS	LEG ONE
CLASS I	
Christophe Auguin/*Sceta Calberson*	42/04/58/04
Steve Pettengill/*Hunter's Child*	40/16/08/54
Jean Luc Van den Heede/*Vendée Entreprises*	42/13/54/12
David Scully/*Coyote*	43/19/34/39
J.J.Provoyeur/*Novell South Africa*	42/22/04/57
Arnet Taylor/*Thursday's Child*	53/23/29/22*
CLASS II	
David Adams/*True Blue*	42/09/50/45
Giovanni Soldini/*Kodak*	43/06/22/28
Chaniah Vaughan/*Jimroda II*	48/18/01/30
Alan Nebauer/*Newcastle Australia*	51/19/41/08*
Robin Davie/*Cornwall*	58/00/45/38*
Minoru Saito/*Shuten-Dohji II*	58/20/28/02
Floyd Romack/*Cardiac 88*	82/03/00/44
Isabelle Autissier/*Ecureuil Poitou Charentes 2*	35/08/52/18
Josh Hall/*Gartmore Investment Managers*	DNF
Neal Petersen/*Protect Our Sealife*	67/16/59/47
Mark Gatehouse/*Queen Anne's Battery*	DNF
Simone Bianchetti/*Town of Cervia, Adriatic Sea*	67/09/33/04
Nigel Rowe/*Sky Catcher*	52/21/04/36
Henry Mitchell/*Henry Hornblower*	69/21/54/00

*Notes corrected times
DNS = Did not start   DNF = Did not finish

994-95 RESULTS

ays/Hours/Minutes/Seconds)

LEG TWO	LEG THREE	LEG FOUR	TOTAL
24/23/40/16	29/16/15/57	24/20/17/29	121/17/11/46
28/02/12/26	31/13/42/09	27/19/59/40	128/04/03/09
27/10/57/24	31/14/13/31	28/02/54/31	129/17/59/38
28/08/04/14	32/19/07/21	28/02/10/21	133/00/56/35
28/20/06/39	31/19/14/10	29/15/45/55	133/05/11/41
55/18/06/19	50/15/22/21	39/16/47/24	200/01/45/26
28/00/28/45*	31/17/51/39	29/00/55/30	131/05/06/39
28/02/27/56	31/16/23/19	30/23/32/57	134/00/46/40
34/22/40/52	42/21/04/13	40/02/19/38	166/16/06/13
34/04/08/50	56/10/35/09	39/03/21/21	181/13/46/28
36/06/55/04	59/09/22/52	43/11/11/54	197/04/15/28
51/15/21/40*	67/08/51/20	45/13/29/51	223/10/10/53
DNS			
DNF			
DNF			
DNF			
44/22/45/42*	DNF		
51/05/11/34	DNF		

THE BOC CHALLENG

	OVERALL RACE
CLASS I	1 Christophe Auguin
	2 Steve Pettengill
	3 Jean Luc Van den Heede
	First on handicap:
	Christophe Auguin
CLASS II	1 David Adams
	2 Giovanni Soldini
	3 Chaniah Vaughan
	First on handicap (in Class
	and overall): David Adams
	First unsponsored:
	Chaniah Vaughan
Seamanship Award	Steve Pettengill
COMSAT Communications Award	Robin Davie
Omega Best 24-hour Run Award (Class I)	Christophe Auguin (350.8 miles)
Omega Best 24-hour Run Award (Class II)	Giovanni Soldini (277 miles)
IBM Performance Award (Class I)	Arnet Taylor
IBM Performance Award (Class II)	Alan Nebauer
Spirit of The BOC Challenge Award	Giovanni Soldini

994-95 PRIZEWINNERS

LEG ONE	LEG TWO	LEG THREE	LEG FOUR
1 Isabelle Autissier	1 Christophe Auguin	1 Christophe Auguin	1 Christophe Auguin
2 Steve Pettengill	2 Jean Luc Van den Heede	2 Steve Pettengill	2 Steve Pettengill
3 Christophe Auguin	3 Steve Pettengill	3 Jean Luc Van den Heede	3 David Scully

LEG ONE	LEG TWO	LEG THREE	LEG FOUR
1 David Adams	1 David Adams	1 Giovanni Soldini	1 David Adams
2 Giovanni Soldini	2 Giovanni Soldini	2 David Adams	2 Giovanni Soldini
3 Chaniah Vaughan	3 Alan Nebauer	3 Chaniah Vaughan	3 Alan Nebauer

LEG ONE	LEG TWO	LEG THREE	LEG FOUR
Alan Nebauer	Arnet Taylor Isabelle Autissier	Alan Nebauer	Giovanni Soldini
Alan Nebauer Josh Hall	Robin Davie	Arnet Taylor	J.J.Provoyeur
Steve Pettengill	Christophe Auguin	Christophe Auguin	Christophe Auguin
David Adams	Robin Davie	Giovanni Soldini	Giovanni Soldini
Isabelle Autissier	Christophe Auguin	Christophe Auguin	Christophe Auguin
David Adams	David Adams	Giovanni Soldini	David Adams

HIGH TECH ON THE HIGH SEAS

THE BOC COMMUNICATIONS REVOLUTION

by Herb McCormick

On the first leg of the first BOC Challenge in 1982-83, French sailor Philippe Jeantot opened up a lead of some eight hundred miles in the opening weeks of the event . . . and he did it under a cloak of silence. Competitors on that opening leg were obliged to report positions just once a week, and Jeantot slipped away on a radical route unbeknownst to his fellow racers. Jeantot's lead – which proved to be insurmountable – was established literally before anyone realized it had happened.

What a difference a decade makes. When Nigel Rowe and the rest of the BOC sailors set out from Charleston, they carried with them an onboard communications and electronics package that was virtually unimaginable for yachts in the BOC size range ten years earlier. Seated before the nav' station aboard his 48-foot *Sky Catcher*, Rowe gazed upon an array of equipment that included a laptop computer interfaced via satellite to send and receive electronic mail, weather files, position reports and other data; a global positioning system (GPS) unit that automatically pinpointed and relayed his location, speed and course heading to race headquarters four times daily; a pair of dedicated emergency beacons that could alert authorities instantly if trouble arose; and yet another distress button linked by satellite to race control.

Rowe, like fellow racers David Adams and Josh Hall, was also equipped with a satellite telephone for making and receiving calls worldwide. Even when struggling against survival conditions deep in the Southern Ocean, he was as accessible as he would have been in the warmth of his office in England.

The heart and soul of the BOC communications network was provided by COMSAT's "C-Link" Inmarsat-C service, coupled with the custom COMSAT Sail Track vessel-tracking service developed especially for the round-the-world race. Taken as a whole, COMSAT provided race organizers with a versatile tool with which they could monitor the fleet's up-to-the-minute progress, offer a safety net, provide rapid two-way communications unaffected even by extreme weather, and exchange relevant data on a regular basis.

For the sailors, it meant having the ability to send messages to sponsors and family as well as to race officials, and to access and use information that would allow them to reach new standards of performance from a tactical, competitive standpoint.

If COMSAT's C-Link service was the "superhighway" on which the information travelled, equipment provided by IBM and Trimble were the vehicles that facilitated the journey through cyberspace. IBM ThinkPad 720s were the laptop of choice for the BOC fleet, bringing the sounds of tapping keyboards to the high-seas music of wind and water. Interfaced with a Trimble Galaxy Inmarsat-C/GPS transceiver, with special software coordinated for use with C-Link technology, the fleet was "plugged in" to shoreside resources in an unprecedented fashion.

COMSAT's C-Link is a "store-and-forward" data messaging service using compact Inmarsat-C satellite terminals for text and data messages. COMSAT's Mobile Link, on the other hand, as employed in the "phone" systems aboard boats sailed by Rowe and Hall, uses Inmarsat-M technology that provides real-time fax and interactive voice communications on vessels so equipped.

The vast potential of this wondrous technology was never better showcased than one month into the race when Hall's *Gartmore Investment Managers* was holed in a collision several hundred miles off the coast of Brazil. Hall instantly hit the distress button on his Galaxy Inmarsat-C transceiver, alerting rescue authorities in England and, moments later, at race headquarters in Charleston, South Carolina. Through COMSAT C-Link service, race officials sent out an instant "fleet poll" to determine which yacht was closest to Hall's position – in this instance, Alan Nebauer's *Newcastle Australia*. Meanwhile, Hall reported via an Inmarsat-M telephone call that he was okay and that, for the time being, his electric pumps were coping with the influx of water.

An intercept point was quickly determined and, again through a C-Link message, Nebauer was diverted towards Hall's boat and provided with position coordinates and a new course to steer. In the past, such communications would have been at the mercy of high-seas radio wave propagation – never a problem with contemporary satellite technology.

As the Australian skipper altered course, COMSAT technicians in Clarksburg, Maryland, remotely modified both boats' position-reporting intervals so their progress could be monitored via Sail Track fleet management software. Nebauer, and other racers keeping an electronic "watch" during the rescue operation, received status reports and updates on a regular basis. Some nine hours after Hall's collision, Nebauer was alongside and assisting his shipwrecked mate onto the safe deck of *Newcastle Australia*.

A more subtle – but also important – benefit to the C-Link connection was the ability it gave race organizers to update media outlets and schools with fresh news from the fleet on a round-the-clock basis. The rich diversity of information assimilated through Sail Track, in conjunction with competitors' C-Link service messages regarding weather conditions, equipment failures and personal observations, provided the BOC media team with stacks of material for daily news releases – which were also available through a COMSAT responding fax service.

Furthermore, with an unprecedented online sponsorship affiliation with CompuServe, the tens of thousands of students following the race worldwide through programs such as the Student Ocean Challenge were able to learn about sailing, geography, oceanography – and computer science – in a timely, fun and completely fresh environment.

The trickle-down effect of BOC technology has long benefited cruising sailors who take the lessons learned from long-distance testing of sail-handling gear, autopilots and other essential equipment and apply them to both coastal sailing and long-distance family- and short-handed voyaging. So, too, the valuable knowledge in communications technology gleaned from the solo racers will also be passed along to recreational and commercial mariners.

The next breakthrough in satellite communications is destined to be in global handheld units, or terminals, that are similar to cellular phones and which will operate through multiple wireless cellular links. For the next round-the-world challenge, full real-time voice communications on a twenty-four-hour basis are not beyond the realm of affordable possibility. Sound inconceivable? No more so than losing a yacht race because you didn't know which way the leader was sailing.